Conducting Hermeneutic Research

critical qualitative research

Shirley R. Steinberg
Series Editor

Vol. 30

The Critical Qualitative Research series is part of the Peter Lang Education list.
Every volume is peer reviewed and meets the highest
quality standards for content and production.

PETER LANG

New York · Berlin · Bruxelles · Chennai · Lausanne · Oxford

Nancy J. Moules, Graham McCaffrey, James C. Field,
Catherine M. Laing and Theodore D. George

Conducting Hermeneutic Research

From Philosophy to Practice
Second Edition

PETER LANG
New York · Berlin · Bruxelles · Chennai · Lausanne · Oxford

Bibliographic information published by the Deutsche Nationalbibliothek.
The German National Library lists this publication in the German National Bibliography; detailed bibliographic data is available on the Internet at http://dnb.d-nb.de.

Library of Congress Cataloging-in-Publication Data
Library of Congress Control Number: 2025015788

Cover design by Peter Lang Group AG
Index by Barbara Cuerden

ISSN 1947-5993
ISBN 978-3-0343-5522-3 (Hardback)
ISBN 978-3-0343-5611-4 (Paperback)
ISBN 978-3-0343-5609-1 (E-PDF)
ISBN 978-3-0343-5610-7 (E-PUB)
DOI 10.3726/b22880

Published by Peter Lang Publishing Inc., New York (USA)
info@peterlang.com

This publication has been peer reviewed.

www.peterlang.com

To the Visiting Scholars of the *Canadian Hermeneutic Institute*:
<http://www.chiannual.com/>

David Jardine, John Caputo, Richard Kearney, James Olthuis, Gail Weiss, Nicholas Davey, Jean Grondin, Kym McLaren, Walter Brogan, Theodore George, James Risser, David Vessey, Dennis Schmidt …

And those yet to come …

Table of Contents

Figures

Foreword to First Edition: The Wisdom of Hermeneutics

By John D. Caputo
(2015 edition)

I am pleased and honored to offer a word in advance to *Conducting Hermeneutic Research*. This is a paradoxical invitation for me because in radical hermeneutics everything turns on saying "come" to the coming of what we cannot see coming, of the unforeseeable. So, without trying to help the reader see too much in advance, without trying to anticipate everything, let me say that what I find so precious in *Conducting Hermeneutic Research* is that it catches hermeneutics in the act. It brings home in the most vivid way just what hermeneutics really is—in the concrete. Its authors are concretely engaged and hermeneutically enlightened practitioners who are describing the difficult and delicate conditions under which concrete hermeneutical work takes place. How are research and writing conducted in such a way as not to become absorbed in a data-driven and objectifying culture? How to show that more is given than data without having one's work dismissed as random, subjectivistic, and impressionistic? How to show that hermeneutics practices a "rigor" that is not reducible to mathematical "exactness," to invoke a distinction from Edmund Husserl (that is put to work in Chapter 9). The task these authors take on is to portray the special place of practice in hermeneutics, to depict the practical wisdom that hermeneutics requires, indeed the practical wisdom that hermeneutics *is*.

As practitioners, the authors understand in their bones what the ancients meant when they said that only individuals exist, while universals are abstractions. In hermeneutics—I offer this as a working definition—it is not a matter of applying universals to cases but instead of applying cases to universals. The only reason that sounds strange is because of the inverted, topsy-turvy nature of the word case. "Case" comes from *cadere, casum*, to fall, as in a casualty, for which we buy insurance. The suggestion is that the individual represents a "fall" from the truth and reality of the universal, a decline into mere particularity. But this is to invert reality. For the individual is what is real. The individual is the first truth, the true being, while universals are abstractions, meaning they are siphoned off (abstract = *ab* + *trahere*) individuals. Universals make handy but relatively empty placeholders, thin, schematic signifiers constituting an efficient shorthand useful for exchanging information. Trading in universals is like passing along linguistic containers which require unpacking to see to what they really contain when we get down to cases. There it is again! We don't get down to cases—we rise to them! We have everything we can do to rise to the occasion of the individual, to ascend to the thick, dense, rich, complexity of the individual situation, instead of lolling lazily amidst the thin transparencies of universals.

In that sense hermeneutics is better served to speak not of the individual case but of the singular situation, not of "cases" but of "singularities," which are always marked by a certain alterity, idiomaticity, idiosyncrasy and conceptual impenetrability. Singularities are not a fall or a defect, but an excess, far too rich ever to be adequately explicated or translated into universals. Just try it for yourself: try to make a list of universals that explicate your feelings for someone you love with a love that surpasses understanding, or that describe an experience that transformed your life, or a work of art that leaves you lost for words. We come up short, but coming up short against singularities is not due to a defect in our language or experience; it is not something to be remedied by building up a still larger stock of universals to draw upon the next time we are confounded by experience. We come up short because of the wealth of the experience. The wisdom of hermeneutics is to have the good sense not to think that reality is a "case" of an abstraction, that the perceptual is a lesser species than the conceptual, that the real is a fall from the ideal, or that "practice" is an imperfect version of the theoretical. Universals are abstracts, extracts, one-sided take outs, a freeze frame, a still which, while serving a purpose, only imperfectly evokes the rush of movement.

In short, in hermeneutics, we proceed from the assumption that practice is the perfect and the theory is the imperfect. The authors of the present volume are practitioners, nurses and educators, who alert us to the delicate art of practice and to the practical wisdom demanded of the practitioner. They face a dilemma like Kierkegaard's, who wrote books which claimed that becoming a Christian is nothing to be found in a book and so tried to write a book as if he had not written a book. These authors are trying to describe a method that is not a method except in the deeper etymological sense of making one's way along (*meta*) the path (*odos*) to truth. To take one of many examples I could choose here, let me say that there is no theory, no body of principles, no rulebook, no set of universal norms that would enable us to "conduct" the interview recorded for us in Chapter 6 with parents who have lost a child to cancer. The situation is steeped in an impenetrable mystery, a question to which there is no answer—why do children die? But while there is no answer, there is a fitting response, a response cut to fit—where there are no mis-fits, just ways of being differently fitted (see the wonderful account of a camp conducted for children with cancer in Chapter 8)—which is compassion. Compassion inscribes a zone of respect around the mystery, is sensitive to the abyss that stirs beneath the cool clinical words "pediatric oncology." Compassion provides for the possibility of the impossible, undertaking to heal an unhealable wound by—in this case—attempting to share this experience with other parents. The interviewer eases into the delicacy of a situation of unimaginable pain with "questions" that do not interrogate or objectify but create a space in which an unbearable suffering, an unspeakable pain, may find words. The words exchanged are gentle, sometimes hardly articulate, words that do not propose or defend theses, words from the heart, from broken hearts. As opposed to the cruelty of introducing a "statistic" about the divorce rate of parents who undergo this nightmare, a shattering number which threatens to crush the spirits of these courageous parents. In this interview we see what the philosophers call the "hermeneutic situation" in the concrete, glowing white hot and jumping off the pages of the philosophy books.

These authors work on the front line of situations where the only rule is that each situation is different. Hermeneutics is not a theory about how to engage in practice. If hermeneutics is a theory at all, it is a theory—which means a "seeing" (*theorein*, as in a theater)—of what we can't see coming, a foreseeing of the unforeseeability of what is coming in the singular situation. Hermeneutics is the theory that practice is not blind but already has its own kind of pretheoretical seeing—rather the way that it is the fingers of the pianist that "know" where the keys are and how to touch them. It is a theory, if it is a theory, about the limits of theory, what Derrida would call a "quasi-transcendental" theory. Unlike a transcendental theory, which lays out the conditions under which something is possible, hermeneutics is a theory that the most important things are possible only under conditions that make them impossible, like the impossible demands of this interview. It deals with limit cases, situations in which we run up against the most impossible things, where we must go where it is impossible to go. Only when we experience this paralysis may we dare proceed. Its greatest difficulty is that it will get too used to such extremes and begin to take the exceptional as business as usual.

Proceeding with the appropriate fear and trembling, understanding that hermeneutics is not a theory that we apply but a practice, they offer us various principles that are not quite principles. "Principles" are constructions drawn from the past whose predictive power depends upon the future being like the past. Principles unfold on the basis of the past, but they fold in the face of what they cannot see coming, of the unexpected. That is why we do not "apply principles to cases." We have the wisdom to know that principles, *principia*, which are sustained by the pretense that they come first (*in principio*), actually come last. Principles come after the fact, after experience has already taken place, and they will be sent scurrying back to the drawing board by the coming of what they do not see coming, by the next unexpected turn of events, by the singularity of something unforeseen—otherwise known as life, where the only preparation is to prepare to be unprepared!

Hermeneutics is wisdom. However postmodern hermeneutics may be, it is also a classical pre-modern wisdom. It goes back to Aristotle who posted himself at the door of ethics and warned all who were about to pass through: if you have come here in search of certainty, look elsewhere. If you come here in search of insurance to keep yourself safe from the "casualties" of concrete ethical life, you've come to the wrong place. Try that place down the street with "mathematics" marked on the door. In mathematics the ideal is the perfect (the perfect triangle is found only in ideal mathematical space) and the real is imperfect (no real triangular thing is ever perfectly triangular). But in ethics, the ideal, say, the definition of courage, is but an imperfect general schema, a finger pointing at the moon, while rising to the demands of the courage called for here and now, in this real and singular situation, is the perfect. Hermeneutics is what Aristotle called the practical wisdom (*phronesis*) which knows that only individuals exist, that individuals are not trimmed down versions of universals but the rich and concretely real, and that our commerce with the reality of singularities cannot be lit in advance by the luminosity of principles.

Hermeneutics is the art of judgment and judgment is the art of the concrete. The person of judgment, Aristotle's *phronimos*, has cultivated the art of discernment, of seeing into the singularity of the situation, into the unexpected demands of the singular, seeing what the situation is calling for, hearing what calls to us in this situation. In exercising a discerning judgment of this sort, we respond to what calls upon us, and we do so in the only responsible way. Hermeneutics is the maximization of responsibility. It recognizes what is called for in the idiosyncratic situation—as opposed to the flight from responsibility which simply follows the rules. What better way to excuse oneself from assuming responsibility than to say that we are only following the rules? "I wish I could do something for you. I sympathize with your situation. It's nothing personal. But I don't make the rules." What is more irresponsible than that? How much injustice has resulted from that? In hermeneutics we are, beyond being responsible to rules, responsible *for* the rules to which we respond.

The universality of hermeneutics means that such discernment is called for in every branch of life—not only in ethics, but in art where the artist is constantly experimenting with the previously untried, and in science which reaches its highest pitch in dealing with the scientific anomalies that throw the received theories into turmoil, and in the various vocations—which means "callings" of course—like the physician and the nurse, the teacher, the therapist, the social worker, the pastor, the judge and jurists. Hermeneutics is not a theory of knowledge but the art of life and death, and it ranges over the length and breadth and depth of life. Hermeneutics does not shy away from the difficulty of life but summons the courage to deal with life in all its ambiguity. Hermeneutics takes the risk of embracing the coming of what we cannot see coming.

To see what I mean, in the concrete, I urge you to keep reading.

John D. Caputo
Thomas J. Watson Professor of Religion Emeritus
Syracuse University
David R. Cook Professor Emeritus of Philosophy
Villanova University

Preface and Acknowledgments

This second edition of *Conducting Hermeneutic Research: From Philosophy to Practice* welcomes a new author to the original collaboration, Professor Theodore George. The original authors remain the same.

In this new edition, we have retained the basic content and structure as well as the original Foreword by John D. Caputo. The first edition was published in 2015 and in the ten years since publication by Peter Lang, we have developed our thinking and understanding, as well as been exposed to new literature and philosophy. We have developed meaningful collaborations with hermeneutic philosophers where we enlighten each other on the important links between philosophy and practice. Reflections of these experiences and connections are integrated throughout. By having a philosopher join us in authorship, we have expanded our philosophy chapters. We have also reconceptualized our chapter on method as this is where we are often questioned on how we distinguish our work from other methodologies such as descriptive phenomenology, interpretive description, interpretive phenomenological analysis (IPA), and thematic analysis.

We have completed many research studies and supervised multiple students who have conducted hermeneutic research guided by our book. We integrate our more recent research, and we proudly feature some of our recent former students' work here—Drs. Michael Lang, Katherine Webber, and Katherine Wong.

In these past ten years, we have also had the privilege of hosting the *Canadian Hermeneutic Institute* and learned from the expertise of philosophers such as Ted George, Walter Brogan, James Risser, David Vessey, and Dennis Schmidt as well as the many papers given by the attendees of our meetings. We cannot understate the relevance these meetings have to our philosophical appreciation of hermeneutics and our commitment to the action of applied hermeneutics in our practice professions of nursing and education. Similarly, our work with the *Journal of Applied Hermeneutics* has given voice to current research and thinking across disciplines. We are continually grateful to Professor Richard Kearney for suggesting the journal at the institute in 2011. Fourteen years of publications are his legacy as well as ours.

Finally, a note as the lead author for both editions of this book: It is meaningful to me that a new edition is being published this year as it will be the end of my teaching career. In July 2025, I start two years of scholarly leave, leading to retirement, and most significantly, I hand off the course I co-developed and taught since 2004, *Hermeneutic Research*, the course after which this book is fashioned. I taught many years of it with my co-author, Dr. Graham McCaffrey. It has been a source of absolute joy and sustainment, and I have learned far more than what I taught. It has been a privilege to teach and learn with so many students around their understandings of the philosophy of hermeneutics and how it can be embraced as a philosophical grounding of conducting excellent research that makes a difference in our human conditions of "living well with and for others in just institutions" (Riceour, 1992, p. 352). This research seeks, encounters, and strives for understanding the frail and human conditions of relationships, mortality, suffering, life, grief, birth, and love.

Professor Nancy J Moules, RN, PhD

Coming to Hermeneutics

... hermeneutics is a lesson in humility ... it has wrestled with the angels of darkness and has not gotten the better of them. It understands the power of the flux to wash away the best-laid schemes of metaphysics. It takes the constructs of metaphysics to be temporary cloud formations which, from a distance, create the appearance of shape and substance but which pass through our fingers upon contact ... and no matter how wantonly they are skewed across the skies there are always hermeneuts who claim to detect a shape ... a bear here, a man with a long nose there. There are always those who claim they can read the clouds and find a pattern and a meaning. Now, it is not the function of ... hermeneutics to put an end to those games, like a cold-blooded, demythologizing scientist who insists that the clouds are but random collections of particles of water ... its function is to keep the games in play, to awaken us to the play, to keep us on the alert that we draw forms in the sand, we read clouds in the sky, but we do not capture deep essences ... if there is anything that we learn in ... hermeneutics it is that we never get the better of the flux.

—CAPUTO (1987, P. 258)

This is a book about the conduct of hermeneutic research in applied disciplines. To describe this conduct is not an easy endeavor any more than is the actual practice of hermeneutic research. Caputo's quote above reminds us of the humility, darkness, flux, and playfulness of hermeneutics. Hermeneutics comes to us as researchers with a long history and ancestry based in philosophy that must first be acknowledged prior to discussing the application of this philosophy to research practice, thus the subtitle of this book—*"From Philosophy to Practice."* Hans-Georg Gadamer (1960/1997) suggested that we cannot step over our shadows; we are connected in a continuous thread with our past, with traditions, and with our ancestors, living out traditions that have been bequeathed to us by others. The echoes of history are always inadvertently *and deliberately* inviting us into both past and new ways of being in the present and, thus, we live in a world that recedes into the past and extends into the future. Rather than pitting ourselves against history, we therefore need to *remember, recollect*, and *recall* it.

Hermeneutic inquiry is a historical and living tradition of interpretation with a rich legacy of theory, philosophy, and practice. This legacy is being lived out differently in varied versions, understandings, and practices of hermeneutics as a research approach or method.

This book is not intended to be a treatise on the *right* way to conduct hermeneutic research but rather, to reveal fresh possibilities for research by weaving legacies of philosophy into practice. In it, we trace the shadows of hermeneutics, an ancestry that leads us to the philosophical hermeneutics of Hans-Georg Gadamer and more contemporary continental philosophers. This is a scaffolding of philosophy that guides us to articulate one possible way to conduct hermeneutic research in contexts of the applied disciplines.

What is Hermeneutics?

Hermeneutics is derived from the Greek verb *hermeneuein*, which means to say, translate, or interpret; the noun *hermeneia*, which is the utterance or explication of thought; and the name *hermeneus*, which refers to the playful, mischievous, "trickster" Hermes (Caputo, 1987, 2018; Grondin, 1994). In bringing the messages of the gods to humans, Hermes entices interpretation. Hermes has the character of complication, multiplicity, lies, jokes, irreverence, indirection, and disdain for rules; however, he is the master of creativity and invention. He has the capacity to see things anew and his power is change, prediction, and the solving of puzzles.

The practice of interpretation known as hermeneutics dates to seventeenth-century biblical and theological textual interpretation and has followed a changing course from rationalism to romanticism, pragmatism to philosophy, and conservatism to radicalization. The Latin word, *hermeneutica*, was introduced in the seventeenth century by the theologian Johann Dannhauer, and it has grown into different schools including the realms of the theological, juridical, and philosophical (Grondin, 1994).

Although it defies definition, in a nutshell, hermeneutics could be described as the tradition, philosophy, and practice of interpretation (Moules, 2002). Hermeneutics has been described as the practice and theory of interpretation and understanding in human contexts; the science, art, and philosophy of interpretation; and the "discipline of thought that aims at (the) unsaid life of our discourses" (Grondin, 1995, p. x). It is considered a reflective inquiry concerned with "our entire understanding of the world and thus … all the various forms in which this understanding manifests itself" (Gadamer, 1976, p. 18). Hermeneutics peers behind language; it ventures into the contextual world of a word, considering "what is said, what is uttered, but at the same time what is silenced" (Grondin, 1995, p. x). Gadamer (1960/1997) offered that the venture into the unsaid involves the speculative dimension in language, the mirroring of meanings, and the belief that the said is always in relationship with the unsaid: "we can understand a text only when we've understood the question to which it is an answer" (p. 370).

Hermeneutics involves recognition of sameness, place, and belonging. Hermeneutic interpretation comprehends the recognition that occurs when something rings "true" of what is said, there is familiarity, kinship, resonance, and likeness as well as difference. It is neither replication nor is it justification. It is an acknowledgment that things come from somewhere; they are not simply fabricated. However, along with sameness and recognition, hermeneutics requires a bringing forth and a bringing to language of something new. We work out this newness by working it into a world of relationships that can sustain it. In these relationships, others start to recognize not only something of themselves, but also of the world; they recognize something old and something new. "Hermeneutics is the art of understanding but also of making oneself understood" (Zimmermann, 2015, p. 54).

At the heart of hermeneutics is the idea of *aletheia*, which we will refer to several times throughout this book. A*letheia* is a Greek word meaning "the event of concealment and unconcealment" (Caputo, 1987, p. 115). *Aletheia* occurs when something opens that was once closed, when something reveals itself or is revealed. *Aletheia* is also connected to the word *Lethe*, which is a mythical river in Hades, when crossed, produces oblivion of the past; thus, it is called the "river of forgetting" (Hoad, 1986). *Lethe* also is tied to the word lethal. *Aletheia* works against what was dead bringing it to life; it remembers and unconceals what was forgotten or lost to the business and "work of simply getting by" (Wallace, 1987 p. 12). It recalls, enlivens, remembers, and reveals. The work of hermeneutics is the work of *aletheia* (Moules, 2015).

In its work of *aletheia*, hermeneutics often takes on a disruption of the clear narrative, always questioning those things that are taken for granted. In this sense, there is a deconstructive element to it but not in a traditionally deconstructive sense as in Foucauldian or Derridean deconstruction. Hermeneutics looks "underneath" what it is trying to understand, it embraces the underbelly of phenomena in the world but with the intention that the understanding it strives for is in the service of a reconstruction of our new knowing of the thing itself. In hermeneutics, there is a striking character of attention to the instance and the particular, rather than an effort to generalize. Interpretation is not a move to relieve the instance from its burden, and though things may be raised out of a strict burden of specificity (Smith, 1991). Rather, there is an effort to conserve the burden and to celebrate the "stubborn particular" (Wallace, 1987). Interpretation moves to represent the particular and to bring it to presence, not essence. Hermeneutics calls forth the ordinary and makes it stand out. In this standing out, however, it does not stand alone, but stands with its history, legacies, and relationships, acknowledging that there are both hidden and apparent traces which constitute and constantly change how something comes to exist. In the end, hermeneutics brings things back home to something that is recognizable and "true."

Paradoxically, hermeneutics is not particularly interested in itself, its own character, or self-definition. Rather, it is more concerned with the "question of human meaning and of how we make sense of our lives in such a way that life can go on … [it] works to rescue the specificities of our lives from the burden of their everydayness … [it] is about finding ourselves, which also, curiously enough, is about losing ourselves" (Smith, 1991, pp. 200–201). "Hermeneutics is less concerned with itself as a philosophy but in the ways we make sense of philosophy within living examples" (Moules, 2022a, p. 376). Gadamer reminds us that our work is about "bringing us before ourselves" (Gadamer, 1988/2016, p. 41).

> Human sciences rather belong to orders that constantly configure and reconfigure themselves through our own concrete participation in them and thereby contribute to our knowledge about the human possibilities and normative commonalities that affect us. Thus, the human sciences bring us before ourselves … Of all the sciences, it is especially the so-called human sciences that contribute the most to the nurturing of these capacities. They force us to confront constantly in all its richness the entire scale of what is human and all too human. (Gadamer, 1988/2016, p. 41)

In this sense,

> Hermeneutics (as a research method) is at its best when it disappears. The philosophy goes quiet and theoretical suppositions fade away. We are examining this topic not by looking at the experience for the sake of the experience, but to interpret it. (Moules, 2022b)

We start here with this claim: *Hermeneutics begins with the premise that the world is interpretable.*

A Brief Note on "Method" in Hermeneutic Inquiry: How We Pursue a Matter

> *Hermeneutics pits itself against the notion that human affairs can finally be formalized into explicit rules which can or should function as a decision-procedure … but … such a view does not throw us back into anarchy and chaos-although a little chaos is a good strategy … Our preoccupation with methodology needs to be replaced with a deeper appreciation of methodos, meta-odos, which is "the way in which we pursue a matter" … The concern with "method" so characteristic of modern science … makes science subservient to method, so that method rules instead of serving, constrains instead of liberating, and fails conspicuously to let science be. (Caputo, 1987, p. 213)*

This quote leads us to the difference we feel the book offers. We make a distinction in this book between the hermeneutic research method we propose and practice, and other methods that are often used in many disciplines A few of these that stand out are: descriptive phenomenology (Giorgi et al., 2017, who drew primarily on Husserl, 1977); interpretive description (Thorne, 2008); Interpretative Phenomenological Analysis (IPA) (Smith et al., 2021); hermeneutic phenomenology according to van Manen (1997) which involves a six step approach; reflexive thematic analysis (Braun & Clarke, 2019); and phenomenological hermeneutic research of lived experience, as taken up by the Swedish nurse researchers Lindseth and Norberg (2004), who have built their four part analysis method based on the philosophy of Ricoeur. In the research we describe here, we are primarily both grounded and freed by the philosophy of Hans-Georg Gadamer (1960/1997). We offer that generally phenomenology is focused on a thick and full description of experience, whereas hermeneutics is interested in the experience as well, but also in how we come to understand the experience, and (we cannot emphasize this enough) *this is through interpretation*. As Caputo reminds us:

> In hermeneutics, we defend the idea that there are no pure facts. Behind every interpretation lies another interpretation. We never reach an understanding of anything that is not an interpretation. We can never peel away the layers to get to some pure, uninterpreted, naked fact of the matter. No matter how loudly you proclaim you are just sticking to the facts, you are only raising the volume of your own interpretation. In hermeneutics, I like to say, interpretation goes all the way down. (Caputo, 2018, p. 4)

Hermeneutics, then, aims to wrest our knowledge and research from pregiven methods in favor of a return to an understanding of the things themselves. Hermeneutic research, like phenomenological research, turns on an attentiveness to our experience but Gadamer's decisive argument is that, precisely because we attend to our experience, what we experience remains opaque and in need of interpretation. Gadamer's hermeneutics departs from the position in classical phenomenology that, when we attend to experience, what appears becomes evident through simple analysis. Gadamer believes, by contrast, that what we experience requires more than simple analysis—it requires interpretation.

If we think of the phenomena we study as the topics we study, then, in hermeneutics, we are guided by, and tethered to, the topics we are investigating. Because different topics call for different approaches, the research may show as methodologically different for different studies. Hermeneutics, thus, offers a substantive philosophy rather than a strategic method to guide the research. In other words, one might say hermeneutics is substantively driven rather than methodologically given. We pursue a matter according to the matter; however, we always start with a phenomenon, something in the world—our topics—living, breathing things that require understanding. We claim that hermeneutics and phenomenology need each other but the difference is that hermeneutics knows this and phenomenology, taken up in the pure sense, does not (Moules, 2002).

> In hermeneutics ... we begin where we *already are*, in the world, up to our ears in an inherited culture, native language, etc. (factical life), not in order to root out but to get to the roots of our presuppositions, back to the living heart of our factical life. (Caputo, 2018, p. 37)

Although hermeneutics does not provide a strict method, it does not ask that we proceed without any guidance at all. This guidance, however, is characterized by different things than other research approaches. Gadamer (1960/1997) suggested that it is not possible to determine a way to proceed without being guided by the topic. At the beginning of interpretive work, there is necessarily a deliberate showing of questionableness, intentionally allowing the topic to guide the direction of the character of the work. This questionableness, however, does not mean that we respond tentatively, but rather that we proceed attentively, recognizing that hermeneutics is a practice of meticulous scholasticism. Although hermeneutics might have a tentativeness about its sense of certainty, it is not timid. It is, in fact, bold and courageous enough to take a "hermeneutic wager" (Kearney, 2010, p. xvii) in understanding. If we translate the notion of method into something of an inheritance, then method is simply a means of knowing one's way around a particular typography. For even though it is not a predetermined step-by-step method, one can cultivate hermeneutics and the questionableness becomes answering these kinds of questions: How can I turn my attention to human life and my topic and not require methods which render it to something else? How can I avoid betraying it and not delivering it unto itself? How do I preserve its character without reducing it? More than anything, hermeneutics is concerned with understanding not explanation.

Koch (1996) suggested that we attend less to method and more to methodology, which is "the process by which insights about the world and the human condition are generated, interpreted and communicated" (p. 174). Therefore, to address methodology means to claim a philosophical ground that guides our research, and which accurately reflects interpretive practices within its philosophical traditions. Given this groundwork, Koch offered that the soundness or rigor of a particular methodology lies in "excursions into the philosophical literature" (p. 175) that supports it. If we claim a tradition, we must be accountable to know it. We live in understanding and interpretation and no amount of measured techniques will save us from the task of interpretation. Hermeneutics has to do with the art of presentation, of drawing people into places where topics live, of making topics compelling, and of "restoring them to their original difficulty" (Caputo, 1987, p. 1). Restoring the difficulty, however, does *not* mean making it impossible to understand. In Chapter 4, we delve more into this idea of method and what it means to the conduct of hermeneutic research.

This Book

This book in its second edition continues to be a response to the question we are often asked as hermeneutic researchers and teachers: "How do I conduct a hermeneutic study?" We are not left abandoned by philosophy or science in hermeneutic research. There *are* ways to proceed in approaching a research topic hermeneutically and it is our belief that this book will serve as a guide and companion in the conduct of sound, rigorous, and valuable research.

In Chapter 2, we trace some of the historical development of hermeneutics, starting with Schleiermacher and working through Dilthey, Husserl, Heidegger, and Gadamer (whose philosophical hermeneutics will be discussed in greater depth in Chapter 3). Throughout, we reference contemporary continental philosophers such as John Caputo, Richard Kearney, Nicholas Davey, Jean Grondin, James Risser, Theodore George, and Dennis Schmidt. There is mention of both the Dutch and the French schools of hermeneutics, but our emphasis is on the German schools of philosophy.

Chapter 3 is focused on the tenets of Gadamerian philosophical hermeneutics and the implications of these tenets for the conduct of hermeneutic research.

In Chapter 4, we return to this complicated question of method, addressing the questionableness and complexity of it in a broader sense and particularly in hermeneutic research. Without being bound to a pre-set unbending method, we offer our ideas of what it means to be "on the trail" in our research endeavors.

Chapter 5 turns to a discussion of research topics and questions. "Hermeneutics begins when something addresses us" (Gadamer, 1960/1997, p. 299). We discuss how a researcher discerns a topic to be studied and, out of that discernment, develops an appropriate research question that will guide how the study will be conducted.

In Chapter 6, we discuss how one might approach recruitment of participants and then engage in the skilled art of conducting strong interviews. The fruitfulness of the analysis in hermeneutic research is highly dependent on the strength of the data collected. Data in this research approach very often arise in the form of unstructured research interviews that are then transcribed to text.

Chapter 7 focuses on the process and conduct of analysis in hermeneutic research, describing ways in which one engages with the data and arrives at interpretations, otherwise known as findings of the study.

Chapter 8 is in response to a frequent question we are asked by beginning hermeneutic researchers: What does good interpretive writing look like? In this chapter, we offer three examples of hermeneutic research (Lang, 2022; Webber, 2024; Wong, 2024). We briefly describe their studies and then include examples of their analyses, which take the form of interpretive writing. Since this is the heart of hermeneutic research and is a learned and practiced art that is often difficult for beginning hermeneutic researchers, we believe it is useful to provide examples of strong interpretive writing.

In Chapter 9, we discuss how one conducts hermeneutic research that has integrity and stands up to rigorous appraisal. Issues of validity, veracity, trustworthiness, and ethical conduct are examined.

Chapter 10 addresses the "so what" question of research. We write about the utility, actionability, and implications of applying the findings of a hermeneutic study to practice with a focus on what is "at stake" (Risser, 1997, 2012) in the research. We discuss issues of dissemination and knowledge transfer and translation.

We conclude with a final chapter, Chapter 11, which leaves the reader with an invitation to proceed with confidence and humility, tentativeness but not timidity in the conduct of hermeneutic research.

Summary

> *In the end ... hermeneutics does not lead us back to safe shores and terra firma; it leaves us twisting slowly in the wind. It leaves us exposed and without grounds, exposed to the groundlessness of the mystery ... this intractable mystery is the final difficulty that hermeneutics is bent on restoring. (Caputo, 1987, p. 267)*

Lethe, or the forgetting and concealment of the mystery, is the constant call to hermeneutics. Hermeneutics strives to keep itself open to the mystery, and it commits to be true to the movement back-and-forth that occurs in play. Hermeneutics aims to keep the play in play and to keep itself in the play while simultaneously trying to uncover what is hiding.

On the surface, hermeneutics can appear to have a charming, ebullient, and almost illiterate face, but there is a deep and long-standing tradition of literacy, rigor, and integrity beneath it. When something is not guided by a rigid procedural method or character, its strength and credibility then lies in its history and ancestry, in being citatious, in being literate, accountable to, and able to speak to these things with competence and grace.

In this book, we offer a way to proceed in the conduct of hermeneutic research as guided by Hans-Georg Gadamer's philosophical hermeneutics. We start with philosophy and end with application in practice, in the anticipation that the book will bridge a gap that is always calling us as hermeneutic researchers in applied disciplines—to make a difference in human lives and living.

References

Braun, V., & Clarke, V. (2019). Reflecting on reflexive thematic analysis. *Qualitative research in sport, exercise and health, 11*(4), 589–597. <https://doi.org/10.1080/2159676X.2019.1628806>

Caputo, J. D. (1987). *Radical hermeneutics: Repetition, deconstruction, and the hermeneutic project*. Indiana University Press.

Caputo, J. D. (2018). *Hermeneutics: Facts and interpretation in the age of information*. Penguin Random House UK.

Gadamer, H.-G. (1960/1997). *Truth and method* (2nd rev. ed.; J. Weinsheimer & D. G. Marshall, Trans.). Continuum.

Gadamer, H.-G. (1976). *Philosophical hermeneutics* (D. E. Lange, Trans.). University of California Press.

Gadamer, H.-G. (1988/2016). The history of the universe and the historicity of human beings. In *Hermeneutics between history and philosophy: The selected writings of Hans-Georg Gadamer Vol. 1* (pp. 25–41; P. Vandervelde & A. Iver, Trans.). Bloomsbury.

Grondin, J. (1994). *Introduction to philosophical hermeneutics* (J. Weinsheimer, Trans.). Yale University Press.

Grondin, J. (1995). *Sources of hermeneutics*. SUNY.

Giorgi, A., Giorgi, B., & Morley, J. (2017). The descriptive phenomenological method. In C. Willig & W. Stainton Rogers (Eds.), *The Sage handbook of qualitative research in psychology* (pp. 176–192). Sage.

Hoad, T. F. (Ed.). (1986). *The concise Oxford dictionary of English etymology*. Harper & Row.

Husserl, E. (1977). *Phenomenological psychology* (J. Scanlon, Trans.). Martinus Nijhoff Publishers. (German original, 1962)

Kearney, R. (2010). *Anatheism {Returning to God after God}*. Columbia University Press.

Koch, T. (1996). Implementation of a hermeneutic inquiry in nursing: Philosophy, rigour and representation. *Journal of Advanced Nursing, 24*, 174–184. <https://doi.org/10.1046/j.1365-2648.1996.17224.x>

Lang, M. J. (2022). *Emerging horizons: Crafting meaning and cultivating understanding through digital storytelling*. [Doctoral thesis, University of Calgary]. Open Theses and Dissertations. <https://prism.ucalgary.ca/handle/1880/100031>. <http://hdl.handle.net/1880/114093>

Lindseth, A., & Norberg, A. (2004). A phenomenological hermeneutical method for researching lived experience. *Journal of Caring Sciences, 18*, 145–157. <https://doi.org/10.1111/j.1471-6712.2004.00258.x>

Moules, N. J. (2002). Hermeneutic inquiry: Paying heed to history and Hermes. An ancestral, substantive, and methodological tale. *International Journal of Qualitative Methods, 1*(3), 1–21. <https://doi.org/10.1177/160940690200100301>

Moules, N. J. (2015). Editorial: *Aletheia*—Remembering and enlivening. *Journal of Applied Hermeneutics*, Editorial 2. <https://doi.org/10.11575/jah.v0i1.53255>

Moules, N. J. (2022a). Hermeneutic practice: What Gadamer has to teach nursing. In T. George & G.-J. van der Heiden (Eds.), *The Gadamerian mind* (pp. 376–386). Routledge.

Moules, N. J. (2022b). *Newly appointed UCalgary Nursing adjunct is faculty's first philosopher.* UToday, University of Calgary. <https://nursing.ucalgary.ca/news/newly-appointed-ucalgary-nursing-adjunct-facultys-first-philosopher>

Risser, J. (1997). *Hermeneutics and the voice of the other.* SUNY.

Risser, J. (2012). *The life of understanding: A contemporary hermeneutics.* Indiana University Press.

Smith, D. G. (1991). Hermeneutic inquiry: The hermeneutic imagination and the pedagogic text. In E. Short (Ed.), *Forms of curriculum inquiry* (pp. 187–209). SUNY.

Smith, J. A., Flowers, P. & Larkin, M. (2021). *Interpretive phenomenological analysis: Theory, method and research.* Sage.

Thorne, S, (2008). *Interpretive description.* Taylor & Francis

van Manen (1997). *Researching lived experience: Human science for an action sensitive pedagogy* (2nd ed.). The Althouse Press.

Wallace, B. (1987). *The stubborn particulars of grace.* McClelland & Stewart.

Wallace, B. (1987). Appeal. In B. Wallace, *The stubborn particulars of grace* (pp. 11–13). McCelland & Stewart.

Webber, K. M. (2024). *"Friendship or whatever it is": Understanding nurse-parent relational complexity in pediatric oncology contexts.* [Doctoral thesis, University of Calgary]. Retrieved from <https://doi.org/10.11575/PRISM/43578> Open Theses and Dissertations. <https://hdl.handle.net/1880/118735>.

Wong, K. L. (2024). *Listening to the voices of dying children: Art, metaphor, and silence.* [Doctoral thesis, University of Calgary]. Retrieved from <https://prism.ucalgary.ca> Open Thesis and Dissertations. <https://hdl.handle.net/1880/120285>

Zimmermann, J. (2015). *Hermeneutics: A very short introduction.* Oxford University Press.

A History of Hermeneutics

For researchers who come from practice disciplines, excursions into continental European philosophy can seem arcane and remote. Practice, after all, implies practicality, and at times impatience with anything perceived as too abstract. Gadamer (2007), however, saw hermeneutics as a practical philosophy since human life is inseparable from understanding, so that a philosophy of understanding itself has direct relevance to how people negotiate all aspects of their existence. Reaching back into the historical development of hermeneutics prior to Gadamer's work helps to understand his thought by identifying important currents of hermeneutic philosophy. Three such currents over the past two hundred years are language, history, and being. How do human beings achieve an understanding of themselves and other beings through language? How do they make sense of what they encounter in a world that is in constant flux, a world, and hence a self, which is historically constituted? These two questions are also central to hermeneutics-as-research, asking questions about complex human situations that emerge through practical involvement in language and in historical spaces. Hence it is worth taking a step back to see how language, history, and being have been taken up in different ways by hermeneutic thinkers and to see how contemporary developments are still part of a living tradition of ideas.

Hermeneutics evolved during the nineteenth and twentieth centuries from a discipline concerned primarily with theological texts, then texts more generally, then to the "human sciences" as a whole, and eventually to Heidegger's understanding of being itself as interpretation of our practical involvement in the world. Gadamer subsequently argued for hermeneutics as philosophy concerned with practice, which is where it becomes most obviously available as a source for research in practice disciplines.

In this chapter, we review some of the historical figures involved in the development of hermeneutics such that it has become a philosophy that can guide the conduct of research. We have chosen to follow a line of development leading up to the philosophy of Hans-Georg Gadamer, which is explored in more detail in Chapter 3. Our choice of this approach is admittedly at the expense of other influential figures whose work is explicitly phenomenological and hermeneutic or has influenced other hermeneutic thinkers. For example, van Manen (1997) is representative of the Dutch school of phenomenology who has described a hermeneutic phenomenological approach to research. Influenced by Heidegger, French thinkers developed ideas in phenomenology including Merleau-Ponty's working out of embodiment and Sartre's existentialism. Ricoeur is a major hermeneutic philosopher who brought other influences including structuralism and psychoanalysis into his thoughts. Gianni Vattimo developed a postmodern hermeneutics influenced by a distinctive interpretation of Nietzsche and Heidegger. Contemporary hermeneutic philosophers including John Caputo and Richard Kearney have been influenced by post-Heideggerian French thinkers, notably Derrida and Levinas, in examining deeply ways in which hermeneutics helps us respond to the voice of the other.

Schleiermacher: Hermeneutics and Understanding

Friedrich Schleiermacher (1768–1834) was a theologian, scholar of languages, and a philosopher. He is "properly regarded as the father of modern hermeneutics as a general study" (Palmer, 1969, p. 97). Schleiermacher believed that, in his time, hermeneutics consisted of a variety of specialized schools of interpretation, in theology or law for example, each of which had its own techniques applicable to a particular type of text. By contrast, he sought to establish a more basic and therefore more universal basis for hermeneutics. "Since the art of speaking and the art of understanding stand in relation to each other, speaking being only the outer side of thinking, hermeneutics is part of the art of thinking, and is therefore philosophical" (Schleiermacher, 1828/1990, p. 74). Grondin (1994) pointed out that universal theories of interpretation had already been put forward but marked Schleiermacher's hermeneutics as a new departure by complicating the work of understanding the world in the light of Kant. By separating phenomena as we perceive them from the unknowable "things in themselves," Kant's *Critique of Pure Reason* called into question the "belief in unproblematical, purely rational access to the world" (Grondin, 1994, p. 64) and created new questions about the relationship between subjectivity and objectivity. Schleiermacher wanted to work out a systematic basis for understanding across disciplines that would take into account the subjective workings of expression while also claiming objective validity. Accordingly, Schleiermacher's hermeneutics provides resources to develop "critical-normative" standards to help clarify what makes an interpretation legitimate, appropriate, or valuable (Gjesdal, 2009, p. 7).

It is not difficult to see the relevance of Schleiermacher's contributions to contemporary interpretive research which, in some quarters, risks summary dismissal as subjective as opposed to the supposed objectivity of quantifiable scientific knowledge. Midgely (2001) made an end-run around this question by the simple expedient of pointing out that in everyday human experience (whether that of a bench scientist or a poet), we move quite easily back and forth between the two positions. A nurse asking a patient to score his pain out of ten, for example, is well aware that one does not *feel* pain in numbered increments, and the unforced expression of pain, subjective yet instantly recognizable to others, sounds more like "Ow"! Hermeneutic philosophy includes ways of examining how it is that people coherently make sense of disparate kinds of knowledge and by deeply exploring meaning-making, it provides a firm basis for sound research.

Schleiermacher identified language as the common denominator behind different applications of hermeneutics. He saw understanding in language as made up of two elements: the expression of a thought by one person, and its reception and comprehension by another. The dialogical relationship is a crucial element for subsequent hermeneutics. It provides one response to the charge of subjectivity, since to be understood, expression has to take place on the grounds of a common language and frame of reference. Dialogue also becomes a trope of the research process, whether metaphorically between reader and text, researcher and disciplinary norms, or literally in interviews and often in the relational work that is a frequent topic of interest for interpretive researchers.

There are two kinds of interpretation in Schleiermacher's hermeneutics which work together with each other: the "grammatical" and the "psychological" (called the "technical" in his earlier work) (Palmer, 1969, p. 88). Psychological interpretation referred to the attempt to reconstruct the thought of a text's author. "By leading the interpreter to transform himself, so to speak, into the author, the divinatory method seeks to gain an immediate comprehension of the author as an individual" (Schleiermacher, 1828/1990, p. 96). Gadamer later cautioned that such an attempt at reconstruction leads to a dead end because, "What is reconstructed, a life brought back from the lost past, is not the original" (2004, p. 159) and can only have interest as spectacle, like a model of a historical figure in a wax museum. Grondin, however, asked, "is it really a mistake to inquire into the subject matter and intended truth that lie behind speech?" (1994, p. 73). The spirit of hermeneutic inquiry is in exploring what lies behind the surface of phenomena, while recognizing that any one source of insight does not stand alone, cut off from other tracks of meaning.

Grammatical interpretation recognizes that the meaning of words is not only a matter of dictionary definitions, but of the context in which they are used. Context includes both the ground of the language to which a word belongs and the whole work in which it is used. Hence:

> A word is never isolated, even when it occurs by itself, for its determination is not derived from itself but its context. We need only to relate this contextual use to this original unity in order to discover the correct meaning in each case. (Schleiermacher, 1828/1990, p. 89)

The grammatical part of interpretation, according to Schleiermacher, depends on the idea of laws governing language that are discoverable. The quotation above reflects such a claim to objectivity in the idea of "correct meaning," even though elsewhere Schleiermacher was much more conscious of the limits to interpretation and argued that hermeneutics started from the prevalence of misunderstanding rather than an assumption that clear understanding is the usual state of affairs.

"There is a more rigorous practice of the art of interpretation that is based on the assumption that misunderstanding occurs as a matter of course, and so understanding must be willed and sought at every point" (Schleiermacher, 1828/1990, p. 82). Schleiermacher's insistence on the primacy of *mis*understanding introduces an important theme into hermeneutics of the finitude, or necessarily limited nature of understanding. The inevitability of misunderstanding does not render understanding impossible or meaningless, only that it demands constant practice directed toward understanding better. In choosing topics for interpretive research, discussed in a later chapter, there is often a felt misfit between the taken-for-granted view of a belief or practice and the researcher's own experience. This discomfort, from which good questions often arise, is one manifestation of Schleiermacher's "misunderstanding."

Although he separated the grammatical and psychological for the purposes of explication and analysis, Schleiermacher saw the two kinds of interpretation as an interactive unity, stating "We must always hold the two sides of interpretation together" (1828/1990, p. 86). Dialectics is a recurrent principle in hermeneutic thought that lies behind the combination of interpretive approaches, as well as the importance of dialogue, and the concept of the hermeneutic circle. Dialectic reasoning goes back to ideas about formal argumentation in ancient Greek philosophy used to arrive at the truth of a statement. The basic back-and-forth movement of dialectics is retained in later usage. From the early nineteenth century onwards, however, dialectics is heavily influenced by Hegel's philosophy. He made use of dialectics as a way of accounting for disparate and conflicting elements of human life in a philosophical system—aiming to demonstrate how such elements comprised mutually conditioning, interdependent, and developmental relationships.

He also famously gave a dialectical account of change in history as the unfolding movement of spirit taking concrete form in political institutions (Forbes, 1975). Merriam-Webster (2014) gives definitions of "the Hegelian process of change in which a concept or its realization passes over into and is preserved and fulfilled by its opposite" and, more generally, "the dialectical tension or opposition between two interacting forces or elements." For our purposes, the important thing about the debts of hermeneutics to Hegelian dialectics is this: hermeneutic research; indeed, all of our efforts to understand, are generative, developmental, perhaps even creative. Understanding results from a back-and-forth process that allows an interpretive perspective to come into view in its clarity and validity. Sometimes, Hegel's conception of how the dialectical development of something is portrayed reductively—no longer as a dynamic process but as a merely mechanical-looking procedure. In this, Hegel's dialectic is depicted as a sequence of three steps that begins with thesis, or initial formation of ideas or practices, that is opposed to an antithesis, that is, an antithetical formation of ideas or practices, whose opposition, in turn, is superseded through their synthesis. In hermeneutics, though, the role of dialectics remains true to the dynamism of Hegel's idea which, as Forbes offers, may best be captured by Hegel's description of the Reichenbach Falls, as a "spectacle of 'free play'" (p. xiv).

Dialectical thinking occurs in various forms in Schleiermacher's work. He even placed it before hermeneutics in relation to dialogue: "Dialectics relies on hermeneutics and rhetoric because the development of all knowledge depends on both speaking and understanding" (1990, p. 74). Grammatical and psychological modes of interpretation rely on each other since individual authors express themselves within the laws of language that makes their work comprehensible in the first instance. Within the psychological mode, Schleiermacher made a further distinction between "a divinatory and a comparative [method]. Since each method refers back to the other, the two should never be separated" (1990, p. 96). Divinatory refers to the interpreter gaining a sense of the author as an individual and the comparative to seeing the author as a representative of a type. Altogether, dialectic for Schleiermacher was "the art of mutual understanding" (Grondin, 1994, p. 73) since the way through misunderstanding lies in sharing ideas with others in order to invite new points of view.

Any discussion of dialectics within hermeneutic philosophy has to include the hermeneutic circle, which is another recurrent concept in the history of hermeneutics from before Schleiermacher onwards and was later taken up by Heidegger and Gadamer. Friedrich Ast (1778–1841), an immediate forerunner of Schleiermacher, saw the hermeneutic circle as a mutual movement between part and whole. For Ast, the whole constituted the unified spirit (*Geist* in German) of a culture in which individual works existed. The spirit as a whole could only be understood by studying it through individual works, and the particular works only came into their full meaning as expressions of the whole (Palmer, 1969). Schleiermacher's contribution was to take the idea of movement between part and whole and to remove the dimension of Ast's grand scheme of unity of spirit. More humbly, in grammatical interpretation, the whole is the genre to which a particular work belongs, and on the psychological side, it is the total life of the author (Grondin, 1994).

Schleiermacher's hermeneutics was innovative in seeking to elucidate the process of understanding itself rather than beginning with texts to be interpreted. His work then focused on the concern to establish standards for interpretations, the importance of language as the medium of understanding, on dialogue as a way of extending understanding, and the hermeneutic circle as a metaphor for understanding works in relation to the context of their production.

Dilthey: Hermeneutics as Methodology

Later in the nineteenth century, two more themes became prominent in the development of hermeneutics. One was the question of historicism and the other the problem of method introduced by Wilhelm Dilthey (1833–1911). Both these currents remain significant for hermeneutics and have implications for research.

Historicism is the idea that phenomena have to be understood in relation to their own time. Human values or belief institutions are not static, and what is normative in one time and place might make no sense in another (see, for e.g., Beiser 2011). It is not the job of a modern historian to pass moral judgment on the ancient Romans, for example, but to try to understand their world as a culture with its own horizons of social norms, ethics, religious beliefs, economic structures and so on. For most people, this is now probably an unexceptional idea. It becomes problematic, however, when the logic of historicism is extended to our own time, rendering our own horizons of cultural meaning contingent and relative against the temporal movement of history. Jean Grondin framed the problem as questions: "Doesn't everything dissolve into present-day perspectives and temporal conditionedness?" and "How, if at all, is it possible to escape from the hermeneutic circle of our historicity?" (1994, p. 77).

One solution for thinkers in the nineteenth century was to look for a unifying principle of reason in history, so that particular events took on a meaning that transcended the context of their own era. In this way, history was seen as a story of human moral progress so that the distinctiveness of different times could be recognized but only in relation to a bigger picture of "humanity's steadily increasing consciousness and awareness of itself" (Grondin, 1994, p. 83). In the twentieth century, after two world wars and the rise of totalitarian political systems, the sense of assurance about historical progress was severely thrown into question, and later thinkers such as Gadamer had to approach historicism in more circumspect ways. For now, however, the salient point is that understanding took on a historical dimension that moved beyond Schleiermacher's focus on the author and the text.

Historicism leads in turn to methodological concerns by raising the question of how to place history and, by extension, the other human sciences on a secure foundation of objective knowledge like the natural sciences. The rapid progress of science and technology in the latter half of the nineteenth century made the relation between the natural sciences and other disciplines a matter of concern for contemporary thinkers. Nietzsche characterized the problem with the image of a double-brain:

> …a higher culture must give to man a double-brain, as it were two brain ventricles, one for the perceptions of science, the other for those of non-science: lying beside one another, not confused together, separable, capable of being shut off; this is a demand of health. (1882/1986, p. 119)

For Dilthey, the distinction between human and natural sciences lay in the inclusion of inner experience, of thoughts, emotions and will in the subject matter of the former (Palmer, 1969). Another way of making the distinction was that the natural sciences were about *explaining* phenomena and the human sciences about *understanding*, establishing meanings of manifestations of human life and culture. The former was objective, standing outside phenomena whereas the latter had to have both objective and subjective aspects. Dilthey attempted to articulate a methodology of the human sciences around "a procedure based on the systematic relation between life, expression, and understanding" (Dilthey, quoted in Palmer, 1969, p. 107). Hence, it was Dilthey who introduced the expression "lived experience" (Dilthey, c.1900/1990, p. 149) to describe the formation of meaning across time by making connections between disparate events. "Life consists of parts, of lived experiences which are inwardly related to each other. Every particular experience refers to a self of which it is a part; it is structurally interrelated to other parts" (p. 151). There is another movement between parts and whole in this recursive relationship between moments of experience and the continuing self that ascribes meaning to them.

The other terms of Dilthey's system follow from this account of life as experience. "Expression" referred to outward manifestations of experience, not only as works of art but as all kinds of cultural forms including law, language, and institutions. In this sense, the human sciences could lay claim to an objective basis since they have these outward, concrete expressions of life as their objects of study. "Understanding," Dilthey's third term, went beyond the usual sense of cognitive sense-making to encompass a deeper apprehension of life, including the experience of another person (Palmer, 1969) through the medium of expressions.

Dilthey's attention to lived experience and the insight that forms of cultural expression could be a conduit to interrelated meanings are important stages in the development of hermeneutics. What delimited his thought, however, was his purpose of trying to establish a methodological foundation for the human sciences. The claim to objectivity came unstuck with his emphasis on the inner aspects of consciousness and of understanding another's lived experience.

The Human Sciences: A Note

"Human sciences" is the English translation most commonly used in hermeneutic literature for the German word *Geisteswissenschaften*. Since human sciences is not a term in common usage in English, it is worth pausing to consider the complexities of the translation, and the applicability of the term to a practice discipline like nursing that historically has no academic standing at all.

Wissenschaft is the German word for science, but it "remains unquestionably broader, as it corresponds to the collective pursuit of knowledge kinds" (Babich, 2009, p. 106). Although science in English has a general meaning, derived from Latin *scientia* meaning knowledge (Barnhart, 1988, p. 968), it has increasingly come to refer primarily to the natural sciences and to scientific method. It is used predominantly in this sense, for example, in public debates in English speaking countries about atheism and religion. *Wissenschaft* to German speakers contains the common root verb *wissen*, to know, and "retains connotations of the 'ways' or conduits of knowing" (Babich, p. 106). Thus, in German, *Wissenschaft* refers broadly to many kinds of knowledge achieved (or pursued) by careful, rigorous, methodical, systematic means.

Wissenschaft is at least equivalent to science, if not exactly, but the first part of the compound noun, *Geist*, does not mean human and is normally translated as "spirit." Thanks to Hegel, for whom historical progress was the self-realization of *Geist*, it is a term that pervades German philosophy and confounds English readers. We are probably most familiar with the German word from *Zeitgeist*, which has entered the English lexicon as shorthand for "spirit of the times." *Geist* also has connotations of mind or consciousness so that for Hegel (1975), "Man is active within [spirit]; and whatever he does, the spirit is also active within him" (p. 44). Dilthey (1990) adopted the term from Hegel, stating "how significant the objective mind [*Geist*] is for the possibility of knowledge in the human studies" (p. 155). The editor of the anthology from which this quotation is taken noted, "Dilthey employs Hegel's term *objektiver Geist* to denote the intersubjective products and creations of human culture as constituted by systems of law or economics, political and social institutions or natural languages" (Mueller-Vollmer, 1990, p. 164).

This comes closer to the idea of "human sciences," historically referring to disciplines such as theology, philology, history, and law that are concerned with human cultural phenomena and would overlap with the humanities and social sciences. Contemporary practice disciplines such as nursing, education, and social work, however, do not fit comfortably into these more traditional categories. Nursing entertains a chronic anxiety about its identity, as science, art, or hybrid. Even then, the terms are contested, and the discipline invites disparate kinds of knowledge from more definitely scientific or humanities sources (McCaffrey, 2020). For hermeneutics, ambiguity is not so much a problem of failed definition as the beginning of possibility for understanding. Resistance to categorization is an asset because the reality of being in the world "lies in its inescapable *existence*, deeper than all its specific properties. We are struck by the world, we care about it. We are implicated in it" (Harman, 2013, p. 43). The indeterminacy of the term human sciences in English is an opportunity to recognize opportunities to take up different areas of knowledge including the arts and humanities. What we think of as academic disciplines in languages, literature, history, religious studies, fine arts, and performing arts all present avenues to deeper understanding of problems arising in human life.

Husserl: Phenomenology and the Turn to the Lifeworld

Edmund Husserl's (1859–1938) work provides a bridge between developments in hermeneutic philosophy in the nineteenth and twentieth centuries. Although not a philosopher of hermeneutics as such, he is credited with developing the first coherent formulation of phenomenology with "conceptual tools unavailable to Dilthey or Nietzsche" (Carman, 2006; Palmer, 1969, p. 124). Like Dilthey, Husserl formulated a response to the increasingly assertive claims of the natural sciences to hold a monopoly on objective, trustworthy, and valuable access to knowledge about the world. Husserl's contributions to phenomenology provided a philosophical framework that has been both appropriated and critiqued within subsequent developments in hermeneutics, and philosophers recognize that the debts of hermeneutics to phenomenology result in difficult, if productive, tensions between the two fields and key figures within the fields (Dostal, 2022; Marion, 2013; Romano 2015).

Husserl's rallying cry was "to the things themselves" (Husserl, 1900, 1901/2001, p. 168; Steeves, 2006) denoting a renewed attention in philosophy to the question of everyday human experience and how to understand it in a rigorous way. It represented Husserl's desire to return the ground of philosophy and inquiry to a direct acquaintance with phenomena, through painstaking attention, careful description, and a rigorous kind of analytic reflection which he described as *phenomenological reduction* or the *epoche*. He asserted the possibility of knowing the world as it is, in which case phenomenological knowledge as he called it would provide the foundation for other kinds of knowledge, including the scientific. Any experiment, for example, designed to produce new knowledge is predicated upon previous assumptions of knowing what things are, in order to be able to organize them into a systematic process.

The term phenomenology captures his focus on phenomena of human knowing, whether through sense perception, memory, or imagination. Husserl was thus interested in the role of human consciousness in all forms of knowing. Early critics of his work accused him of recycling philosophical idealism, but he was clear that he distinguished between phenomenological knowing of things-in-the-world and knowing products of the mind independent of immediate sensory input. Husserl responded to his critics in his preface to the 1931 English translation of his book *Ideas* (1931/2012), which was first published in German in 1913. "Our phenomenological idealism does not deny the positive existence of the real world and of Nature" (p. xlii) and "the real world indeed exists, but in respect of essence is relative to transcendental subjectivity, and in such a way that it can have its meaning as existing reality only as the intentional meaning-product of transcendental subjectivity" (p. xliii). For Husserl, it made no sense to choose between realism or idealism and his philosophy was dedicated to working out what he meant by "transcendental subjectivity," or what it is for human beings to know the world.

Intentionality

Intentionality is a basic theme of Husserl's phenomenology, "the unique peculiarity of experiences to be 'the consciousness *of* something'" (Husserl, 1931/20122012, p. 171). Thus, it follows, depending on the nature of the "something," that "perceiving is the perceiving of something, maybe a thing; judging, the judging of a certain matter; valuation, the valuing of a value; wish, the wish for the content wished, and so on" (p. 171). Intentionality is what binds us, inescapably, to the world and constantly provides meaning. Note, this is not intentional in the conventional sense of making a conscious effort but rather is a meaning-making inherent in all our thoughts and perceptions. Once Husserl established the idea of intentionality to describe the way in which humans are primordially committed to a world of meaning (not necessarily to particular values or rationality—a nihilistic belief that life is meaningless, or a state of psychotic mental chaos are still forms of "meaning" as kinds of human experience) he elaborated how it is that we can place knowledge of experience on to a philosophical—and according to Husserl, a scientific—basis.

The Natural Attitude and Phenomenological Method

Husserl distinguished the natural attitude, which is our normal everyday awareness, from the phenomenological attitude, which permits a systematic, deliberate analysis of phenomena. From the natural standpoint:

> I am aware of [a world], that means, first of all, I discover it immediately, intuitively. I experience it. Through sight, touch, hearing, etc., in the different ways of sensory perception, corporeal things somehow spatially distributed are *for me simply there*, in verbal or figurative sense "present," whether or not I pay them special attention by busying myself with them, considering, thinking, feeling, willing. (Husserl, 1931/2012, p. 51)

In order to study the world of phenomena, however, it is not enough simply to go on experiencing things without subjecting them to sustained attention, which requires the phenomenological method. Husserl's phenomenology required a process of reduction, of taking away everything extraneous, by which phenomena could become known in their essence. Rather than constructing and testing hypotheses, formulating cause and effect explanations, or building models and theories, as science is wanting to do, Husserl thought that, through a careful method of peeling back the layers of appearances, one could get to the true nature of things: stable invariant *essences*, manifested as unchanging characteristics and/or structures. This conception of the way the world is, and Husserl's life-long dream of establishing a singular, unified science, one that would account for all knowledge, locates him squarely in the spirit of Western thinking, a lineage easily traced from Plato through Descartes and Kant (Madison 1977).

Essence

Eidos is a Greek word meaning essence that Husserl used to denote the essential qualities of an object, the distinguishable characteristics that make a thing recognizably itself and not something else. "*The essence (Eidos) is an object of a new type. Just as the datum of individual or empirical intuition is an individual object, so the datum of essential intuition is a pure essence*" [italics in original] (Husserl, 1931/2012, p. 12). This conception of essence is important to understand, in the first place to follow Husserl's idea of "eidetic reduction" and then to see some of the ways that his students, Heidegger and Gadamer, diverged from his phenomenology.

The essence of a thing (which can be an object of experience, perception, memory or even the imagination), following from the idea of intentionality, is bound up with human consciousness. Husserl gave the example of a tree, which could be reduced to its chemical elements, but that would not reveal the essence of the tree as such since, "the meaning—the meaning of this perception, something that belongs necessarily to its essence—cannot burn away; it has no chemical elements, no forces, no real properties" (Husserl, 1931/2012, p. 187). Although this sounds antithetical to the reductionism of the natural sciences at one level, Husserl was also trying to place phenomenology on a scientific footing. His insistence on the purity of essences required a method of knowing things as separate and stable, which he called the eidetic, or phenomenological reduction.

Phenomenological Reduction and Bracketing

Reduction was the term Husserl used for the process of consciously setting aside extraneous factors to arrive at the essence of a thing, just as in the culinary sense of the word a cook reduces a sauce by boiling away superfluous liquid. The goal is "the absolutely faithful description of that which really lies before one in phenomenological purity, and in keeping at a distance all interpretations that transcend the given" (Husserl, 1931/2012, p. 188). To move from the "thesis" of the natural attitude to a phenomenological attitude, "the thesis undergoes a modification—while remaining in itself what it is, *we set it as it were 'out of action,'* we *'disconnect it,' 'bracket it'*"[italics in original] (p. 57). Thus, presuppositions about experience are put out of play, including the findings of the natural sciences, which still belong to the natural attitude. Bracketing therefore implies both a rational agent who is confident in knowing the range and limits of his or her presuppositions, and that objects of whatever kind are sufficiently distinct to stand out once the natural attitude is stripped away.

The following example may help to give some idea of what Husserl was getting at with his phenomenological way of seeing applied to a tree:

> "In" the reduced perception (in the phenomenologically pure experience) we find, as belonging to its essence indissolubly, the perceived as such, and under such titles as "material thing," "plant," "tree," "blossoming," and so forth. The *inverted commas* are clearly significant; they express that change of signature, the corresponding radical modification of the meaning of the words. The *tree plain and simple*, the thing in nature, is as different as it can be from this perceived tree as such, which as perceptual meaning belongs to the perception, and that inseparably. [Italics in original] (Husserl, 1931/2012, p. 187)

One observation is that it is probably easier to illustrate phenomenological reduction using an example of a discrete object, like a tree, than an experience-in-the-world, which is more often the object of research. Contemporary phenomenologists, who have addressed research practice have argued that bracketing is a concept with a narrow philosophical meaning that is not relevant or useful to research (Carel, 2016; Zahavi & Martiny, 2019).

The Lifeworld

The main principles of Husserl's phenomenology are laid out in his earlier work, but he introduced one further important concept as late as 1936, the *Lebenswelt* or "lifeworld" (Føllesdal, 2005, p. 424). The idea of the lifeworld was a further working out of the idea of the natural attitude, of the world of everyday things and experiences. The lifeworld conveys the sense of unthinking immersion in the world, in the way that we pass through a door without stopping to think about the door-ness of the door, its mechanism, its history, or its symbolism. Husserl wrote that, "The lifeworld … is always there, existing in advance for us, the 'ground' of all praxis, whether theoretical or pretheoretical. The world is pregiven to us …" (cited in Føllesdal, p. 425). The idea of the lifeworld more clearly delivers a sense of the world as connected experience, of meanings combined into a flow of being and functioning in the world. Husserl also used the lifeworld concept to link back to science, by explaining that scientific knowledge too has to derive meaning from a prior givenness of a world in which knowledge becomes possible at all.

Madison (1990) referred to this contribution by Husserl as "the great archeological-hermeneutic discovery: the *Lebenswelt*" (p. 40):

> The *Lebenswelt* is nothing other than the immediate flow of un-reflective life, the ground out of which arises all scientific thematization and theorizing. It is the world as we actually live it (what Heidegger called "factical life"), a world which therefore precedes the Galilean and modern distinction between subjective and objective … It is the *prescientific* world of lived experience upon which all scientific constructs are based, and which they necessarily presuppose… The "objective" world of science is but an *interpretation* of the world of our immediate experience, the life-world, which transcends all objectivistic and subjectivistic categories. (p. 44)

The lifeworld provides hermeneutics with its phenomenological base, which, once Heidegger critically appropriated Husserl's concept of the lifeworld, is grasped with Heidegger's successor-concept of *being-in-the-world*.

Phenomenology and Hermeneutics

Phenomenology brings to hermeneutics a philosophically robust way of trying to articulate everyday life and experience. In this, it is a product of its time, recognizing a need to find rigorous ways of understanding the human experience of living in the world, which the pure logic of positivism and even the great advances in the natural sciences of the nineteenth century simply could not address. In one sense, Husserl worked to substantiate Nietzsche's typically terse assertion that, "the great problems are to be encountered in the street" (1881/1982, p. 78). In the introduction to *Ideas*, Husserl wrote, "We shall start from the standpoint of everyday life, from the world as it confronts us…" (2012, p. 3). Perhaps it is the second part of this sentence that betrays the underlying scientific outlook that still affected Husserl's work. The world confronts us, requiring methods of examination that will bring it to understanding in the unambiguous light of human reason. Palmer (1969), placing Husserl into the context of hermeneutics, pointed out the very different attitudes toward science between him and his student, Heidegger "which seemed to follow logically from the earlier training of the former in mathematics and the latter in theology" (p. 6).

Heidegger: From Phenomenology to Hermeneutics

Martin Heidegger (1889–1976) was a "star" student and apprentice of Husserl, who took phenomenology in a radically different direction and went on to become one of the most influential philosophers of the twentieth century, publishing his magnum opus of *Being and Time* in 1927. Heidegger's project was to bring the ontology of the subject into the "experience of something." Removing the brackets, Heidegger acknowledged that "we are in the matter and not simply enclosed in ourselves" (Gadamer, 1984, p. 59). For Heidegger, experience was already out in the world; experience is not a thing, but a movement in the world. As a result, understanding is deeply entrenched in the profound ontological makeup of *Dasein*: care, existence, temporality, and being (Heidegger, 1927/1996). Heidegger identified *Dasein*, or being-in-the-world, as a thereness of being that is distinguished by the capacity for self-reflection; people are situated in, and constituted by, their worlds.

Gadamer (1984) took up from Heidegger the notion that interpretation is never an isolated human activity, but something enacted through an experience: "we are always taking something *as* something" (p. 58). Heidegger (1927/1996) maintained that human life is not given to us as a phenomenon which requires our explication, but as a question, an address, as something which is revealing and concealing, coming and going, present absent, a thrownness—and the work of hermeneutics is entering into the interpretation of these things.

Heidegger did not believe that we can establish direct primitive contact with things "underneath" interpretation but rather was devoted to a disciplined form of paying attention and to using language carefully to describe the rich, nuanced, layered, and relational character of life as it is lived. This remains a central commitment of hermeneutic work today. Husserl's concept of the "lifeworld" provided Heidegger a hermeneutics with a phenomenological base. Unlike Husserl and Hegel's concern about that which appears in consciousness, though, Heidegger regarded the lifeworld not as being grounded in transcendental subjectivity but rather as a matter of *being-in-the-world*. As such, his work was committed to staying as close as possible to examining practical life and ascribing to *phronesis*, practical wisdom, as the form of knowledge arising from experience that undergirds hermeneutic phenomenology.

Heidegger, Understanding, and Truth

Heidegger distinguished between two kinds of truth. This distinction is important, for it is Heidegger's second kind of truth, truth as disclosure or unconcealment *(aletheia)* that we are after in hermeneutic work (Davey, 2006). The traditional sense of truth involves the discovery of some fact about the world, and Heidegger did not deny that this kind of truth exists or is not important in our lives (Wrathall, 2011). Heidegger described this sense of truth as a matter of correctness. However, without a deep sense of connectedness and purpose, such correctness about the facts in themselves is meaningless. Hoy (2006) arrived at this with this explication of what Heidegger meant by truth as disclosure:

> The contrasting term (to factual truth) "disclosedness" (*Erschlossenheit*) suggests that the total context is opened up through understanding. Understanding thus does not consist only of making assertion about the world, but also of grasping the entire mode of being-in-the-world. Understanding grasps the world as such, without which the discovery of particular features of the world would not be possible ... the isolated, atomistic discovery of one fact after another would not generate and understanding of the world that was significant and intelligible, but only of a disconnected aggregate. An interpretation is precisely not a heap of facts, but an account of how these facts are *possible*. (p. 184)

The world does not exist, as Heidegger pointed out, as a thing or a set of things, but as an event, an event we must participate in to understand through language (Heidegger, 1927/1967; Wrathall, 2013). This is the fundamental difference between Husserl and Heidegger (Wrathall, 2013): this move from the world as a set of things with fixed properties or essences, to the world as a set of interrelated and layered events that happen to us, that in turn, are revealed to us through our practical involvement. It represents Heidegger's radicalization of phenomenology, and the end of foundational notions of being and understanding, as well as Husserlian idealism (Ricoeur, 1981). No longer were things "given in consciousness," as Husserl had posited, but rather existed as *beings in motion*, in a world in motion, beings constantly being made, unmade and remade, in a world undergoing the same kind of ceaseless constitution and reconstitution. It is not enough to reflectively analyze what we find in given to us in our consciousness; rather, what is called for is to interpret ourselves, things, and others, as we participate in the complex movement of the world. The character of our being in the world also gave hermeneutic understanding its "unquiet" nature (Davey, 2006), or as Gadamer would say "doomed" understanding to be constantly caught up in the play of question and answer.

Heidegger set thinking in motion, so to speak, and tied it inseparably to action in the world. At the same time, he tore it loose from Cartesian science and neo-Kantian constructivism:

> ...a concept is not a schema, but rather a possibility of being, of how matters look in the moment, i.e., is constitutive of the moment—a meaning drawn out of something-points to a for-having, i.e., transports us into a fundamental experience-points to a foreconception, i.e., calls for a how of addressing and interrogating. (Heidegger, 1923/1999, p. 12)

Heidegger also placed the ground of hermeneutic inquiry "inside" phenomena themselves, that is, there were no two separate entities, "things to be investigated" and "methods to be applied," but living phenomena that addressed us, revealing in their address how to inquire, and the path to understanding that opened in their appearance.

> What is revealed in it (the phenomenon) is how the *anticipatory leap forward and running in advance* should be undertaken and can only be undertaken. The anticipatory leap forward: not positing an end, but reckoning with being on the way, giving it free play, holding fast to *being possible*. (Heidegger,1923/1999, p. 12)

To repeat a little differently, because it is tantamount to conducting hermeneutic research:

> ... *phenomenon* means the constant preparation of *the path to be travelled*. This thematic category has the function of a critical, cautionary guidance of seeing... (Heidegger, 1923/1999, p. 60)

Therefore, when we say that hermeneutics is committed to the phenomenon, and not a predetermined method, we do not mean that anything goes, or as Heidegger (1923/1999) would say, it is not something simply given in advance, nor is it something arbitrary. A "phenomenon" is a dynamic composite of material objects and environments, and embodied, meaning-seeking human beings.

We are addressed by possibilities for inquiry in the experience of the phenomenon itself. Again, these exist as possible beginnings, not as given, as Husserl believed, and not as full-blown procedures, as science believes. Both must be worked out *in practice*, that is, in the practice of understanding, in the ceaseless revealing and concealing of truth, and in the dialectic of question and answer. What is required in the beginning on our part is what Heidegger (1923/1999) called a "radical wakefulness," a holding out for possibility, and a "whiling" or living with a phenomenon in a state of "questionableness" (Heidegger 1923/1999, p. 62).

Heidegger and the Hermeneutic Circle

It was Heidegger who made the decisive connection between phenomenology and hermeneutics in his exploration of Dasein as a state and process of having to make sense of the world in which we find ourselves. He did not pursue hermeneutics as a dedicated theme, but it appears early in *Being and Time* as one of his starting points for his own revaluation of phenomenology. "Our investigation itself will show that the meaning of phenomenological description as a method lies in *interpretation*" (Heidegger, 1962, p. 61, italics in original). Heidegger's best-known reference to hermeneutics is in regard to the hermeneutic circle. This was not a new term, having been used since the nineteenth century in textual hermeneutics to refer to reading a text by understanding one part in reference to the whole, or one work in reference to its context. Reading interpretively thus involves a dialectical movement where greater understanding of each part of a text can emerge in light of its place within a larger work, and at the same time, understanding of the whole work shifts in light of each part. Heidegger took up the sense of dialectic back-and-forth and absorbed it into his hermeneutical phenomenology to mean not just studying a text but making sense of the world as we live as part of it. However, Heidegger was not suggesting this remains at the level of a natural, involuntary process, like breathing in and out, but that it gives us opportunity to actively interpret the world. "It is not to be reduced to the level of a vicious circle, or even of a circle which is merely tolerated … our first, last, and constant task is never to allow our fore-having, fore-sight and fore-conception to be presented to us by fancies and popular conceptions, but rather to make the scientific theme secure by working out these forestructures in terms of the things themselves" (p. 195). Here one can see how Heidegger is still working within phenomenology, by his attention to the things themselves. However, he was asserting that we always, necessarily, bring to bear prior assumptions of various kinds in what we make of those things. We are not trapped by those assumptions, because the back-and-forth between ourselves and the world opens up space for working out, for reflective attention to what is going on, even while we are part of the picture. Heidegger's conception of the hermeneutic circle is a crucial link between his philosophy and the full development of philosophical hermeneutics by Gadamer, as we will discuss in Chapter 3.

After Heidegger

Heidegger's work has inspired many thinkers who came after him, certainly after *Being and Time* in 1927. We devote the next chapter to the way Gadamer picked up his clues about hermeneutics and developed a dedicated philosophy of how it is we understand things at all, and how we can understand anew. In this section, we briefly introduce other thinkers in the phenomenological and hermeneutic tradition who have influenced researchers in practice disciplines.

Maurice Merleau-Ponty was a French philosopher best known for his attention to embodiment as our primary mode of contact with the world. Heidegger's Dasein never attains the feel of the flesh-and-blood creatures we are. Heidegger, in response to Husserl, recognized that the meaning of things is disclosed to us not through reflective analysis of what is given in our consciousness but through our concrete being-in-the-world. However, as Merleau-Ponty's approach suggests, Heidegger did not take his breakthrough far enough; concrete existence is much more concrete than Heidegger himself described it to be. "Heideggerian Dasein has no real sense of a living body: Dasein does not eat, sleep or have sex" (Kearney, 2010, p. 88). Merleau-Ponty (1945/2012) set out to make our embodied existence central to his phenomenology. Husserl observed that we know the body in two ways, as object and as lived self. He used two German words to make the distinction, *Leib* and *Körper*, where *Leib* refers to the lived body, as we know our own bodies subjectively and in constant contact with the world, and *Körper* to the objective body that can be measured and considered externally (Carel, 2016). His insight was extended by Merleau-Ponty and has since been taken up by numerous phenomenological thinkers. Havi Carel (2016), for example, is a contemporary phenomenologist who has written about illness, using her own experience of a severe progressive lung disease. Carel adds refinements to the two-way distinction by noting that we can consider our own body objectively (for e.g., monitoring one's own heart rate while exercising), and that although clinicians are concerned with *Körper*, they also relate to patients with a second-person (I-you) perspective that personalizes the objective dimension.

Another development building from Merleau-Ponty's work is in the interdisciplinary field of embodied cognition. Derived from phenomenology and neuroscience, this body of thinking known as enactivism has a view of cognition as distributed through the sensing body, and in constant interaction with the environment (Gallagher, 2017; Varela et al., 2016). Authors in health disciplines have begun to explore its possible applications to how clinicians and patients make sense of their physical, emotional, and social experience of illness (McCaffrey, 2024: Stilwell & Harman, 2019).

Richard Kearney (2015), a contemporary philosopher, coined the term "carnal hermeneutics" to link embodiment to interrelated modes of physical and cultural sense-making. He argued that hermeneutic thought has drifted too far into seeing language as the ultimate field of interpretation, at the expense of our primordial way of knowing the world through the senses. He pointed out the multiple meanings of the word "sense," beginning with our five physical senses, and then our interpretive orientation to our environments, physically, cognitively, socially, and culturally.

Another work of Kearney's that belongs to the hermeneutic tradition and has resonance for researchers in applied disciplines is his book, *Strangers, Gods and Monsters* (Kearney, 2003). He explored the moment of encounter with the other, drawing on an array of philosophical, religious, and literary sources to draw out the complexity of working out what to do in the face of a stranger. For applied disciplines, that invariably require constant interactions with others, in settings that already set up expectations like schools and hospitals, Kearney's work has valuable insights.

Kearney was a student of Paul Ricoeur, a French philosopher and along with Gadamer, the other major figure in developing the possibilities of hermeneutics in the late twentieth century. Ricoeur and Gadamer arrived at hermeneutics independently of each other around the same time, in the early 1960s (Grondin, 2014). They were both influenced by Heidegger, seeing understanding and interpretations as integral to human life. They both emphasized the role of language and the way in which our understanding is fundamentally shaped by our historical situation. There are differences in emphasis, however. Ricoeur was more interested in how understanding happens and held on to a more sympathetic interest in methods of interpretation (Grondin, 2014). Ricoeur advocated for a hermeneutics of what he called a "long route" that began with Heidegger's hermeneutical phenomenology of existence but that included considerations of the contributions made to our understanding of existence by the many and often conflicting interpretations of the human condition found across disciplines and other areas of philosophy (Ricoeur, 1974, p. 6). At different points in his extensive writings, this led him to discuss the importance of symbol, metaphor, and narrative, as well as institutions, and textual structures for working out understanding (Kearney, 2004). In his treatment of narrative, he stressed the role that storytelling, for example through emplotment, can help us mark out, organize, and clarify the meaning of our temporal experience (Ricoeur, 1985–88).

Ricoeur made far greater use of mediators in his phenomenology of understanding. These included the figures of Marx, Freud, and Nietzsche, who all in their way questioned our certainty in our transparency to ourselves, by pointing out how we are influenced by our socio-economic or class position, our unconscious drives, and our will to power respectively. These "masters of suspicion" figured in Ricoeur's "hermeneutics of suspicion" (Ricoeur, 2013, p. 8) which was a way of opening up interpretive space around texts or our own understandings of them. Grondin (2014) pointed out that this hermeneutics of suspicion was always in dialectical play with a hermeneutics of trust; the goal was always to secure a more robust understanding of truth, not to undermine any possibility of truth. The play between reading of surface and hidden meanings occurs again in Ricoeur's (1986/2008) work on reading texts. Unlike Gadamer, he was influenced by structuralism, looking to explain the structure of a text as one step in understanding. He distinguished "between a naïve interpretation and a critical interpretation, between a surface interpretation and a depth interpretation" (p. 160). Ricoeur's dialectic of explanation and understanding has been taken up as an analytic tool by Scandinavian researchers using an approach they call "lifeworld hermeneutics" (Palmér et al., 2024).

Ricoeur's hermeneutics, leading through symbols and history is always concerned with how meaning is created socially. The title of his book about textual interpretation is entitled *From Text to Action* (2008), recognizing that understanding is not an interior, private experience but part of what determines how we choose to act in the world. In a later work about selfhood as a social and ethical hermeneutic process, he commented on how our social relations in modern life are often instantiated in institutions (Ricoeur, 1992). The theme of institutions as shaping our possibilities, and limits, for understanding is an important one for applied hermeneutic research which invariably takes place within highly structured institutions where complex social demands for healthcare, education, social support, or justice are met (how effectively they are met, or appropriately, for whom, or from whose point of view are all good hermeneutic questions). The hermeneutic significance of institutions is emphasized by John Caputo, a contemporary hermeneutic philosopher. He takes this up from the point of view of the institutional setting for any interaction between a professional practitioner and client, be it clinic, classroom, consulting room, or courtroom. "Interpretation is not a free-floating, immaterial spirit. It is stubbornly stuck in the glue of institutional life…" and "Events do not take place in mid-air; they happen in institutional settings" (Caputo, 2018, p. 220).

These quotations come from Caputo's 2018 introduction to contemporary hermeneutics which includes a chapter dedicated to applied hermeneutic research.

He eloquently captures the flesh-and-blood buzzing of experience through which we all navigate the world, while not ignoring how this is necessarily entangled with scientific objectivity and its encompassing material effects in technology. "Hermeneutics describes the experiential world that is running all the time, beneath the radar of rules, algorithms and objectifying knowledge…" (Caputo, 2018, p. 233).

Summary

In this chapter, we have traced the development of hermeneutics as a distinct strand in philosophy, which evolved partly in response to the growth in the power of science during the nineteenth and twentieth centuries. The combination of a hermeneutic tradition extending the reach of interpretation beyond texts, and of phenomenology centering primary human experience had enormous effects on how we can think about interpretation. Inspired by Heidegger, there have been many different though related ways of exploring interpretation. Having noted some of the significant thinkers in this tradition in the next chapter we focus on Hans-Georg Gadamer's philosophical hermeneutics.

References

Babich, B. E. (2009). Nietzsche's "gay" science. In K. Ansell-Pearson (Ed.), *A companion to Nietzsche* (pp. 97–114). Wiley-Blackwell.

Beiser, F. (2011). *The German historicist tradition*. Oxford University Press.

Caputo, J. D. (1987). *Radical hermeneutics: Repetition, deconstruction and the hermeneutic project*. Indiana University Press.

Caputo, J. D. (2018). *Hermeneutics: Facts and interpretation in the age of information*. Pelican.

Carel, H. (2016). *Phenomenology of illness*. Oxford University Press.

Carman, T. (2006). The principle of phenomenology. In C. Guignon (Ed.), *The Cambridge companion to Heidegger* (pp. 97–119). Cambridge University Press.

Davey, N. (2006). *Unquiet understanding*. SUNY.

Derrida, J. (1978). *Spurs: Nietzsche's styles* (B. Harlow, Trans.). University of Chicago.

Dostal, R. J. (2022). *Gadamer's hermeneutics: Between phenomenology and dialectic*. Northwestern University Press.

Dilthey, W. (1990). The hermeneutics of the human sciences. In K. Mueller-Vollmer (Ed.), *The hermeneutics reader* (pp. 148–164). Continuum.

Føllesdal, D. (2005). Husserl, Edmund. In E. Craig (Ed.), *The shorter Routledge encyclopedia of philosophy* (pp. 415–427). Routledge.

Forbes, D. (1975). Introduction. In G. W. F. Hegel, *Lectures on the philosophy of world history: Introduction* (pp. vii–xxxv). Cambridge University Press.
Gadamer, H.-G. (1984). The hermeneutics of suspicion. In G. Shapiro & A. Sica (Eds.), *Hermeneutics: Questions and prospects* (pp. 177–193). MIT Press.
Gallagher, S. (2017). *Enactivist interventions: Rethinking the mind*. Oxford University Press.
Gjesdal, K. (2009). *Gadamer and the legacy of German idealism*. Cambridge University Press.
Grondin, J. (1994). *Introduction to philosophical hermeneutics*. Yale University Press.
Grondin, J. (1995). *Sources of hermeneutics*. SUNY.
Grondin, J. (2014). Do Gadamer and Ricoeur have the same understanding of hermeneutics? In M. Xie (Ed.), *The agon of interpretations: Towards a critical intercultural hermeneutics* (pp. 43–64). University of Toronto Press. <https://doi.org/10.3138/9781442696303-004>
Habermas, J. (1990). *The philosophical discourse of modernity* (F. G. Lawrence, Trans.). Yale University Press.
Hegel G. W. F. (1975). *Lectures on the philosophy of world history: Introduction*. (H.B. Nisbet, Trans.). Cambridge University Press.
Heidegger, M. (1927/1962). *Being and time* (J. Macquarrie & E. Robinson, Trans.). HarperCollins.
Heidegger, M. (1927/1996). *Being and time* (J. Stambaugh, Trans.). SUNY.
Heidegger, M. (1929/1999). *Ontology—The hermeneutics of facticity*. University of Indiana Press.
Hoy, D. (2006). Heidegger and the hermeneutic turn. In C. Guignon (Ed.), *The Cambridge companion to Heidegger* (pp. 177–201). Cambridge University Press.
Husserl, E. (2001). *Logical investigations* (Vol. 2) (D. Moran, Ed., 2nd ed.). Routledge. Original work published in 1900/1901.
Husserl, E. (2012). *Ideas: General introduction to a pure phenomenology*. (W. R. Boyce-Gibson, Trans.). Routledge. Original work published in 1931.
Kearney R. (2003). *Strangers, gods and monsters*. Routledge.
Kearney, R. (2004). *On Paul Ricoeur: The owl of Minerva*. Ashgate.
Kearney, R. (2010). *Anatheism: Returning to God after God*. Columbia University Press.
Kearney, R. (2015). The wager of carnal hermeneutics. In R. Kearney & B. Treanor (Eds.), *Carnal hermeneutics* (pp. 15–56). Fordham University Press.
Madison, G. B. (1977). Phenomenology and existentialism: Husserl and the end of idealism. In F. Elliston & P. McCormick (Eds.), *Husserl: Expositions and appraisals* (pp. 247–268). Notre Dame University Press.

Madison, G. B. (1988). *The hermeneutics of postmodernity: Figures and themes*. Indiana University Press.
Marion, J.-L. (2013). *Givenness & hermeneutics*. Marquette University Press
McCaffrey, G. (2020). *Nursing and humanities*. Routledge.
McCaffrey, G. (2024). Enactivism: Embodied cognition, sense-making, and nursing. *Nursing Inquiry, 2024; e12672*. <https://doi.org/10.1111/nin.12672>
Merleau-Ponty, M. (2012). *Phenomenology of perception* (D. A. Landes, Trans.). Routledge.
Merriam-Webster. (2014). *Dialectic*. Retrieved from <http://www.merriam-webster.com/dictionary/dialectic>
Midgley, M. (2001). *Science and poetry*. Routledge.
Mueller-Vollmer, K. (Ed.). (1990). *The hermeneutics reader*. Continuum.
Nietzsche, F. (1982). *Daybreak: Thoughts on the prejudices of morality*. (R. J. Hollingdale, Trans). Cambridge University Press.
Nietzsche, F. (1986). *Human, all too human: A book for free spirits* (R. J. Hollingdale, Trans.). Cambridge University Press.
Palmer, R. E. (1969). *Hermeneutics*. Northwestern University Press.
Palmér, L., Nyström, M., & Karlsson, K. (2024). Lifeworld hermeneutics: An approach and a method for research on existential issues in caring science. *Scandinavian Journal of Caring Sciences (38), 200–209*. <https://doi.org/10.1111/scs.13201>
Ricoeur, P. (1981). *Hermeneutics and the human sciences: Essays on language, action and interpretation*. Cambridge University Press.
Ricoeur, P. (1985–88). *Time and narrative*. University of Chicago Press.
Ricoeur, P. (1992). *Oneself as another* (K. Blamey, Trans.). The University of Chicago Press.
Ricoeur, P. (2008). *From text to action: Essays in hermeneutics, II* (K. Blamey & J. B. Thompson, Trans.). Continuum.
Ricoeur, P. (2013). *Hermeneutics: Writings and lectures, volume 2*. (D. Pellauer, Trans.). Polity Press.
Romano, C. (2015). *At the heart of reason*. Northwestern University Press.
Schleiermacher, F. D. E. (1990). Foundations: General theory and art of interpretation. In K. Mueller-Vollmer (Ed.), *The hermeneutics reader* (pp. 72–97). Continuum.
Steeves, H. P. (2006). *The things themselves: Phenomenology and the return to the everyday*. SUNY.

Stilwell, P., & Harman, K. (2019). An enactive approach to pain: Beyond the biopsychosocial model. *Phenomenology and the Cognitive Sciences, 18*, 637–665. <https://doi.org/10.1007/s11097-019-09624-7>
van Manen, M. (1997). *Researching lived experience: Human science for an action sensitive pedagogy*. The Althouse Press.
Varela, F., Thompson, E., & Rosch, E.. (2016). *The embodied mind: Cognitive science and human experience*. MIT Press.
Wrathall, M. (2001). *Heidegger and unconcealment: Truth language and history*. Cambridge University Press.
Wrathall, M. (2013). *The Cambridge companion to Heidegger's Being and Time*. Cambridge University Press.
Zahavi, D., & Martiny, M. M. (2019). Phenomenology in nursing studies: New perspectives. *International Journal of Nursing Studies, 93*, 155–162. <https://doi.org/10.1016/j.ijnurstu.2019.01.014>

Gadamer's Philosophical Hermeneutics

Hans-Georg Gadamer (1900–2002) was one of the leading hermeneutic philosophers of the twentieth century, who took up linguistic and ontological themes from Heidegger to work out a thoroughgoing philosophy of how it is that human beings come to understanding. He drew on earlier developments in hermeneutics and on Heidegger's ideas about how human being-in-the-world is itself interpretive to develop a complex philosophical hermeneutics. One of Gadamer's distinctive contributions was his emphasis on dialogue as a means of addressing difference. "Stylistically and substantively, the difference between their two modes of thought is the difference between a meditative thinker (Heidegger) and a dialogical one (Gadamer)" (Dostal, 2002, p. 247). Gadamer's hermeneutics not only incorporates an account of changing understanding but also leads us to expect it. Indeed, Gadamer argued that to understand something always means to have come to understand it "in a *different way*" (Gadamer, 2013, p. 307). It is perhaps Gadamer's focus on how understanding changes that partly explains how it is that his philosophy has been so readily adapted to research in practice disciplines.

Gadamer was born in 1900, the year Nietzsche died, and the year Freud first published the *Interpretation of Dreams*. He was born into Imperial Germany, saw its collapse in 1918, then the Weimar Republic, the Third Reich, communist East Germany, democratic West Germany and in the last twenty years of his life German re-unification. He experienced the extraordinary technological advances of the twentieth century, for example in transport, communications and medicine, and among the effects of which have to be counted Hiroshima and Treblinka. His work can be seen against this background as a deeply humane project to articulate the very possibility of understanding in the face of ideological and technological threats to individual life and expression in shared social spaces.

Our intent in this chapter is to introduce a number of significant concepts in Gadamer's work that have a bearing on all that follows in later chapters about the conduct of research. By examining a series of concepts in the light of our particular application, we have lost the architecture of his major work, *Truth and Method*. We hope that what we have sacrificed in structural cohesion we have gained in clarity and focus on the purpose of this book. What follow is—it hardly needs saying in this context—our interpretation. There is, of course, no substitute for reading Gadamer's own work, which has been extensively translated into English and first we offer a brief guide to some of the available works.

Guide to Gadamer's Work

Gadamer's major work is *Truth and Method*, which first appeared in German in 1960 when he was 60 years old. He formally retired from the University of Heidelberg in 1968, but lived until 2002 and continued to publish, teach, and attend conferences up until the last couple of years of his long life (Grondin, 2003b). Consequently, he had many years to reflect on his account of hermeneutics, respond to critics, refine his ideas, and communicate them to numerous audiences.

Truth and Method is a long, dense philosophical work but is by no means as difficult to penetrate as Heidegger's *Being and Time*. It is divided into three parts, pursuing the theme of coming to a truth about something in understanding. Part one is concerned with truth "as it emerges in the experience of art" (Gadamer, 2004, p. 1) since art is a locus of social and historical meaning, even though accessed subjectively. Part two takes up truth in the human sciences, including Gadamer's account of his predecessors including Schleiermacher, Dilthey, Husserl, and Heidegger. The third section draws on Heidegger's language ontology to concentrate on language as "the medium of hermeneutic experience" (Gadamer, 2004, p. 384).

Other works translated into English consist mostly of collections of papers and lectures that were written after the appearance of *Truth and Method*. Gadamer stuck closely to his central project of hermeneutics, so the benefit to the reader of these later works is that they often focus on particular aspects or applications of the ideas in *Truth and Method* (see, for e.g., Gadamer, 1977, 1981, 1996, 2007). His later writings also include important engagements with critical theory (see for e.g., Gadamer 1981b, 1990) and deconstruction (see for e.g., Gadamer 2007). One volume of note to researchers in health-related fields is *The Enigma of Health* (1996), which collects writings about the problems of negotiating technology and humanist concerns in health care. A more recently published major collection is *The Gadamer Reader* (2007), which contains many well-translated pieces organized clearly around themes including language, aesthetics, and hermeneutics as practical philosophy. A good introduction to Gadamer's philosophy is the short book *Gadamer in Conversation* (2001). It is, as it says in the title, a collection of transcribed conversations in which Gadamer responds to questions about his work, often explaining it with refreshing directness. Of note too are the books edited and translated by Pol Vandevelde and Arun Iyer entitled *Hermeneutics Between History and Philosophy: The Selected Writings of Hans-Georg Gadamer, Volume 1* (2016) and *Ethics, Aesthetics and the Historical Dimension of Language: The Selected Writings of Hans-Georg Gadamer, Volume II* (2022). A collection of works that pertain to Gadamer and his influence exist in *The Gadamerian Mind* edited by Theodore George and Gert-Jan Van Der Heiden (2022).

We note, as well, that although nothing should replace reading Gadamer's original work, there is a decided advantage to reading, too, the work of others who have studied, and in some ways extended, Gadamer's philosophy. In this regard, we refer to the work of Donatella di Cesare (2013), Nicholas Davey (2006, 2013), Jean Grondin (1994, 1995, 2003a, 2003b), Georgia Warnke (2002), Richard Palmer (1969), James Risser (1997, 2012), Rod Coltman (1998), Dennis Schmidt (2008, 2012a, 2012b, 2015, 2016), or Charles Taylor (2002) to name a few.

Concepts of Gadamer's Hermeneutics

We begin this section with three fundamental aspects of Gadamer's philosophy, his assertion of the universality of hermeneutics, and then the intrinsically historical and linguistic aspects of understanding. The third of these includes brief discussions of conversation and questions, two kinds of language that have special bearing on research interviews. The subsequent sections introduce concepts by which Gadamer explained the working out of understanding in human life, among the exigencies of historical and linguistic being.

Universality and Finitude

Gadamer made a bold claim for hermeneutics as universal and also stressed the finitude, or incompleteness of understanding. Clarifying how these two claims relate to one another serves to introduce Gadamer's distinctive hermeneutic philosophy and to position it in within the context of the contemporary landscape of research in practice disciplines.

Gadamer maintained that hermeneutics involves a claim to universality because everything we encounter, even the things we are already familiar with or take ourselves to know well, remain always in need of being understood. Accordingly, in hermeneutics, what is universal is first and foremost the hermeneutic "problem," namely, that the need to interpret is ubiquitous (Gadamer 2007b). Universality is the focus of the final section of *Truth and Method*, and it refers to the point that understanding happens in language and that this "points to a universal ontological structure" (Gadamer, 2004, p. 470). To live in a world of meaning in the first place is to live in a world that is understood and interpreted through language. For Gadamer, this does not mean that things do not exist until they are put into words but that "[t]he speculative mode of being of language has a universal ontological significance" (p. 470). It is not the verbalization of this or that object of experience that points to universality, but the basic intelligibility of the world for human beings. Understood in this way, universality clearly does not imply special knowledge or lay claim to any particular truth about the world. In fact, the opposite is true, since the interpretability of the world implies that, "the knowledge of experience will be foreign to all dogmatism" (Grondin, 2003a, p. 118).

Understanding-in-language presents a horizon of infinite possibility—not as a system of signs that can be endlessly reorganized but as "an act that is linguistically creative and world-experiencing" (Gadamer, 2007, p. 87). Precisely because language as such is endlessly proliferative, any given word, statement, text, or interpretation is finite within the world of meaning. Finitude provides one of the compositional principles of hermeneutic work. As a researcher, one has to start somewhere and one has to finish somewhere, while the life of the topic—already present before the researcher arrived—continues on beyond each interpretation.

In *Truth and Method* and the 1965 lecture, *The Universality of the Hermeneutical Problem* (in Gadamer, 1977 & 2007), Gadamer addressed what he meant by universality in relation to science and technology. He drew a distinction between the internal logic of science, its adherence to method and striving for objectivity, and the historical fact that science too exists within "the great horizon of the past, out of which our culture and our present live, influenc[ing] us in everything we want, hope for, or fear in our future" (Gadamer, 2007, p. 82). While science and technology will continue to produce new knowledge and have powerful effects on our lives, that is not the same as concluding that scientific method must therefore be the sole recourse to answer questions arising from human life. Rather, the very power of science has a distorting effect because the onrush of scientific progress leaves its own presuppositions "half in the dark" (p. 83). Using the example of statistics, Gadamer observed that, "what is established by statistics seems to be a language of facts, but which questions these facts answer and which facts would begin to speak if other questions are asked are hermeneutical questions" (p. 84).

Scientific research, properly conducted, may be objective but the questions it addresses are "always already" implicated in networks of historical and value-laden meaning. Jean Grondin glossed this aspect of Gadamer's thought:

> In stressing the universality of the hermeneutic aspect, Gadamer's fundamental idea is to mark the limits of objectivizing thought, which seeks to gain a hold on the being, for the purpose of domination. So that there is no mistake, this objectification is indispensable in science. But science has acquired an authority and a monopoly so uncontested in our civilization that we have come to think that all knowledge, all relationship to being, resorts to objectification. (Grondin, 2003a, p. 149)

Unlike some postmodern critiques, Gadamerian hermeneutics is not about undermining scientific knowledge in itself, nor relativizing it, but establishing a context of human understanding in which science occupies a significant space, but not the whole space. Prior to—and present with—the method-governed realm of science is the *Lebenswelt*, the human home of being, meaning, and language. The argument from universality thus provides an answer to the questions: why hermeneutic research, and why in practice disciplines that are often heavily dependent on science and technology, yet (so far) continue to be conducted and sustained within networks of human relationships? These relationships, in the hermeneutic reading, "draw for their intelligibility on our ordinary understanding of what it is to be a human agent, live in society, have moral convictions, aspire to happiness, and so forth" (Taylor, 2002, p. 131). Taylor made the point that there is an intellectual divide between those who do find important questions that can only be answered "at this level of cultural difference" (p. 129) and those who believe in the goal—if they think they have not already got there—of securing an account of what it is to be human at a basic, pre-cultural level. Against this dichotomy, hermeneutic researchers often find themselves having to articulate firmly, if not defend, the basis for their work.

History—"Historically Effected Consciousness"

Understanding has a temporal dimension, which is central to Gadamer's hermeneutics. If interpretation can only ever enter into a conversation that is already going on—there has to be something already there to interpret—then good interpretation attends to the history of the topic. Not only that, but we are in the flux of history, under the multifarious influences of our time and place. We can conscientiously do our best to clarify our understanding from within the flux, but what we cannot do is step out of history into a "view from nowhere." Hermeneutics consequently demands respect for historical awareness, which is again in contrast to the scientific and technological outlook of linear progress whereby old hypotheses can be rendered obsolete, and next year's model is always promised to be better than this year's.

Gadamer's (2004) term for such historical awareness is "historically effected consciousness" which is "primarily consciousness of the hermeneutical *situation*" (p. 301, italics in original). Being within our own historical horizon sets another condition of finitude:

> The illumination of this situation—reflection on effective history—can never be completely achieved; yet the fact that it cannot be completed is not due to a deficiency in reflection but to the essence of the historical being that we are. (p. 301)

We can never fully catch ourselves as the historically effected beings that we are because to do so would require a separate point of view. Understanding again is partial in relation to the field of possibility, and also partial because things change in time. Not only do events keep happening, but we (both in the personal sense and as members of larger, cultural units) are also moving and changing so that our position in relation to events is forever becoming, rather than static.

Related to his idea of historically effected consciousness, Gadamer placed great emphasis on tradition—a position that has left him with a lingering, if undeserved, reputation as a conservative thinker. His point was not that tradition ought to be venerated simply because it is tradition, but that we are fooling ourselves if we think we can simply discard tradition and start from a blank slate. Given that understanding is effected historically, it is only when we achieve some awareness of the traditions of which we are already a part that we can begin to evaluate them and think clearly and critically about where to go next.

> Tradition as conceived by philosophical hermeneutics is not just a stock of inert ideas or values but a manner or style of becoming critically engaged with (and thus continuing if not extending) the influence of a set of questions or subject matters. (Davey, 2006, p. 53)

Approaching a topic of research historically does not therefore mean writing a history of it (though it could), but of establishing a context for the terms of understanding by which the researcher, and readers, can enter into a fresh understanding. McCaffrey, for example, studied therapeutic relationships in mental health nursing. This is by no means a new topic, going back at least to Hildegaard Peplau's work in the 1950s. The persistence of the topic in the literature, with similar themes of advocacy and resistance among nurses, suggested an important interpretive avenue when finding nurses in the research interviews talking about working alongside colleagues with dramatically different approaches to care. Keeping in mind the historical dimension, however, acted as a caution against jumping to any ready conclusions about "fixing the problem" and helped to reframe questioning about what perpetuated an apparent division about therapeutic relationships. For example, there is a thread in the literature of exhortation, of advocating that nurses in acute care should work in a more consciously therapeutic way. Clearly however, the persistence of the theme itself reveals that there have been, and continue to be, other forces at work that inhibit or resist the practice of therapeutic relationship. Reading the literature in the light of this historical understanding led to questions about how competing forces play out in both nurses' attitudes and social environments. "We learn something about ourselves, about the meaning of being human, when we study history; indeed, when we study any of the humanities. The fusion of horizons is a third thing, neither the past nor the present but something new, something that has not and could not have existed before" (Caputo, 2018, p. 103).

Language and Linguistic Being

Language is fundamental to Gadamerian hermeneutics, as discussed above, because it has the universal significance of being the air that understanding breathes. Language, in Grondin's (2003a) phrase, has an "uncanny nearness" (p. 123). Its nearness is its universality, and it is uncanny because it remains unstable and carries within it, reminders of its limits, of insecurity and possibilities of meaning breaking down. (Uncanny = *unheimlich* in German, a Heideggerian word with the root *Heim* which means "home"—language has the naturalness of being at home and yet is filled with possibilities of uneasiness and interruption. Think how many horror films revolve around the home that turns out to be full of uncanny events that turn the security of home upside down). There is an important distinction between the projection into the possibility of understanding and the finitude of actual expression and understanding:

> knowledge lives in everybody who speaks when he looks for the *mot juste*—to know the word which can reach the other—but it always knows at the same time that it has not completely found it. The wanting-to-say, the intention, always goes above or slantwise to, what can be truly encircled by a language or in words that go to rejoin the other. (Gadamer, cited in Grondin, 2003a, p. 129)

Language impels toward understanding in the face of its limits, even because of its limits that always leave understanding incomplete. Gadamer recognized that there are parts of human experience that are not immediately linguistic, including sensory experiences such as viewing an artwork or listening to music. He argued, however, against the Kantian view of aesthetic experience as a privileged and separate form of experience. The impact of a painting is primarily visual, of course, and yet it only makes sense as an experience in relation to the dense fabric of meaning that the viewer brings to the experience related to the meaning woven into the work. One reason why certain artworks persist and take on the mantle of a masterpiece is that they forever run ahead of definition and interpretation—but not for any lack of trying. If we invoke, as an example, the Mona Lisa (by its name, note), readers can instantly bring to mind an impression of the painting, but not without some association of Leonardo da Vinci, or the Renaissance, or perhaps the Louvre, or an opinion of the work. By introducing aesthetics at the start of *Truth and Method*, Gadamer established the idea of interpretation as a mode of being that animates the human world, linguistically and ceaselessly.

Movement is a vital characteristic of language for Gadamer, which leads to a caution against too great an insistence upon conceptual or terminological fixity. Even in philosophy:

> The words that carry its concepts ... are not firm markers and signals through which something can be univocally designated, as in the systems of symbols in mathematics and logic and their applications ... They originate in the communicative movement of human interpretation of the world, a movement that takes place in language. (Gadamer, 2007, p. 66)

Similarly, technical terms with well-defined applications serve a narrow purpose, but "in the highly artificial form of terminology we encounter only the ossified crust of the living stream of thinking and speaking" (p. 67). The tension between these two approaches to language surfaces in presenting hermeneutics to audiences who are used to, perhaps unquestioningly, expecting language to behave like a mechanical symbolic system. Usually, it is incumbent upon the hermeneutic researcher to choose his or her words carefully, explaining what is, after all methodical, rational, and rigorous about this approach.

Conversation

Perhaps the most distinctive of Gadamer's ideas about language, and the most obviously relevant to research, is the central place he gives to conversation: "All living together in community is living together in language, and language exists only in conversation" (Gadamer, 2001, p. 56). Conversation is a natural, social form of the open dialectic that lets new understanding appear as each one speaks—and more importantly, listens—to the other. Setting out the structural potential of conversation in this way obviously does not mean to say that all conversations are mutual and productive. Gadamer was laying out the conditions for understanding, not describing a general phenomenon that applies to every actual conversation. He specified that in "every true conversation ... each person opens himself up to the other [and] truly accepts his point of view as valid" (Gadamer, 2004, p. 387).

He differentiated genuine mutuality from situations such as a therapeutic interview in which the participants' roles and the pregiven purpose of the exchange prevent the possibility of "genuine" (Gadamer, 2004, p. 385) conversation. This has implications for research interviews in which the researcher is in the position of asking questions of the participant in the name of a previously established topic and goal. Since Gadamer never wrote about hermeneutics with this kind of application in mind, here is a point where we offer our own interpretation. One of the characteristics of genuine conversation is that both participants find themselves subordinated to the flow of the conversation itself, so that it is the subject matter that leads. We discuss this in more detail in Chapter 6, but wish to state here that, in spite of the researcher's intent and guidance, in successful interviews, there is a lively interchange in which the researcher becomes both attentive listener to the other as well as self-conscious questioner. The structure of understanding through conversation is discernible even though the ideal conditions of the genuine conversation are not met. In the text of a 1989 speech to psychiatrists, Gadamer (1996) wrote of "the capacity to attend to another human being" (pp. 166–167), which suggests he was not dogmatic about his own distinction when faced with a concrete form of practice and certainly had no wish to bar particular spheres of activity from interpretive life.

There is something attractive and approachable in the way Gadamer discussed conversation as the everyday occurrence of two people talking. Behind the straightforward image, however, stands his linguistic ontology and historically effected consciousness. Participants in a conversation are not two separate rational agents starting every conversation as if from nothing, but beings who are speaking out of traditions that precede them, using words that are already saturated in cultural meanings. Conversation is "a life process in which a community of life is lived out" (Gadamer, 2004, p. 443). As such, a research interview is not just a question of extracting information from a participant, but a joining with the participant in an exploration of a community, or culture of which they are a part and have expertise to share.

Questions

Interviews or conversations are kept going by asking questions. We go into more detail about asking good questions in research interviews in Chapter 6. Our concern here is with how Gadamer considered questioning as one of the impulses of dialogue and thus of understanding. He noted that a question, when not a leading, rhetorical, or trick question, is based on a negative, not knowing. When we say that someone asks a leading question, for example, we mean that this person already anticipates a certain kind of answer and is perhaps even looking for such an answer. With a genuine question, however, things are different. One asks a genuine question because one does not know something, perhaps because one does not yet know even what the right question to ask is, or how to formulate it. As such, a question is another mark of finitude.

Questions bear this mark even though they may not have any hermeneutical intent behind them. They may, for example, be part of everyday conversation, with a superficial desire for knowledge (how are you?), or surrounded by a distinct power imbalance (interrogation). Hermeneutical questioning is informed by a humility toward one's own not knowing, a genuine curiosity toward what the other might have to say, and the goal of shared understanding—not simply taking information for one's own ends. Asking questions of a topic in this way renders the topic questionable: "The significance of questioning consists in revealing the questionability of what is questioned. It has to be brought into this state of indeterminacy" (Gadamer, 2004, p. 357). Thus, the importance of a well-formed research question is that it identifies a topic clearly while also leaving it open.

In the following sections in this chapter, we pursue a number of additional concepts in Gadamer's work that address aspects of how history and language are mobilized in individual encounters with an art object or text, or in the present context, a matter of importance to researchers.

Play

Gadamer took up play as one of the explanatory ideas in his aesthetics, which in turn modeled his interpretive framework. Play appears in the epigraph at the start of *Truth and Method*, in lines from a poem by Rilke about becoming "the catcher of a ball / thrown by an eternal partner" (Gadamer, 2004, p. v). Grondin (2003b, p. 315), in his biography of Gadamer, related his choice of these lines to his love of tennis. For Gadamer, the significance of play is that when one is fully involved in play, it takes one outside of oneself and the game becomes more than a subjective experience. Play at the same time requires seriousness to be properly absorbing but also frees the player into responsiveness to the flow of the game. Play is not random: it has rules, participants, and a field of play but its possible outcome is open (which is why it is such an offense to fix a game—it corrupts its very nature). What anyone will make of a work of art is likewise unknowable in advance and any outcome—if one plays properly—comes out of a period of uncertainty in which impressions, experiences, opinions, viewpoints (literal and metaphorical) are given free play. Play is thus another example of the movement of interpretation, of its vitality and contrast to prescribed formulae. It is important, in addition, to stress Gadamer's (2004) observation that the play goes beyond the players, that "the *primacy of play over the consciousness of the player* is fundamentally acknowledged" (p. 105, italics in original). To be caught up in the play of possible meanings demands more than merely forming a subjective opinion but letting the artwork—or research topic—stand amidst the cross currents of its presence in the world so that the self is being reinterpreted in the light of the work even while the work is interpreted.

Prejudices

Understanding is always about something that is already there, which means we can never start as if with a blank slate. Thus, Gadamer introduced the notion of prejudices, of those prior understandings that we already bring to the topic (or perhaps more accurately, that bring us to the topic). Gadamer's considerations of the theme of prejudice, then, are closely related to his ideas that understanding is effected historically and that we experience such effects as tradition. Prejudice is the most problematic term of Gadamer's because of its primarily pejorative meaning in English usage. All he meant by it is that we never approach a text, experience, or topic as a completely blank slate—we already have a fabric of meaning into which we accommodate, with more or less difficulty, the next new event. Gadamer (2004) felt that prejudice was so important that, "[t]he recognition that all understanding inevitably involves some prejudice gives the hermeneutic problem its real thrust" (p. 272). Interpretation happens in dialogue, and it is our prior commitments that give us something to say in dialogue with new experience. So far, this idea of prejudice is neutral in that it is only making the point that we always bring existing understandings to bear on a topic. There are, however, good and bad prejudices, those that leave us open to dialogue and new possibilities and those that would close off dialogue, taking new information only as either confirmation or contradiction of an established position. Hence, Gadamer called for "the foregrounding and appropriation of one's own fore-meanings and prejudices, [since] the important thing is to be aware of one's own bias" (p. 271). Given that prejudices are always in play in hermeneutic understanding, it is incumbent upon us to reflect actively on our own angles of concern for a topic and to remain open to the possible surprise of stumbling over our own prejudices or having someone else stumble on them and point them out to us.

The Hermeneutic Circle

The movement of existing understanding, or prejudice, into constructive interchange with another is described by the image of the hermeneutic circle. In the nineteenth century, as noted in the previous chapter, the hermeneutic circle referred to the dialectic of part and whole in a narrow sense of an actual text. Heidegger gave the circle an existential spin in *Being and Time* by making it about the back-and-forth of understanding for *Dasein*. Gadamer held on to the implication of the latter sense, that the being of the interpreter is implicated in the process of understanding, and also retrieved the meaning of part and whole:

> Fundamentally, understanding is always a movement in this kind of circle, which is why the repeated return from the whole to the parts, and vice versa, is essential. Moreover, this circle is constantly expanding, since the concept of the whole is relative, and being integrated in ever larger contexts always affects the understanding of the individual part. (Gadamer, 2004, p. 189)

The circle is sometimes visualized as a spiral to represent this widening of the "whole" as it is informed and shaped by each partial understanding or viewpoint that lends a new association to the topic and adds to its connectedness in the world. This also means that the whole is not a fixed quantity, a puzzle that only needs all the pieces in the right places to be complete, but more of a complex and living assemblage of meaning. As his thought developed, and in part in response to Derrida's approach to deconstruction, Gadamer came to reassess some aspects of his conception of the hermeneutical circle. He suggested that the pursuit of understanding is captured perhaps not foremost by the image of the circle, but instead of being on the trail. With this new image, he stresses that in the pursuit of understanding, we never quite have the whole of our topic in view, but, instead, follow the trail of our topic, and that, therefore, we do not encounter parts as much as we follow tracks or traces (2007). This idea is developed further in Chapter 4.

Experience—*Erlebnis* and *Erfahrung*

Experience, as we discussed in the previous chapter, is one of the routes that phenomenology takes in its attempt to get at the immediacy of what it is to be a human being in the world. In *Truth and Method*, Gadamer used two different German words for experience that expand the sense of the word. He discussed them in the context of aesthetics, but taking the experience of art as exemplary of how events of understanding are not merely subjective. *Erlebnis*, which was used by Dilthey, refers to an intense experience that stands out from the usual run of events as something remarkable that lingers in the memory as an object of reflection and contemplation. The problem with this kind of experience is that it risks being detached from participation in the world. It carries traces of both nineteenth-century romanticism and love of the sublime and of early twentieth-century phenomenology with its hankering after positivist separation and definition. *Erfahrung*, from the verb *fahren*, which means to travel or journey, has the connotation of raw experience taking one more deeply into the world. *Erfarhung* has a "binding quality" (Gadamer, 2004, p. 84) whereby experience happens along with the networks of meaning that are already present. A research participant might, for example, describe a memorable experience of walking into a classroom for the first time as a new teacher. It may have been an intense experience that the teacher has recalled and recounted many times but in itself it has more of the character of *Erlebnis*. When the singular experience is brought into a form of developmental life, through reflection, association, and dialogue—for example, with other teachers, with research literature, with fictional or artistic representations, with similar experiences of other professionals—the experience takes on the character of *Erfahrung*. In the research context, participants will have varying degrees of reflection to offer about their experience, but it is certainly the task of the researcher to locate experiences in ecologies of meaning.

"There is a world already interpreted, already organized in its basic relations, into which experience steps as something new, upsetting what has led our expectations and undergoing reorganization itself in the upheaval" (Gadamer, 2007, p. 87). One implication of Gadamer's emphasis on experience is that there is a dialectical movement between the world as it comes to meet us and what we are then able to make of it. In this relationship lies another example of the humility in hermeneutics: that we are not all-comprehending masters of the world (nor can become so). Indeed, he believed that, as we become increasingly experienced, we not only expand our understanding of the world, things, and others, but, crucially, we achieve the self-understanding that whatever we have learned is limited, temporary, and corrigible.

Experience is accordingly another example of finitude because, properly understood, it means that one cannot know what is coming. There is a negativity to experience because in order to stand receptive to otherness and the unknown, one has to hold the already familiar as potentially questionable and open to revision. This philosophical principle has clear relevance to research and provides a rationale, for example, for the practice of the semi-structured interview, which needs to be topic-focused but cannot be determined in advance as in a survey.

Bildung

Bildung is another German word that can be translated as "cultivation," which is related to experience. *Bildung* is the kind of cultivation or development that a person achieves who is open to experience in the above sense of continually revealing new possibilities. It implies the continuing formation of the self in the light of experience, beyond the sheer acquisition of experiences. "The result of *Bildung* is not achieved in the manner of a technical construction but grows out of an inner process of formation and cultivation" (Gadamer, 2004, p. 10) and thus is a process that can never be declared completed.

This helps to articulate how it is that the researcher is changed by doing the research. Experiences—of reading, discovering new sources, interviewing participants and reviewing transcripts, conversations about the work and so on—alter the researcher's own field of understanding as she or he becomes more *gebildet*, cultivated. It is not only a matter of expertise but of a complex relationship with one's own expertise in which unlearning and relearning are part of learning. Davey (2006) wrote that "the process of becoming 'experienced' (*gebildet*) involves the assimilation of a body of ideas, it does not entail the acquisition or the imposition of a *determinate* set of ideas" (p. 49, italics in original).

What we mostly call the "topic" in this book, referring to a worthwhile subject matter for research, can be translated by the German word, *Sache*, which Davey (2006) took up from Gadamer in his elaboration of *Bildung*. Reiterating the point that cultivation takes place within a context, Davey described it as "becoming literate with regard to the *Sachen* that form a given culture" (p. 69). Here is another place where extension of the argument into practice disciplines is justified. Davey was careful to rebut the critique of Gadamer as conservative by separating *Bildung* from its historic associations with a particular idea of what a cultivated person might look like. He argued that, hermeneutically, *Bildung* takes on meaning and value in relation to a particular *Sache*, and not according to a predetermined standard of social values. Given this flexibility, it makes sense to talk about subject matters as they belong within a social, institutional, or professional culture. The topic of therapeutic relationship, for example, will appear differently according to whether the cultural context is nursing, mental health, palliative care, education, psychotherapy, or hospitals. In this example, it is more than likely that all the examples are related, but each will have its own literature, its own set of associations and cultural nuances. *Sachen* that are worth investigating have a generative effect because they are not comfortably defined and restricted—looking closely at one part of a topic, associations become apparent, either obviously so or in peripheral vision. "Indeed, for a *Sache* to function, that is, for it to become historically effective, it must shade into meanings different to those associated with its first appearance" (Davey, 2006, p. 72). Hermeneutic research demands the ability to find a culturally lively subject matter to start with, and then to follow where it leads.

Fusion of Horizons

Horizontverschmelzung, the German word for "fusion of horizons," once came up in a hermeneutic research class for graduate students taught by two of the authors. One of the students, who spoke German, said *Verschmelzung* brought up for her the image of melting butter. Melting is one of the meanings of the English "fusion" too, along with blending and bonding together (Fusion, 1993). Fusion of horizons is a frequently cited concept in Gadamer's hermeneutics, but it is complicated both by the multivalent meanings of fusion and by his using it in different contexts. At first sight, the phrase can evoke the sense of horizons becoming bonded together into one. What Gadamer had in mind, however, is that in our experience, our own horizons become less rigid, loosening, melting, and flowing into larger and more complex streams of horizons of meaning thanks to our encounter with the other (George, 2020b).

The first place the phrase occurs in *Truth and Method* is in relation to history, where the horizons in question are those of the past and the present. Our horizon of the present—formed by the values, assumptions, concerns that condition how we look out on the world—is inextricably influenced by horizons of the past. Further, the horizon of the present is always changing in the light of new circumstances and new knowledge. It would be a mistake, however, to conclude from this that progress is all we need to worry about, and to dismiss the past. The past, the other horizon, is always shaping our consciousness of the world and it too changes since we are always interpreting the past from the horizon of the present.

> In fact the horizon of the present is continually in the process of being formed because we are continually having to test all our prejudices. An important part of this testing occurs in encountering the past in understanding the tradition from which we come. Hence the horizon of the present cannot be formed without the past. (Gadamer, 2004, p. 305)

There is then a fusion, a coming together of horizons to achieve new understanding (of the present and of the past, depending on the focus of inquiry) but it is always provisional, never finalized. The fusion of horizons, as when a researcher draws conclusions about the history of a concept, is a point of understanding that has validity since it is based upon an informed reading of the past. It can be used to inform present understanding and future decisions. It cannot, however, be declared unchangeable in the light of as yet unknown shifts in horizons.

Further on, Gadamer came back to the fusion of horizons in relation to reading texts, as a more concrete example of where we encounter the horizon of the past. Texts, after all, unlike speech, carry their time of origin with them into the present. A few exceptional texts continue to speak to readers for centuries—bookshops in the English-speaking world often have several different translations of Dante's *Divine Comedy* on their shelves, for example—a work from fourteenth-century Italy that portrays a fundamentally different view of the world and the cosmos from modernity and yet continues to be translated and re-translated and published in popular editions for a contemporary readership. To take a less extreme example from the disciplinary literature of mental health nursing, the pioneering work of Peplau (1952/1988), mentioned above, continues to be cited as a source of understanding of working therapeutically through relationship. There are aspects of her early work, however, that reflect the predominance of psychoanalytic thinking in the mental health care of the 1950s that have to be thought about differently in the changed standards of contemporary psychiatry and mental health care. The continued, if changing, value of a work like Peplau's underlines Gadamer's point that some insights do not wear out easily and continue to generate meaningful and worthwhile understanding even though understanding has to be vigilantly re-examined and renewed in the light of the always-moving horizon of the present.

Gadamer (2004) argued that to fully engage with the meaning of the text, the reader brings his or her own horizon into play. There is not one ultimate, true meaning hidden in the text but unavoidably one reads from the horizon of the present. As with prejudices, this can be enabling when the horizon is held "more as an opinion and a possibility that one brings into play and puts at risk, and that helps one truly to make one's own what the text says" (p. 390). It is an interesting claim—that one reads and understands the otherness of a text *better* by having an angle of commitment of one's own, but only provided that one can hold that angle as a possibility open to change. Gadamer applied this point also to the play of conversation, "in which something is expressed that is not only mine or my author's, but common" (p. 390).

Fusion of horizons applies then to three of Gadamer's areas of chief concern: history, text, and by extension, conversation. It is one form in which he discussed the encounter with otherness and how it is possible for understanding to move, expand, and change in the light of encounter with the other. The term neither implies that one side surrenders understanding to the other, nor that the fusion involves complete sublimation of both. In fact, there are many possibilities of combining and blending prior understandings or holding on to differences—but in a new constellation in relation to each other.

Die Sache or the Topic

Understanding is always about *something* that pulls us toward the world and invites interpretation in order to make sense of it (George, 2020). The German word *Sache* can be translated as matter, in the sense of "the matter at hand," or in terms of research, a topic. George (2020) took up Figal's "realistic hermeneutics" (p. 16) to emphasize the substantiveness of hermeneutic understanding, which is brought about in the first instance by our encounters with something that is outside of ourselves, that "stands over against us, such that it may demand our attention" (p. 17). Problems that lend themselves to hermeneutic research present us with something difficult and intransigent. If they were easily solved, if they were not all that complicated, or simply required yet one more training module or poster to fix, then they would be in no need to work at them.

We have chosen to highlight George's advocacy of realistic hermeneutics, in preference to postmodern interpretations of Gadamer that lean into language and make it the determining factor, not the matter itself. For Figal and George, language is referential, our interpretations refer to, and direct, our attention toward something in the world. This is salient for research in practice professions, where topics are always about a matter, or topics that reside in reference to a world that is already structured by the needs of professional work (teachers needs schools to teach in, teaching materials, students, an infrastructure that enables communication between teachers and students; nurses need buildings, equipment, patients, and an infrastructure that, among other things, licenses the modification of social norms of asking questions about personal matters and physical contact). This version of hermeneutics supports two elements of research. One is the commons of reference, that the significance of the topic, and new interpretations of the topic, are communicable to other professionals or indeed anyone with sufficient familiarity with the referential frame (e.g., in healthcare, patients, family members); second, research stays connected to the stubbornness of everyday reality, where research problems are seen. Hermeneutic research grants a high degree of interpretive creativity, potentially bringing in many diverse kinds of sources, but at the center of the resultant network of meanings, lies the topic, the matter at hand, *die Sache selbst*.

Application and *Phronesis*

One of the appeals of hermeneutic philosophy for researchers in practice disciplines is that, in spite of its complexity, it is rooted in the phenomenological lifeworld, and what is at stake in understanding for everyday human, social activities. It is this rootedness that makes hermeneutics, as we argue throughout this book, naturally movable from the traditional concerns (in *Truth and Method*) of legal, theological, and textual interpretation to problems of classrooms and clinics. Application is one of Gadamer's concepts that serves the purpose of substantiating the extension, and it leads to another idea, that of *phronesis*, or practical wisdom.

Gadamer (2004) used the law as the clearest example of "recognizing application as an integral element of all understanding" (p. 307) since laws live through application that is, at the same time, interpretation. Application, however, does not mean taking an abstract principle and imposing it upon a situation since "means are in general determined by ends, and rules are determined by, or even abstracted from, behavior" (Gadamer, 2007, p. 61). Application, as part of the structure of understanding, has to be conditioned by historically effected consciousness. The intention here is not to restrict application to repetition of what is already known and done, but to seek out possibilities for application that are comprehensible within the horizon of present understandings. Hermeneutical awareness, far from being conservative, encourages restless questioning of what appears obvious and inevitable through sensitivity to impermanence. Application is situational and flexible since it is interpretation within a concrete situation. Warnke (2002) highlighted an ethical dimension to application: "Our application of the ethical knowledge we possess occurs within a history that is unceasing in its demand that we apply it, however much or little of it we may possess" (p. 84).

Application can be seen as a matter of practice, of reinterpreting principles in the light of circumstances, and reinterpreting circumstances in the light of principles. Practice disciplines like education, social work, or nursing that have at their core personal interrelationships within schemas of technical knowledge and ethical values are clearly sites of hermeneutic application. For application to be done well requires a disposition on the part of the agent—the teacher, social worker, or nurse for example—which Gadamer (2004) referred to as *phronesis*, translated both as "practical knowledge" (p. 19) and "moral knowledge" (p. 312)[1]. Aristotle used the word *phronesis* to distinguish contextualized knowledge from objective knowledge that does not change. One of the features of practical knowledge is that it demands judgment and action within a situation, where "the knower

1 There are other variant translations of *phronesis*, including Risser's (1997) "practical reasoning," Sachs' (2002) "practical judgment" and Schwarz's (2010) "practical wisdom." For convenience, we have used the versions found in the 2004 translation of *Truth and Method*.

is not standing over against a situation that he merely observes; he is directly confronted with what he sees. It is something that he has to do" (Gadamer, 2004, p. 312). Practical knowledge is different from technical knowledge that can be determined in advance because, however complex, it requires exact and repeatable action. Practical knowledge is also moral knowledge because, as Warnke noted, it functions within the flow of the moment in which values as well as technical skills are operative.

Application and *phronesis* provide a valuable explanatory framework for the complex work of practice disciplines. As such, they may be helpful to researchers in trying to describe phenomena of practice, as well as referring to the conduct of interpretive research itself.

Transformation Into Structure

We want to borrow one final term from Gadamer's aesthetics, which we believe illuminates the stage of writing up the finished interpretive findings in hermeneutic research. Gadamer (2004) intended "transformation into structure" (p. 110) to mean the point at which creative play comes to an end through the achievement of the work of art. The artwork is transformative because it takes up the play and, in capturing a vision of the world, re-presents the world in new alignments of possibility. The response to an artwork is at the same time the recognition of something known, a self-recognition on the part of the viewer, and "the joy of knowing *more* than is already familiar" (p. 113). Writing a finished version of hermeneutic research similarly brings to an end the play of interpretation, at least for the moment and, in doing so, it reconstitutes the topic in ways that bring to the fore new possibilities for practice. Writing in hermeneutics is, of course, not separable from the writer, so that it is not just that the researcher presents a novel arrangement of the facts, but that the researcher writes from within an altered horizon of the self. "The transformation into structure … allows a subject to see its world differently and to become different to itself" (Davey, 2006, p. 135). As with the image of fusion, however, structure does not mean finality. Davey described transformation into structure "as the disclosure of meaning within a given cycle of events" so that "what was incomplete and fragmentary emerges as a meaningful whole" (p. 136). Structure is necessary as a point in a cycle of interpretation and understanding in which meaning comes together as a unit of articulation and in doing so, the newly articulated meaning becomes available in itself for questioning, reappraisal, deconstruction, and interpretation.

Summary

In his 1972 essay, *Hermeneutics as Practical Philosophy* (Gadamer, 2007, pp. 227–245), Gadamer laid out his view of hermeneutics as a practice. He based this on a foundation of Aristotelian practical philosophy of how citizens ought to live in the community of the *polis*, oriented toward the good. Practice in this broad sense thus takes account of contingency, of the human situation of having to choose with discernment amidst the currents of history and messiness of events. By using the word practice, however, he indicated that humans are not helpless in the face of the world, that we have choice, reason, and knowledge—however finite and mutable—in forming our values and actions.

Hermeneutics as a practice suggests obvious comparisons with practice disciplines such as teaching, social work, counseling, nursing, or medicine. Practice in these contexts too has an underlying moral orientation toward the good of communities. In addition, however, practice disciplines to varying degrees and in different ways make use of science and technology requiring specific technical expertise. Research and management too strive to bring scientific methods and uniformity to the governance and conduct of practitioners. The tension between generalizable scientific knowledge and application in the particular situation thus takes on a particular immediacy for practice disciplines. Practice is constituted in the continual negotiation of "applying this [general] knowledge in the concrete case" (Gadamer, 1996, p. 16). Gadamer discussed this tension in his addresses to medical audiences, and emphasized the importance of keeping open the space of practice as a practice of human responsiveness:

> What we need to do is to learn to build a bridge over the existing divide between the theoretician who knows the general rule and the person involved in practice who wishes to deal with the unique situation of this patient who is in need of care. (p. 94)

In reality, of course, there is no absolute separation between the theoretician and the practitioner, and the negotiation between the two is experienced as an internal as well as social or institutional matter. This only underlines the hermeneutic sense of practice for which the exercise of judgment is primary:

> Being an experienced practitioner does not strictly speaking impose limits on deployable methodical devices or tactics. To the contrary, becoming an experienced practitioner entails sharpening if not acquiring a guiding *sense* for judging which approach to a task is more plausible or appropriate than another. (Davey, 2006, p. 17, italics in original)

This brief introduction to important concepts in Gadamer's philosophy is intended to provide a framework for what follows in the working out of a coherent and effective approach to research, but it can only point toward the practice to come.

References

Caputo, J. D. (2018). *Hermeneutics: Facts and interpretation in the age of information*. Pelican.

Coltman, R. (1998). *The language of hermeneutics: Gadamer and Heidegger in dialogue*. SUNY.

Davey, N. (2006). *Unquiet understanding: Gadamer's philosophical hermeneutics*. SUNY.

Davey, N. (2013). *Unfinished worlds: Hermeneutics, aesthetics and Gadamer.* Edinburgh University Press.

di Cesare, D. (2013). *Gadamer: A philosophical portrait*. Indiana University Press.

Dostal, R. J. (2002). Gadamer's relation to Heidegger and phenomenology. In R. J. Dostal (Ed.), *The Cambridge companion to Gadamer* (pp. 247–266). Cambridge University Press.

Fusion. (1993). In L. Brown (Ed.), *The new shorter Oxford dictionary* (Vol. 1, p. 1047). Oxford University Press.

Gadamer, H.-G. (1977). *Philosophical hermeneutics* (D. E. Linge, Ed. & Trans.). University of California Press.

Gadamer, H.-G. (1981). *Reason in the age of science* (F. G. Lawrence, Trans.). MIT Press.

Gadamer, H.-G. (1981b). What is practice? The conditions of social reason. In *Reason in the age of science* (pp. 69–87; F. G. Lawrence, Trans.). Cambridge University Press.

Gadamer, H.-G. (1990). Reply to my critics. In *The hermeneutic tradition from Ast to Ricoeur* (pp. 273–297). State University of New York Press.

Gadamer, H.-G. (1996). *The enigma of health* (J. Gaiger & N. Walker, Trans.). Stanford University Press.

Gadamer, H.-G. (2001). *Gadamer in conversation* (R. E. Palmer, Ed. & Trans.). Yale University Press.

Gadamer, H.-G. (2004). *Truth and method* (J. Weinsheimer & D. G. Marshall, Trans.). Continuum. Original work in 1960.

Gadamer, H.-G. (2007). *The Gadamer reader: A bouquet of the later writings* (R. E. Palmer, Ed.). Northwestern University Press.

Gadamer, H.-G. (2007b). Hermeneutics tracking the trace [On Derrida]. In R. E. Palmer (Ed. & Trans,), *The Gadamer reader: A bouquet of the later writings*, (pp. 372–406). Northwestern University Press.

Gadamer, H.-G. (2013). *Truth and method* (J. Weinsheimer & D. G. Marshall, Trans.). Bloomsbury. Original work 1960.

Gadamer, H.-G. (2016). *Hermeneutics between history and philosophy: The selected writings of Hans-Georg Gadamer, Volume 1*, (P. Vandevelde & A. Iyer, Eds. & Trans.). Bloomsbury.

Gadamer, H.-G. (2022). *Ethics aesthetics and the historical dimension of language: The selected writings of Hans-Georg Gadamer, Volume II* (P. Vandevelde & A. Iyer, Eds. & Trans.). Bloomsbury.

George, T. (2020). *The responsibility to understand: Hermeneutical contours of ethical life*. Edinburgh University Press.

George, T. (2020b). Hermeneutics. *Stanford encyclopedia of philosophy* <https://plato.stanford.edu/cgi-bin/encyclopedia/archinfo.cgi?entry=hermeneutics>

George, T., & Van Der Heiden, G.-J. (2022). *The Gadamerian mind*. Routledge.

Grondin, J. (1994). *Introduction to philosophical hermeneutics* (J. Weinsheimer, Trans.). Yale University Press.

Grondin, J. (1995). *Sources of hermeneutics*. SUNY.

Grondin, J. (2003a). *The philosophy of Gadamer* (K. Plant, Trans.). McGill-Queen's University Press.

Grondin, J. (2003b). *Hans-Georg Gadamer: A biography* (J. Weinsheimer, Trans.). Yale University Press.

Palmer, R. E. (1969). *Hermeneutics*. Northwestern University Press.

Peplau, H. (1988). *Interpersonal relations in nursing*. Palgrave Macmillan.

Risser, J. C. (1997). *Hermeneutics and the voice of the other: Re-reading Hans-Georg Gadamer's philosophical hermeneutics*. SUNY.

Risser, J. C. (2012). *The life of understanding: A contemporary hermeneutics*. Indiana University press.

Sachs, J. (2002). *Aristotle. Nicomachean ethics* (J. Sachs, Trans.). Focus.

Schmidt, D. J. (2008). Hermeneutics as original ethics. In S. Sullivan & D. J. Schmidt (Eds.), *Difficulties of ethical life* (pp. 35–47). Fordham University Press.

Schmidt, D. J. (2012a). The idiom of the ethical. *Epoché: A Journal of the History of Philosophy, 17*(1), 15–24. <https://doi.org/10.5840/epoche201217120>

Schmidt, D. J. (2012b). On the sources of ethical life. *Research in Phenomenology, 41*(1), 35–48. <https://doi.org/10.1163/156916412X628739>

Schmidt, D. J. (2015). Text and translation. In J. Malpas & H.-H. Gander (Eds.), *The Routledge companion to hermeneutics* (pp. 345–353). Routledge.

Schmidt, D. J. (2016). Hermeneutics and ethical life: On the return of factical life. In N. Keane & C. Lawn (Eds.), *The Blackwell companion to hermeneutics*. (pp. 65–71). John Wiley & Sons.

Schwarz, B. (2010). *Practical wisdom: The right way to do the right thing*. Riverhead.

Taylor, C. (2002). Gadamer on the human sciences. In R. J. Dostal (Ed.), *The Cambridge companion to Gadamer* (pp. 126–142). Cambridge University Press.

Warnke, G. (2002). Hermeneutics, ethics, and politics. In R. J. Dostal (Ed.), *The Cambridge companion to Gadamer* (pp. 79–101). Cambridge University Press.

"Hermeneutics on the Trail": The Way of Being in Hermeneutic Inquiry

We borrowed Gadamer's (2016) pithy phrase "hermeneutics on the trail" (p. 179) because we thought it an apt description of hermeneutic inquiry. Of course, Gadamer meant something much wider and deeper than doing research, that is, nothing less than the way we cope skillfully in the world through understanding. *Coping skillfully through understanding*, though, is an excellent way to name what is at the heart of hermeneutic inquiry. In addition, the phrase opens onto a rich semantic field of interrelated phenomenological constructs, such as attunement, perception, the event, the trace, and wayfinding, which allow us to further describe what doing hermeneutic research entails. Before moving on, let us elaborate on this phrase, bursting as it is with *movement* and *engagement*:

> For Gadamer, being on the trail as hermeneutics is, is to be in constant contact *through* dialogue, asking questions, answering, being asked other questions, led astray, led toward dead ends, but never giving up on the prospect of meaning itself, which is for him the cornerstone of shared existence. (Vandevelde & Iyer, 2016, p. 302)

It is interesting to note that the title has also been translated as "tracking the trace," from an earlier version (Gadamer, 2007) of the piece. In here, Gadamer extended Derrida's notion of the trace that gets at the essence of being on the trail:

> Someone who finds a trace/clue certainly also knows that something has existed before and is now left behind. But one does not just take note of this. One begins to search and to ask oneself where it leads. Only for a person who is on his way and in search of a right path, does the trace stand in the context of seeking and detecting [*des Spurens*], only then does picking up that trace mark his beginning. (pp. 390–391)

Traces for Gadamer (2007) are freighted with meaning, that is, they are interpreted—something we will deal with further in the section on perception.

Gadamer thinks that the trace provides the same kind of sense that a question does, that is, "with it one finds a first direction, something is disclosed … One allows it to lead" (p. 391). The main concern of this chapter is to set out guidelines for "being on the trail."

Guidelines for a Hermeneutic Inquiry

The term "guidelines" was chosen carefully to signal an older meaning of the term, that is, "that which serves to steady the motion of a thing or journey" (OED, p. 491) *not determine it*. Guidelines are not methodological imperatives, nor protocols. They are in the service of steady, dependable movement. They are not meant to displace good judgment or set aside the knowledge of an experienced practitioner. They do not absolve someone of being careful or responsible for the conduct of the inquiry. They will not, indeed cannot, tell a researcher how to respond appropriately to an encounter on the trail, interpret a particular trace, decide on the best direction to be taken, or guarantee, through following them, that understanding will occur. Guidelines are there to simply orient the researcher, to help them make responsible, dependable, and defensible decisions. They operate much like stars do for navigation. One does not sail toward the stars; they do not tell when to sail, or how, and certainly not where to sail. In other words, stars do not cause someone to sail. All that careful practice of sailing depends upon locally determined, mutually interacting conditions, which need constant consideration and re-consideration: the nature of the vessel, the swell of the ocean, the unfolding weather conditions, the experience, skill, and character of the navigators, to name but a few. Many ways can be made from the stars; they generate possibilities for navigation, allow for a diversity of paths. However, the stars do serve to properly "steady" the sailing, to provide important traces to the question of where we are now, and from this, for the navigators to decide, steadily, methodically, interpretively, the answer to the question: where do we head next?

It might be best to think of these guidelines offered below then as traces, left behind as lessons learned from our work. As is the case with all traces, they will need to be interpreted anew.

1. Hermeneutic Inquiry Is Not a Method, a Cluster of Methods, nor a Methodology, but Rather a Practice

We contend that Gadamer had no real quarrel with method per se. He did think it inadequate for hermeneutic inquiry, but he was much more concerned with the dominant worldview that scientific method was the only legitimate path to dependable, legitimate knowledge, understanding, and action. Gadamer (1960/1997) himself claimed that his work "is phenomenological in its method" (p. xxxvi), but by this he did not mean method as a prescriptive procedure or protocol for doing hermeneutics. Rather, he was referring to *being disciplined by and attentive to the events* that happen to us "on the trail." Dostal (2002) elaborated:

> By referring to his method, Gadamer means, not a procedural set of rules, but rather the *discipline of attending to things* (our emphasis). By calling his method phenomenological, he does not thereby subscribe to Husserl's method of phenomenology, but rather indicates that the task of the enterprise is descriptive, in this case descriptive of the human experience of understanding, i.e., of hermeneutical experience. (p. 251)

A further clue to this was given by Gadamer (1960/1997) himself, in the closing statement of *Truth and Method*, as if he knew what lay ahead for those wishing to take up the work of hermeneutics: "what the tool of method cannot achieve must—and really can—be achieved by a discipline of questioning and inquiring" (p. 491). What Gadamer's words refer to here is *being disciplined*—by the topic, by the questions that arise, and most importantly perhaps by what we encounter "on the trail." This is why he urges us not to "conceive understanding as a methodic activity of the subject, but as something that the thing itself does, and which thought 'suffers.' This activity of the thing itself is the real speculative movement that takes hold of the speaker" (p. 474).

> Commonly, in qualitative work, *method* is conceived of in this way:
> In the everyday ordinary usage of the term in qualitative studies (and social inquiry more generally), *method* denotes a procedure, tool, or technique used by the inquirer to generate and analyze data ... method contributes to the generation and growth of knowledge but is itself transparent or neutral or at least the effects of a method on the object of understanding are determinable or controllable. (Schwandt, 2007, p. 191)

There is no heart, flesh, and blood to method, no indication that it is a *thoughtful, embodied activity with other willful, sentient beings*, who are often unpredictable in what they will say, do, or most importantly *require of us beyond what we have planned*. Neither is there any context in methods—they are placeless, depopulated, and timeless, stripped of the history and the understanding of the participants—as well as what is already at work "in place." There is no landscape in methods—a world in which we can dwell. In addition, there are no events in methods—no sudden reversals of understanding, nothing mysterious is at work. The course of inquiry is completely "determinable and controllable"; no one must suffer unpredictable events.

However, we need to emphasize that it is not the case that hermeneutics does not employ methods—interviewing, observation, textual analysis, interpretation, and the like. To be sure it does, but the notion of method does not begin to capture the complex way that we come to an understanding of the world and the things in it, including what is most mysterious to us—who we are.

Much more than a method, Gadamer considers hermeneutics to be a way of life, which is a *praxis* or practice, and this for us captures the fullness and complexity of hermeneutic research in a way that the terms method and methodology do not. For Gadamer (2001):

> The word "praxis" points to the totality of our practical life, all our human action and behavior, the self-adaptation of the human being as a whole in this world... Our praxis, in short, is our "form of life." (p. 78)

As teachers, nurses, psychologists—as *practitioners*, pedagogical practice refers to a way of life in the classroom with our students or in the hospital room, or therapy session, something much more complex, difficult, and "astonishing" than enacting this or that method. Practice includes our relationship with our students, patients, and clients, with the subject matter we teach, with how we respond to events in practice, with whom we understand ourselves to be as practitioners. Most importantly perhaps, practice is deeply affected by who our students or clients think we are—how *we show up for them* and *respond to them* in the classroom or the hospital room. As sensitive practitioners, we must "suffer" life itself, as Scott (2002) wrote:

> The robustness of energy, feelings of power (and powerlessness), measures of delight, and dark sadness, movements of decay, bodily effects of rhythms ... excitations and tranquilizations, instincts, enforcements, forms of deception, manipulations, expressions of pride (and shame), desire, pleasure, and joy. (p. 170)

All of this can be said about hermeneutic research—our relationship with the topic, with our participants, with who we think they are, with how we respond to what we hear, see, and feel—*to what touches us*, and especially *moves us to think and act differently* are all part of the practice, of "being on the trail" in hermeneutic work. We must be finely attuned and responsive, and *response-able* to what is occurring around us, something that no method can deliver.

Another fundamental difference between method and hermeneutic practice is outlined by Davey (2006):

> ... the practice of philosophical hermeneutics pursues dialogue and dialectical encounter with the other. It seeks a disciplined openness to the strange and foreign. It encourages a creative tension between the assumptions and expectancies of our own horizons and those that are different. (p. 4)

This "disciplined openness to the strange and foreign"—to what is different to the way we are in the world, is what Lipari (2014) called a practice oriented by "ethical attunement." This "entails the recognition of another self, the startling presence of another being … (it) brings a recognition of an unknown order to whom we are bound and about who we feel care and concern" (p. 176). This is the ethics that guides the response and responsibility in hermeneutic practice.

It should be apparent now that hermeneutic practice is saturated with what Gadamer has aptly called "deliberation and decision-making." No one can escape from the task of choosing well, to paraphrase Aristotle—to do the right thing, at the right time, in the right way, for the right amount, and for the right reason. All those "rights" must be worked out interpretively during an inquiry. One can never say, for example, "well, ethnography or grounded theory made me do it. I simply followed the steps it prescribes." There is no way to shift the burden and capacity to respond and be responsible to a predetermined script. Hermeneutics is a method of choosing appropriately.

If context matters in hermeneutic practice, so does the character of the hermeneutic practitioner. The ability to be ethically attuned requires, primarily, a fundamental vulnerability to what is other. It requires *epistemological humility*, in that we know that our knowledge is limited and in need of revision. It requires *courtesy*, or better perhaps what Derrida and others call *hospitality*, in that we acknowledge our indebtedness to others, and welcome their capacity to teach us something new. It requires that we *suffer* having our understanding overturned, our expectations for what is possible thwarted, our ways called into question. Even more difficult, it requires that we simply do not set being taken aback aside, or conquer it with "better methods," but rather that we are transformed by what we encounter. It requires *tact*, what Gadamer (1960/1997) described as "a special sensitivity and sensitiveness to situations and how to behave in them, for which knowledge from general principles does not suffice" (p. 16). Tact involves both sense and feeling, but also a kind of knowledge—knowing how to orient ourselves in a situation, recognizing, as James Risser (1997) says, "what's at stake in a situation"(p. 97), discerning which resources to draw upon to understand what we encounter, knowing which questions to ask next, knowing when to probe, and when to let the silence speak for itself. Method, on the other hand, in its strictest sense is "tact-less" since the procedures are universally applicable and one need not be concerned with whether they apply, for they always apply, everywhere. Tact cannot be acquired in the abstract because it does not have to do with abstract rules. It can only be learned in and through experience, that is, by being practiced, from encounter to encounter, from case to case, to learn, as Caputo (1987) has said, from a series of "intentionally frustrated expectations" (p. 58). From this, we can see that hermeneutics hopes to generate something more than theory, knowledge, or efficient technique. It hopes that, in coming to an understanding, we become cultivated human beings, that we "live well with and for others in just institutions" (Ricoeur, 1996, p. 265). What hermeneutic researchers are drawn toward is a larger ideal, both in their research, but beyond that, in their life-worlds: "cultivating the kind of dialogical communities in which *phronesis*, judgment and practical discourse become concretely embodied in our everyday practices" (Bernstein, 1983, p. 224).

It is worth noting, given that many qualitative methodologies claim to be inductive, that hermeneutic practice is neither deductive nor inductive, but rather *dialogic*. Induction involves the "upward" generation of theory and general principles from data, a key process in approaches like grounded theory. As mentioned, induction leads to general principles, and in doing so, tends to come to rest in theory, leaving the lifeworld in all its rich textured meanings behind. When this happens, the generative power of hermeneutic insight that would help us see what is at stake in a situation (Risser, 1997), that would help us understand differently, disappears in a set of affirmed principles. Worse, hermeneutic experience—the things that come to matter in people's concrete lives—get extinguished. Gone are the differences, disappointments, and the events of understanding—the overturning of what one believes, of what is already known and taken for granted, of the way forward. Gone also is what Gadamer (2007) called "a kind of communality in virtue of which the reciprocal taking of council, the giving and taking of advice, is meaningful in the first place" (p. 261). When that happens, our methods are in danger of devolving into a "vicious circle": we reinforce beliefs we already hold, we simply find what we expect to find, we fill out already existing schemata, but our *enframing* stays in place. Nothing revolutionary in our being-in-the-world happens. We fail to understand.

If hermeneutics does not involve induction, it is equally true that it does not involve deduction either—the "downward" logic of deriving practice from theory or subsuming the particular under the general. It is not simply about applying the rules. Rather, hermeneutic analysis requires a dynamic interaction between the general and the particular, between the perceiver and the perceived, between self and other, or to use a favorite example, the case and the law. What arises from such back-and-forth is a more nuanced understanding of the concrete situation, and the topic, a better set of questions and possibilities for seeing, thinking, and acting in the future. Generating an array of possibilities for future concrete action through understanding is vastly different from generating theory inductively or a set of "best practices" deductively. Thus, hermeneutics is not vertical, but "horizontal" in its movement, from the back-and-forth of dialogue to the temporal or historical understanding it generates. Hermeneutics involves utilizing the resources of the past, what is known, to interpret the present, it depends upon the event encountered in the moment, and our response to it. All of which is "for the sake of being" to help us choose the most appropriate action required to fulfill the requirement of being well with and for others. The view provided is not either "up" (inductive) or "down" (deductive), but forward, "not positing an end, but reckoning with being on the way, giving *it* free play, disclosing it, holding fast to *being possible*" (Heidegger, 1999, p. 13).

In hermeneutic practice, one proceeds based on understanding what is at stake in the situation, attuned perception, concrete discovery and the imagining and re-imaging of possible meanings and courses of action. This does not mean that anything goes in hermeneutics—warranted courses of action, chains of evidence, and persuasive arguments must be established during the investigation, and all of this must stand up to scrutiny and thorough going critique *in a dialogue with others*. Cases for and against must be made and subjected to rigorous argumentation. Clear, retrospective "answerability" for what one understands and how one proceeds is required.

2. The Way of Hermeneutic Inquiry Is Guided by the Topic (Phenomenon) and Driven by the Dialectic of Question and Answer

A word first about the choice of the word topic instead of phenomenon. A topic (from the Latin *topos*) refers to a place, and more specifically for hermeneutics, *a place where meaningful things show up*, and better yet perhaps "defined as an open area of possibilities in which a historical people dwell" (Guignon, 2006, p. 19). Topics are alive, as Ingold (2002) said about the *topos*,

"It is an immensely variegated terrain of comings and goings, which is continually taking shape around the traveler even as the latter's movements contribute to its formation" (Ingold, 2002, p. 237). When we say that topics are alive, we mean also that they have agency—that is, they have the power to speak to us, to seize us even when they are ungraspable, to astonish us, and most importantly, to move us to be otherwise. Topics are more than a single phenomenon—they are "always at once dense and resonant with passing life" (Scott, 2002, p. 21). With them, "a world of interwoven meanings comes tumbling in" (p. 19), and these have the potential to overwhelm us, and most importantly *generate questions that call for a response*. There is an intimate, reciprocal, and dynamic relationship between questions that arise and how we answer or respond to those questions that is fundamental to hermeneutic inquiry. Gadamer (1960/1997) named this the "dialectic of question and answer" to capture its evocative power. Further he claimed that this dialectic *constituted the very basis of interpretation itself*:

> The apparent thetic beginning of interpretation is, in fact, a response; and the sense of the interpretation is determined, like every response, by the question asked. *Thus, the dialectic of question and answer always precedes the dialectic of interpretation. It is what determines understanding as an event.* (p. 472)

A strong claim indeed, from which Gadamer does not back down, but rather strengthens: "We cannot have experiences without asking questions" (p. 362), and further still, "the path of all knowledge leads through the question" (p. 363).

By questions Gadamer does not mean any kind of question generated from our imagination. Genuine questions in fact come from outside of us, from our encounters with the topic. They occur to us as events. They also stand in a specific relationship with the topic. That is, to count as genuine questions they must "break open the topic"– they occur as events. That means that questions are *revelatory*, they make previously unavailable aspects of the topic available for our scrutiny. That does not mean we understand questions fully when they occur—we are not masters over our own questions; they can bewilder us, and have a sense of mystery about them, but as Gadamer (1960/1997) wrote "the essence of the question is to have sense. Now sense involves a *sense of direction*" (our emphasis, p. 362). Such an interpretive sense is tantamount to being on the trail.

One cannot be in a hurry on the trail. In hermeneutic work, being called by a topic does not immediately license one scurry on to the trail, but rather, calls for careful probing and questioning of what appears. One must learn from the topic, both about what it is a case of, but also about what this one case requires of us to deepen understanding of both the instance and its context. This careful consideration with what appears before us is an *interpretive learning process*, as Gadamer (1960/1997) has stated above, focused on "learning how to ask questions" (p. 365) that will drive our understanding and subsequently the course of our investigation. Before rushing to an interpretation, we need to ask: What is this thing that appears before us? Why does it appear like this? Most importantly, we are called upon to respond to the fundamental interpretive question: *What are we seeing this as*? Are we being called upon to see things *otherwise*? How should we proceed? Being on the trail requires that we "while" as well as that we move. The requirement of "learning how to ask questions" is never extinguished in a single round of asking questions, every encounter with the topic requires close scrutiny, every experience of learning from the topic requires a new set of questions to be generated, because if the encounter "works" hermeneutically, it produces new understanding, and possibly a different course of action. Action follows the logic of the question and answer—this is how we make our way on the trail. This means also that we must have the courage and perseverance to "suffer" all the (unpredictable) twists and turns required to stay on the trail, to take on the *response-ability* required by hermeneutic work. Hermeneutic responsibility is closely tied to the question-and-answer dialectic of the *event of the question*. Conversely, the modern sense of the word is tied, according to Raffoul (2010) to Aristotle and makes some basic, non-hermeneutic assumptions. First, of these is that we are *autonomous agents*, *self-owned* and *self-legislating* as Raffoul says. In this understanding, responsibility is voluntary, the agent operates from a position of power. Hermeneutic responsibility is quite the opposite, in fact. It entails:

> Having to respond to a call, exposure to the vulnerability of the other (or to the other *as* vulnerability), openness to the event of being as my own "to be," having to take upon oneself the weight of responsibility (whether that weight is finitude, otherness, or an essenceless existence). (Raffoul, 2010, p. 19).

Responsibility, in hermeneutic work, might be thought of as *answerability*, signaling a close, dynamic relationship with the question-and-answer dialectic.

3. Hermeneutic Inquiry Requires a Finely Attuned Attentiveness and Ever-Evolving Response to What Is Happening on the Trail

If it is the case that understanding guides all our efforts in hermeneutic work, it is also the case that all our efforts to understand depend upon our ability to perceive, and to attune our perception, in the first place. It must be said that perception in hermeneutics is not simply the registering of bare, brute phenomenon, something the senses provide as fodder to be operated on by the mind—fitted into a scheme of things through a cognitive act. Perception, then, in hermeneutics is not a prerequisite for action but rather interpretive action itself. As Hoy (2006) maintained:

> Seeing is not simply perceiving the properties of external objects with the bodily eyes. Instead of construing seeing *that* an object has such and such a property, Heidegger construes seeing *as* already interpreting something as something... we grasp entities in their webs of relation to other entities, not as aggregates of perceptual properties. (pp. 189–190)

Perception then is an active, exploratory, deeply interpretive process. Without interpretation, there is no access to the intelligibility of what is there, and no sense of direction becomes available for exploring the topic. "Seeing what is at stake" (Risser, 1997), or as Heidegger (1999) put it, being on "the right path of looking" (p. 62) requires knowledge and skill, as well as active engagement. Perception should be thought of then as a way that we "*enact* the perceptual world by skillful exploration" (Noe, 2012, p. 59), or better yet, perhaps, of interpretive grappling with the traces that appear to us on the trail.

A simple example should help illustrate. When student teachers arrive in our classroom fresh from academe, we often begin our conversations about teaching and learning around the question, "What did you notice?" Often what would come to the fore, especially in their first instances of teaching, are things like "The lesson went pretty much as planned" or "Most of the students were able to finish the assigned activity," or "I should have had more for them to do" and even more sweetly, "This is a really nice class." All of this is true but lies on the surface of what was *happening*: You taught the lesson but *lost* the class. What was missing was an attuned perception to the students, and the important "traces" of learning, and more importantly, of not learning, that were occurring under the surface of the smooth roll out of the plan. The heads-in-hand, or quiet sighs, or fiddling with pens, or shifting bodies are traces that needed probing, to find out if students were struggling, or stymied, or disengaged, or even deeply engaged. None of these behaviors, by themselves, can be taken as given that something is wrong, or right for that matter. They could simply mean that the student is tired, or thinking deeply while twirling their pen, or shifting at their desk from stiffness incurred from sitting. They could mean that nothing really is at stake, or everything is at stake. This is to say that these kinds of traces call for investigation into what they mean. They raise important questions about what is happening, or not, as students live through the lesson. Should we intervene, or let things be? Probing carefully, *tactfully*, could lead to deeper insight into learning or the lack of it, into the force and the direction the teaching needs to take, even that that an entire halt to things needs to occur—that we are lost, or dead-ended and need to circle back to find our way.

However, this is where rigorous practice in hermeneutics, what Gadamer (1960/1997) called "uninterrupted listening" (p. 465) is essential. What might that mean? Uninterrupted does not mean that we never stop listening, but that when we listen it is not interrupted by our expectations, or that we already know—we are open to hearing otherwise. Second, when we listen it is not simply with our ears, but rather as Lipari (2014) claimed,

> I listen not only to words with my mind, but also to the music of the voice in my ears, the posture and gesture of the body with my eyes, the vibrational rhythm of the others' pulsations, movements and intonation in my body … Listening itself is a form of speaking that resonates with echoes of everything we have ever heard, thought, seen, touched, said, and read throughout our lives. (p. 9)

We are not simply listening to words or for information, or to fill in our topics, but rather,

> A rhetorically and ethically sensitive listener keeps an ear out for places of silence, erasure, misrecognition. Such a listener notices gaps and fissures, the elisions that occur when one voice speaks in place of another or when another is silenced. Who speaks? Who is heard? Whose voice rendered unintelligible? (Lipari, 2010, p. 121)

Uninterrupted listening does not freeze us in place, either. Quite the opposite, it "allows oneself to be conducted by the subject matter to which the partners in the dialog are oriented" (Gadamer, 1960/1997, p. 367). The task in hermeneutic listening is one of "cultivating an *interpretive ea*r for the suggestive resonances of words in their *relationship* to things studied" (Przanowska, 2019, p. 82).

4. More Than Method, *Wayfinding* Is a Way of Life for Hermeneutics on the Trail

We are making the claim here that doing hermeneutic work involves *wayfinding*, the essence of being on the trail. Wayfinding is a complex, dynamic process, involving seeing what is at stake, interpreting the trace, engaging in the question-and-answer dialectic, "knowing as you go" and even getting lost and finding oneself, repeatedly.

Some of the foregoing will require further explanation. We should set the scene with the notion of wayfinding. We begin with Ingold's (2002) important insight hearkening back to Gadamer's understanding of hermeneutics as a "way of life."

> Contrary to the assumptions of cartographers and cognitive map theorists, life is not contained within things, nor is it transported about. It is rather laid down along paths of movement, of action and perception. Every living being, accordingly, grows and reaches out into the environment along the sum of its paths. To find one's way is to advance along a line of growth, in a world which is never quite the same from one moment to the next, and whose future configuration can never be fully known. Ways of life are not therefore determined in advance, as routes to be followed, but have continually to be worked out anew. (p. 242)

"Continually to be worked out anew" is the essence of wayfinding, and we would argue hermeneutic inquiry but a careful word about what this does not mean is required. It does not mean proceeding "willy-nilly," without insight and discipline. Ingold borrowed the idea from ancient Micronesian sailors who found their way, even as far as Canada, without maps. They did not simply jump in their vessels and start paddling, unprepared. They did not proceed without an understanding of the stars, and without being perceptive about the wind, the waves, the ocean, and the weather, that is, without depending upon the dynamic relationship between the stars (the universal), and the immediate conditions unfolding around them (the particular). Another way of saying this is that they were guided by a deep understanding derived from their practice. They had to be careful and disciplined, rigorous and perceptive—dispositions acquired from the right kind of experience. So, when Ingold claims that wayfaring is "knowing as we go," he does not mean simply mean winging it, or as a colleague of ours who is critical of hermeneutics says, "going down in our basements and making stuff up." Neither does it mean that those early mariners did not plan or employ methods, but rather that their plans, methods, and practices were vulnerable and open. As Ingold (2002) wrote, "above all, wayfinding depends upon the attunement of the traveler's movements in response to the movements in his or her surroundings" (p. 241).

Similarly, in hermeneutic inquiry, "knowing as we go" arises because of the dynamic relation between the topic, the traces it offers, the questions and the answers that arise about those traces, and the other. What is it that knowing as we go yields? Nothing other than a good interpretation. What is a good interpretation when one is on the trail? It is one that helps us see "what is at stake in the situation" (Risser, 1997), one that yields new understanding of the topic and ourselves as wayfarers, and importantly, in Gadamer's (2016) words, "for those who are on their way and looking for their way ... one is pointed in a direction, and thus bound to follow" (p. 192).

Summary

It may seem as though hermeneutic inquiry is beyond the ken of mortal practitioners, especially for those who are just beginning to learn about engaging in hermeneutic inquiry. Given that the way of inquiry has not been mapped out in advance, there is not a set of fixed steps to follow, that the path and the way along it must be made and not simply followed it can seem to many to be too complicated, too onerous, and far too risky to undertake successfully. Gadamer (2018) himself signaled the difficulty of being on the trail when he spoke of losing the trace, of hitting dead ends and of getting lost. Our many graduate students over the years, most of them novice hermeneutic inquirers when they began their research, would heartily disagree. First, as experienced teachers and nurses—successful practitioners—they know that practice can break down, children do not always learn, patients do not always get better, we are as often stymied as we are successful. This is to say that nurse and teacher practitioners beginning to do hermeneutic inquiry soon realize that they, as Gadamer (2016) wrote, "are always already on the trail and never find ourselves at a distance from where we can see the immeasurable world of signs lying fully spread out before our eyes" (pp. 194–195). Our students might be beginning anew, as we often do in the classroom and the hospital, but they are not beginning *tabula raza*. Careful practice has taught important hermeneutic lessons and cultivated crucial dispositions for doing hermeneutic work—being tactful, being open to what finely attuned perception makes available to them, being able to answer the call of their students, patients (and topics) in being responsible.

The phrase "being on *the* trail" can be a little misleading—as if the topic is traversed just once, as if there is only one trail, as if we get only one chance at finding our way. That is not the case in hermeneutic work—we crisscross the topic countless times during the course of an inquiry. We see, hear, and feel from many different perspectives and vistas—with the help of the other, whether that other is our participants, our "dissertation buddies," our colleagues, our supervisors and even, (with deep gratitude for their tolerance) our spouses. We should not forget to mention one of our favorite interlocutors, whom we return to again and again, often as a group, for his insight and advice—Hans-Georg Gadamer. This "being on the trail together" is the enduring practice of the *Canadian Hermeneutic Institute* (chiannual.com). In hermeneutic inquiry, newcomers and old hands alike take great comfort in the fact that we are not on the trail alone, and just as importantly, that we do not, and cannot, "get it right" the first time. "Miss-takes" are an essential part of any hermeneutic inquiry. For what is "being pulled up short" if not a miss-take that interrupts our taken-for-granted path? To suffer these mistakes, to be open and vulnerable to what arrives, is to bear the weight of responsibility for "being on the trail" in hermeneutic inquiry.

References

Caputo, J. D. (1987). *Radical hermeneutics: Repetition, deconstruction, and the hermeneutic project*. Indiana University Press.

Davey, N. (2006). *Unquiet understanding: Gadamer's philosophical hermeneutics*. SUNY.

Dostal, R. J. (2002). Gadamer's relation to Heidegger and phenomenology. In C. Guignon (Ed.), *The Cambridge companion to Gadamer* (pp. 247–266). Cambridge University Press.

Gadamer, H.-G. (1960/1997). *Truth and method* (2nd rev. ed.; J. Weinsheimer & D. G. Marshall, Trans.). Continuum.

Gadamer, H.-G. (2001). *Gadamer in conversation: Reflections and commentary* (R. Palmer, Ed.). Yale University Press.

Gadamer, H.-G. (2007). *The Gadamer reader: A bouquet of later writings* (R. Palmer, Ed. & Trans.). Northwestern University Press.

Gadamer, H.-G. (2016) *Hermeneutics between history and philosophy. The selected writings of Hans-Georg Gadamer, Vol. 1* (P. Vandevelde & A. Iyer, Eds. & Trans.). Bloomsbury Academic.

Heidegger, M. (1999). *Ontology: The hermeneutics of facticity*. Indiana University Press.

Hoy, D. (2006). Heidegger and the hermeneutic turn. In C. Guignon (Ed.), *The Cambridge companion to Heidegger* (2nd ed.). Cambridge University Press.

Ingold, T. (2002). *The perception of the environment: Essays on livelihood, dwelling and skill*. Routledge.

Lipari, L. (2004). Listening for the other: Ethical implications of the Buber-Levinas encounter. *Communication Theory*, *14*(2), 122–141. <https://doi.org/10.1111/j.1468-2885.2004.tb00308.x>
Lipari, L. (2014). *Listening, thinking, being: Towards an ethics of attunement*. Pennsylvania State University Press.
Noe, A. (2012). *Varieties of presence*. Harvard University Press.
Przanowska, M. (2019). *Listening and acouological education*. University of Warsaw Press.
Ricoeur, P. (1996). *Oneself as another*. University of Chicago Press.
Risser, J. (1997). *Hermeneutics and the voice of the oth*er. SUNY Press.
Raffoul, F. (2010). *The origins of responsibility*. Indiana University Pres
Schwandt, T. (2007). *The Sage dictionary of qualitative inquiry*. Sage Publications.
Scott, C. (2002). *The lives of things*. Indiana University Press.
Vandevelde, P., & Iyer, A., Eds. & Trans. (2016). *Hermeneutics between history and philosophy: The selected writings of Hans-Georg Gadamer, Vol.1*. Bloomsbury Academic.

The Address of the Topic[1]

"Understanding begins when something addresses us" (Gadamer, 1960/1997, p. 299). The conduct of a research study guided by the tenets of Gadamerian philosophical hermeneutics rarely has a definitive starting point or endpoint, but if one had to delineate a place where inquiry begins, it is often around the experience of being addressed personally about something at work in one's life or practice. An address is the feeling of being caught in some aspect of the world's regard, of being called or summoned. In this chapter, we speak about the experience and importance of the address of a topic in the working out of a hermeneutic inquiry.

What Is an Address?

Addresses catch us off guard and break through our regular routines. They cause us to pause and take note, ask not that we speak or do something immediately, but rather that we stop and listen. It is through this process of listening, or what Bruns (1992) called "reading with our ears" (p. 157), that the topic of inquiry often arrives. To listen when we are addressed means that we are vulnerable and open, that we are prepared to be guided by a topic and its own form of address, rather than assumed versions of it, or by a predetermined method. As stated previously in this book, it is not the case that there is not a method in hermeneutics, but rather, that *method serves the topic and is informed by the topic*. The question becomes one of how we serve the topic in a disciplined way. How are we to be disciplined by the topic? In other words, the topic asks for rigor from us, attentiveness, and discipline to stay with it and stay true to it.

An address functions to interrupt or unsettle our everyday taken-for-grantedness of things. This is why it arrives typically in the form of a question or set of questions. As Dunne (1993) explained: "There is often a *suddenness* about it that makes us say that a question 'comes' to us, that it 'arises,' or 'presents itself'"

(p. 135). There is a case though that an address might not always be sudden; instead, it may have lingered for years and nagged in maybe not quite noticeable ways. However, there is a process of actually "waking up" to this or starting to pay attention to it and to begin to question. Bergum (1991) explained what it is that generates questions, and the effects they have:

> Questioning indicates the existence of an unsettled issue, a difficult matter, an uncertainty, a matter for discussion. It also invites a reply, a dialogue, a searching out of opportunities and similarities. It opens possibilities and leads, in some sense, to uncertainty, for it throws what may have been thought secure into dis-equilibrium or imbalance. (p. 57)

The address that occurs is a substantive one. We are hailed by subject matter, or better stated perhaps, *a subject that matters* so that, when we are addressed, we are obligated to respond, not in "any old fashion," but to respond to the best of our abilities, to do the right thing, in the right way, as Gadamer would say.

When a topic shows itself, *it haunts us*, because it also "hides" itself. It is, as Bergum has alluded to, shrouded in mystery. As a result, we are called to the mystery of the topic, to do justice to the questions that it can raise in us, to approach it care-fully, with both curiosity and suspicion, suspense, and intent, discipline and free play. In hermeneutics, tenants with proper names inhabit topics; they are things of human concern, and also, things that have concern for us, that is, living things that literally make a difference in our lives.

Address, as experienced, can be a breathtaking and breath-sustaining gift. When it arrives, it asks that the researcher suffer the mysteries of the topic—and this means to put what they believe at risk, to be open to learning from risking what matters, and most importantly, to speak of this in human terms, to do well by "the tenants" that greet you at the portal. Thus, the servitude demanded by a topic is not primarily methodical, but rather ethical in nature (Caputo, 1993); it is a call of our conscience, that comes with an obligation to respond to the call of *what should be done*, and not simply, as can occur in the natural sciences, *what can be done*.

> Obligation is the event of someone; of something personal in the midst of this inarticulate hum … Events happen anonymously, like the roar of the surf, while obligation is like the cry of a small child who has lost his way on the beach calling for help. (Caputo, 1993, p. 246)

The obligation to respond to the call of the topic is not simply a question of "how do I broach my topic?" but rather, "how do I cultivate what is already there?" — existing, speaking, opinionated, teasing and teeming with mystery. In responding to this address, there is a sense of an opening, or as Heidegger might have suggested, a clearing, and the promise of being transformed by a living, provocative conversation that was already underway. Conversational topics, then, have entrails; they are historically located, and we must listen carefully to pick up on the entrails. In this way, the topics are not new; they are already at play. Hermeneutic inquiry demands that, as late arrivers to a conversation, we both let what is at play move us forward, and that we join in moving it forward.

This demands attention. Davey (2013) suggested that "being attentive … implies that one knows one is being addressed and that one's self-understanding is caught up in the entailments of that address" (p. 80). He further offered that attentiveness has aspects of passivity and activity in the vulnerability to the topic and the responsiveness of addressing it with "patience and focus" (p. 80). Akin to the notion of obligation, Davey claimed that "attending is also profoundly ethical: it is a practice through which the one who attends changes" (p. 83).

The Substance of a Topic

What constitutes a topic? In practice professions, such as nursing, social work, psychology, and education, topics are often grounded in the field of practice. They have a place, a geographical territory, so to speak, in which they dwell. For example, a psychologist might be struck by the notion of shame in eating disorders, a nurse by the experiences of having nursed children who sometimes die, an educator by the coding and naming of "slow learners," or a social worker by the issue of child abuse. Practitioners *suffer these things in their practice.*

Within each practice, there are as many topics as there are questions, but not all topics are experienced as a form of address. Even the ones that do address us are partially hidden from us because of our *prejudices*, as Gadamer (1969/1997) would say, or to paraphrase Heidegger (1927/1962), by our practical involvement with the things themselves. To use Heidegger's example, one cannot properly notice or understand running for the bus when one is running for the bus. One starts to notice a topic, when one is "pulled up short" (Gadamer, 1969/1997), when we miss the bus, so to speak, and are left breathless in its disappearing exhaust. In the same way, one is not often aware of health except in its absence (Gadamer, 1996). Unless something like this happens to us—*and* we do not *will* it to happen—we often continue in our practices in unquestioning ways, assuming taken-for-granted discourses and ways of being around what we do in everyday practice. It is, however, the disruption of success in our everyday practices that allows a topic to emerge, in completely familiar, but also strange and disruptive ways.

For example, one of the authors (Moules, 2002, 2003, 2009a, 2009b) was involved in family therapy work and practiced using therapeutic letters as a routine part of the clinical work. It continued to amaze her to witness the power of written communication in a practice that had its tradition in the power of talk, and yet the written communication seemed to have a different and sometimes even stronger influence. She was struck with how even family members who might not immediately been seen as particularly "literary," were captivated by the letters and moved to extremes of keeping them in bedside drawers or, in one case, framing them. This disruption of the familiar and the kind of amazement that goes with it, a puzzlement, wondering, and passion for understanding, represents the call of topics.

As we have said, discerning what constitutes a topic requires that we first listen to its call, and then work out how we might best answer. At times, the topics are too immense and unanswerable; these do not lend themselves to a hermeneutic study. If the topic is, for example, "why do children die?" one can imagine that this is not a question that any amount of hermeneutic research (or any other kind of research) could offer an answer. However, inside of that existential and unanswerable question lies other topics and questions that can be addressed, such as "How might we understand oncology nurses' experiences of working with children who sometimes die?" or "What is it like for the parents of children who die, or the grandparents of children who die?" Each of these topics is different, but the same in this way: each requires the "voice of the other" (Risser, 1997). For us to understand, each requires that we engage with those who have lived through the experience so that we might learn from them. Davey (2006) suggested that this also involves speculative thought, and speculative thought involves being "caught up in the motion of ideas, and ...arrested by them" (p. 113).

Topics involve a phenomenon or sometimes many phenomena, yet hermeneutic research is not the same as pure phenomenological research in that the goal is not to essentialize, define, or even simply describe the topic. The goal is not to carve away at all the extremities of the phenomenon of interest to reach an essence or core, to achieve an uncontaminated description of it stripped of its context. Rather, the desire is to conserve the topic in all of its complexity, in the words of Caputo, "to restore it to its original difficulty" (1987, p. 1). As stated, very often our practices go unnoticed and unexamined, lost to discourse, assumption, and involvement; often they remain in the state of being taken for granted. When the address of a topic arrives, it troubles something and problematizes it. When this happens, the work becomes about "exoticizing the domestic" (White, 1993, p. 35), taking what is assumed and unquestioned and looking at it as something new and exotic. This involves looking at it from fresh perspectives, trying to understand it differently, while still preserving the topic's integrity, the whole of it, as it lives in the world.

In looking to a topic, to understand a topic while conserving its complexity, we are not searching for an essence; rather this is an act of truth-seeking—of looking for what might be true in and of the topic. This does not mean to imply that there is one "Truth" to be known about topics but rather that we stay true to the work of *aletheia* in unconcealing topics in all of their messiness and richness.

The Hermeneutic Notion of Truth

We admit, up front, that any discussion of truth is difficult and tricky, partly because truth in research, and this holds for a lot of inquiry that would be called "qualitative," is often thought of *only* as correspondence between thought and world, between an "inner" and "outer" representation of the thing itself. There is no inner and outer in hermeneutic research, in the sense of an unbridgeable chasm between self and world. We are, as Heidegger (1927/1962) maintained, always in the world, and hermeneutic research is always about understanding, about what it means to be in the world in a particular way. This is to say that, as practitioners, we are deeply involved in our practices, and it is only through our practical, everyday involvement that the truth, that is, *the meaning of something*, becomes available at all (Heidegger, 1927/1962; Wrathall, 2013).

Truth, at least the truth about being human and human practice, is also tricky because it is located in time and place. It can and does change (and stay the same) over time and between places. Hermeneutic truth is plural, not singular, in this way: There is not one right way to help all patients recover from cancer, for example, or a single method for helping every child learn to read. At the same time, *not every way is right*. We *can* get it wrong; we can make people sicker by trying to help them heal. We can make learning to read impossible; while trying to teach, we can deceive ourselves thoroughly and fall into untruth (Wrathall, 2013) in the very pursuit of truth. The history of nursing and education is littered with such examples. Finally (here at least), truth is tricky in hermeneutic work because it disappears as it appears. We never get "the whole truth and nothing but the truth," because *truth is both revealed to us and concealed from us at once*. This is why Gadamer, following his teacher Heidegger, appropriated the notion of truth as *aletheia* for hermeneutic work.

Hermeneutic work is more about conservation than preservation. To preserve something is to hold it in all its sameness, to protect and save it from spoiling, and changing, *to kill it*, whereas to conserve something means *to keep it alive*, to keep it from being damaged, lost, or wasted (Merriam-Webster online, n.d.). In our efforts to conserve a topic, to not allow it to be lost or forgotten as something simply accepted, the unconcealment and enlivening that comes with truth necessarily comes into play. As mentioned earlier, hermeneutics is the practice of *aletheia*, the event of unconcealment and unhiddenness (Caputo, 1987, p. 115; Coltman, 1998). *Aletheia* first occurs when we are addressed, when something opens which was once closed, when we become aware of something that was not there as being there. *Aletheia* can be represented by the metaphor of opening the lid of a well, of flipping the lid open and letting it rest so one can look into what lies beneath it. In this opening of one side, another side is closed, for with every opening there is closure, and some things are necessarily left behind. The opposite of Lethe and lethal, a*letheia* works against what is dead or forgotten; it enlivens and remembers. *Aletheia* is the clearing of things into the mystery beneath; it is the "ongoing, historical, epochal process by which things emerge from concealment into unconcealment" (Caputo, 1987, p. 177). The four meanings then of *aletheia* are a portal or opening, an enlivening, a remembering, and unconcealment. When topics address us, they open something, they call on us to remember why it is that certain things matter, and they ask us to bring these things alive in the here and now of our lives.

The Centrality of the Notion of Phronesis to Hermeneutic Work

Gadamer was committed to staying close to concrete, factual life. His approach focused on *understanding life as it is lived* and, for Gadamer, that meant achieving an understanding of how to act well in concrete, particular circumstances. This is why he based his notion of understanding on the form of knowledge the Greeks called *phronesis*, because it provided him with a notion of practical knowledge, knowledge in action, which remains *experiential* through and through (Davey, 2006). Dunne (1993) elaborated:

> ...phronesis is a habit of *attentivenesss* that makes the resources of one's past experience flexibly available to one, and at the same time allows the present situation to "unconceal" its own particular significance—which it may do comfortably within the terms of one's experience or else only by evincing as insight, which while it could not occur without one's past experience, still transcends, and so enriches it. (pp. 305–306)

So, while it is true that we can be struck by something, addressed in a way that opens a topic for us, it is only through a "habit of attentiveness" that we can keep the topic open, that we can follow the direction implied in the questions that arise, and learn from the event of being addressed. The role of deliberation in this process is key and holds an important position in Gadamer's (1997) description of phronesis. In the following, we offer examples of the work of phronesis in its experiential understanding of "life as it is lived" in everyday practices.

Examples of Topics and How They Arrived

The hermeneutic experience of being addressed, of grasping that there is clearly something true about what is being said, involves, first: recognizing something that one was already acquainted with but had not fully grasped, and second: in reappropriating what had not been initially grasped, coming to realize its significance for the first time.
—Davey (2006, p. 117)

Example A

Doubled and Silenced: Grandparents' Experiences of Childhood Cancer (Moules, Laing et al., 2012; Moules, McCaffrey et al., 2012).

Working in pediatric oncology, both Laing and Moules knew firsthand how cancer is a family affair. Childhood cancer affects not only cells, but the body, life, relationships, and communities. There has been much research done on the experiences of siblings of children with cancer and parents, but very little attention to the extended family, in this case, the grandparents. A part of the address of this topic was that, a few years ago, Moules had the experience of having her only child in the Intensive Care Unit due to an acute cardiac crisis. He is also the only grandchild of her parents, and she became aware of how her parents were not only suffering and worrying for their grandson, but also their own daughter and her fears and concerns. They, however, did not want to burden her with their worries so this doubled concern was suffered silently and alone. Grandparents of children with cancer live this duality and the study invited voice to an experience that had been, to some extent, silenced.

Example B

"It's Not Just Camp": Understanding the Meaning of Children's Cancer Camps for Children and Families (Laing, 2012; Laing, 2013; Laing & Moules, 2013; Laing & Moules, 2014a; Laing & Moules, 2014b; Laing & Moules, 2015).

Laing credits a short film about cancer camp, shown in the second year of her undergraduate nursing degree, as the impetus to get into the field of pediatric oncology. It was a simple film showing children with cancer attending camp, supplemented by interviews with several children, and nurses who were attending as camp counselors. While the details are forgettable, she never forgot that moment in time when, as she described, "pediatric oncology chose me." As she traversed through her clinical career in pediatric oncology, Laing was struck by how important camp was for kids with cancer and their families. She never understood why camp was so important, why the kids started talking about summer camp shortly after Christmas trying to gauge the likelihood they could go the same week as their friends, or that they would not be too sick to go for one of the weeks. While she did not understand why, the fact that camp seemed such a profound experience for most kids and families always stuck with her. After deciding to pursue doctoral studies and struggling at first to identify a topic for research, Laing eventually came back to the idea of camp. She wanted to understand what it was that made camp so special, so important for these families, and why it mattered. It was camp, after all, that had claimed her in the first place.

Example C

The Case of the Disappearing/Appearing "Slow Learner" An Interpretive Mystery (Williamson, 2012; 2015; Williamson & Field, 2014a, 2014b; Williamson & Paul, 2012a, 2012b).

As someone who, as a student, struggled academically in ways that would align with Alberta's current definitions of educational disability, as a parent of a child with a Down Syndrome, and as a teacher/coordinator of disability services at a large urban high school, Williamson had been experiencing disability for most of his life. His impetus for entering doctoral studies was to interpret the assumptions and practices involved in working with slow learners, a particular category of students who are predicted by way of intelligence testing to struggle in school but for whom the Albertan special education system has granted no formal support. Williamson had been teaching in an instructional tier aimed at these students for many years and had come to see how this category on the border of disability exposes the frequent rigidity of educational thinking about disability and intellectual potential. Tools meant to address student diversity and disability categories can, ironically, become unwieldy, imposing further restraint on a system that is already too inflexible for all students. Despite this, Williamson has also been privileged to bear witness to the transcendent moments when generous teaching practices meet engaged learners, and disability categories, at least in their deficit framings, disappear. It is the appearance and disappearance of categories that finally called out to Williamson, who is also a life-long fan of detective fiction, as way of framing the complexities of this topic. He chose to present his research in this area as a "hard-boiled" detective story: "*The Case of the Disappearing/Appearing Slow Learner.*"

Example D

Understanding Nurse-Patient Relationships on Acute Mental Health Units, Buddhist Perspectives (McCaffrey, 2012; McCaffrey et al., 2012).

While working in an interdisciplinary position on a mental health unit, McCaffrey was struck by contrasting perceptions of how nurses did their work. Nurses saw themselves as having good therapeutic relationships with patients, while team members including occupational therapists, social workers, and psychiatrists often felt frustrated that nurses seemed under-informed about patients, and their work with them was undirected. After starting to explore more deeply the question of how nurses work with patients on mental health units, McCaffrey became aware of how much his nursing practice was informed by an earlier experience of working in a therapeutic community, in which relationship was the medium of care and change was paramount. The topic was, at the same time, formed by a study of Zen Buddhist traditions of thought and practice, which offered new ways of looking at nursing. Obvious affinities between Buddhism and nursing, such as practicing with suffering and compassion, became a starting point for deeper and more complex exploration.

Example E

"Do You Think the Angels Will Speak Spanish?": Nurses' Experiences of Death in Pediatric Oncology (Morck, 2014).

Morck's (2009) previous work, which will be described in the following section in this chapter, was looking at the emotional marks that happen to psychiatric nurses after hearing stories of trauma and suffering. As her clinical work shifted to the area of oncology rather than mental health, she became addressed by the impact on pediatric oncology nurses when children die as they can do in this population. The work of Rashotte (2005) in *Dwelling With the Stories That Haunt Us* spoke to her about the ways that loss haunts and marks, not just the family of children with cancer, but also those professionals who care for them.

Example F

The Public Face of Grief: Parental Bereavement and Social Media (Moules et al., 2024)

Having studied grief for years, Moules, Laing, and Neimeyer became fascinated with the societal shift that was happening in the world of bereavement. Like every other aspect of life, social media is becoming more and more prominent in bereavement practices. The number of people choosing to publicly air things about their deceased loved one or their feelings of grief was noticed by the researchers. They invited hermeneutic philosopher, Professor Theodore George, to join them in conducting a hermeneutic study to try to reach some understanding of what this choice might mean to both bereaved individuals and those who post on social media sites of bereavement.

Speaking for the Address

How do you write about address? Topics start somewhere and most often they start with an instance. This instance needs to be described in the work as a way of locating and populating the topic with a living example that shows it for all its power. An example of this is the paper published in the *Journal of Applied Hermeneutics*, "Isn't All Oncology Hermeneutic?" (Moules et al., 2013). Although the paper does not reflect a research study, it is a response to the critique that has been made about the relatively small numbers of participants that often appear in hermeneutic research, and an argument about the fit of hermeneutics as a research method that attempts to understand practice and phenomena that arise within practice. The authors of this work start by describing an instance that gave rise to the discussion—an arrival of the topic. In this case, the topic was about hermeneutics, numbers, power, and verification through numbers in contrast to the "fecundity of the individual case" (Jardine, 1992). Throughout the paper then, the discussion of theory and philosophy had to also be instantiated and Moules et al. did so through two very powerful descriptions of the experience of an oncologist and his patients.

In the introduction of topics in hermeneutic research, most often there is a story around the arrival of the topic, a narrative of dialectic with the topic and a reason as to why the topic matters to the researcher, and an instantiation of the meaningfulness and call of the topic. In a master's thesis hermeneutic study by Morck (2009) entitled *"Right There, in the Midst of it with Them": Impacts of the Therapeutic Relationship on Nurses*, she was attempting to understand the topic of the impact on mental health nurses of hearing stories of pain, suffering, and trauma. In the thesis, she recounted being a young, new nurse and starting her work in a hospital inpatient mental health unit. Very early in her career, she recalled encountering one of the patients she was working with cowering in the corner of her room. As she approached and engaged in conversation with the patient, she was to hear a terrible story of abuse where the patient claimed that the rain outside the window smelled of urine. Following this seemingly incomprehensible statement, Morck knelt with the patient and gently asked her more about how the rain smelled like urine. The patient proceeded to tell her an event she remembered: she was five years old, just raped by her father and his friend, thrown down the steps, urinated on, and then they left out the door. It was raining outside. Morck discussed how this instance was one of many that had a profound impact on her as a new and young nurse hearing of such suffering. Hearing stories like this one and countless others was then the address that called her to her research, a topic full of complexity and obligation to do well with it.

Topics cannot just matter to the researcher alone; they must be something relevant in the world. They are not selfish indulgences, trying to work out something individually for individual curiosity, gain, or even therapy, but rather a working out that is meaningful in relation to the phenomena that surround it. It is not just Morck who experienced the weight of hearing and bearing stories of pain and suffering but other psychiatric nurses who hear and bear the same responsibility—and it is not just psychiatric nurses. Social workers bear witness to stories of violence and abuse. Teachers hear stories of children's child abuse, stories of torture and escape from war torn counties. No one profession owns what has been referred to as "vicarious trauma" (see for e.g., Figley, 1995; Mathieu, 2011).

Asking Questions of the Address: Developing Research Questions

Out of topics, one needs to narrow and focus on a research question. In hermeneutics, there is a particular kind of flavor to the question. One would not necessarily seek an ontological question such as "What is something," as hermeneutics is not in search of phenomenological essences. It is not intended to shave off extremities to narrow something down to a definition of what it is or is not. Rather than definition or explanation, it is in search of understanding and interpretation, looking for possible and good ways to understand a particular topic.

More hermeneutic in intent than a "what is" question are questions that imply interpretation. A question such as "how might we understand the meaning of children's cancer camps for children and families?" would be a question that aims for meaning, interpretation, and understanding rather than assessment or measurement of impact.

In a similar way, hermeneutics does not set out to develop theories or templates so a research topic that might be described as, for example, "Developing a Theory of New Social Workers Learning" would not be consistent with the way we have taken up hermeneutic research. The title of the study and the guiding research question then must show integrity with the philosophy that informs it. This is an important point of congruency. If one develops a question that is unanswerable from a hermeneutic perspective, such as "Why do children die?," the credibility of the work is compromised and incomprehensible.

The process of determining one definitive research question is often one that is under the gaze and demand of funding bodies and granting bodies, but in many ways, it is counterintuitive to hermeneutics. Questions beget questions and the answer to a question is only one response. We are reminded that Gadamer (1960/1997) suggested that hermeneutics is the answer to a question that could have been answered differently. The research question that began the research is sometimes forced to change, given the shifts in thinking that arise as the researcher engages with the data. Research questions are only intended to guide the research and serve the topic and, often as the study progresses, the question becomes clearer.

Speaking to the Address: What Constitutes Data in Hermeneutic Research?

Understanding *begins* with an address, but it only begins there. Understanding a topic must be cultivated. Everything is potential data if it helps to further the interpretation of the questionability of the topic. Data may come in the form of photographs, art, poetry, textbooks, policy, newspaper articles, scholarly literature, philosophical texts, literary texts, conversations, or any other medium. Address spreads outwards as the interconnections of the topic become apparent. It is another mark of the relevance of effective hermeneutic work when a topic is seen to live in worlds of shared cultures.

One can conduct a hermeneutic study without the traditional qualitative method of interviewing participants, but there has to be a good demonstration that researchers have gone beyond only their own perception and reflections of the topic. Very often, however, this kind of research strives toward involving conversation, the Latin of which is "conversa" which means to turn around together. Gadamer (1960/1997) took up the notion of dialogue as central to hermeneutics. Hermeneutics is dialectic, a "fusion of horizons" which cannot happen alone. For example, to understand a topic such as grandparents' experiences of childhood cancer, there are many portals of understanding but the most obvious is by engaging in research conversations with grandparents directly.

Once a topic has emerged, it opens up to a process of inquiry that attempts to conserve it in all its complexity and pursues it through its associations and connections to the world—with the conscientious intention to remain rooted in the original human situation and to bring back to those involved some new and sustaining ways of understanding themselves. Address signals the complexity that lies beneath the surface of everyday activity. Borrowing from the lexicon of grounded theory, where data "saturation" indicates an end to data collection, by contrast, *hermeneutic inquiry begins in saturation, with a topic that is already overloaded.*

> From a philosophical perspective, there is a poverty of understanding, but there is an excess of meaning in what we are studying. There is data saturation when it comes to most research, but when looking at something from a hermeneutics lens, you really can't over-exhaust a topic. (George, 2022)

As mentioned, often in hermeneutic research, data is collected through interviews. Understanding only begins with an address; the address then summons the researcher to move into the conduct of the study to obtain answers to the questions that arise. In the next chapter, we discuss the selection of participants, the nature, skill, and focus of interviews to collect rich data, fertile for interpretive analysis and very necessary in the conduct of this kind of research.

Summary

In the bigger picture of the conduct of hermeneutic inquiry, we start here with the experience of "address"—the ways one is called by topics, invited into positions of curiosity and wonder, tethered by what is known, and untethered by the possibilities of what remains to be discovered. Address is the call to dis- and un-covery as well as the call to recovery of what was forgotten. It is the beacon that summons and lures us to topics, but also the quiet warning and reminder that we are obligated to do well by them.

Note

1. A version of this chapter has been previously published in the *Journal of Applied Hermeneutics* and is reprinted with permission.

References

Bergum, V. (1991). Being a phenomenological researcher. In J. Morse (Ed.), *Qualitative nursing research* (pp. 43–57). Sage.

Bruns, G. L. (1992). *Hermeneutics ancient and modern*. Yale University Press.

Caputo, J. D. (1987). *Radical hermeneutics: Repetition, deconstruction and the hermeneutic project*. Indiana University Press.

Caputo, J. D. (1993). *Against ethics: Contributions to a poetics of obligation with constant reference to deconstruction*. Indiana University Press.

Coltman, R. (1998). *The language of hermeneutics: Gadamer and Heidegger in dialogue*. SUNY.

Conserve. (n.d.). In *Merriam-Webster's online dictionary*. Retrieved from <http://www.merriam-webster.com/dictionary/conserve>

Davey, N. (2006). *Unquiet understanding: Gadamer's philosophical hermeneutics*. SUNY.

Davey, N. (2013). *Unfinished worlds: Hermeneutics, aesthetics and Gadamer*. Edinburgh University Press.

Dunne, J. (1993). *Back to the rough ground: Practical judgment and the lure of technique*. University of Notre Dame Press.

Figley, C. R. (1995). *Compassion fatigue: Coping with secondary traumatic stress disorder in those who treat the traumatized*. Routledge, Taylor & Francis Group.

Gadamer, H.-G. (1960/1997). *Truth and method* (2nd rev. ed.; J. Weinshemer & D. G. Marshall, Trans.). Continuum.

Gadamer, H.-G. (1996). *The enigma of health: The art of healing in a scientific age*. Stanford University Press.

George, T. (2022). *Newly appointed UCalgary Nursing adjunct is faculty first philosopher*. UToday, University of Calgary. <https://nursing.ucalgary.ca/news/newly-appointed-ucalgary-nursing-adjunct-facultys-first-philosopher>

Heidegger, M. (1927/1962). *Being and time* (J. M. E. Robinson, Trans.). Harper and Row.

Hoad, T. F (Ed.). (1986). *The concise Oxford dictionary of English etymology*. Oxford University Press.

Jardine, D. W. (1992). The fecundity of the individual case: Considerations of the pedagogic heart of interpretive work. *Journal of Philosophy of Education, 26*(1), 51–61. <https://doi.org/10.1111/j.1467-9752.1992.tb00264.x>

Laing, C. M. (2012). At play, In play. *Journal of Applied Hermeneutics*, Article 6, <https://doi.org/10.11575/jah.v0i0.53197>

Laing, C. M. (2013). *"It's not just camp": Understanding the meaning of children's cancer camps for children and families*. Unpublished doctoral research, University of Calgary, Calgary, AB, Canada.

Laing, C. M., & Moules, N. J. (2013). The island of misfit toys. *Journal of Applied Hermeneutics, Article 8*, <http://hdl.handle.net/10515/sy5js9hq4>

Laing, C. M., & Moules, N. J. (2014a). Stories from cancer camp: Tales of glitter and gratitude. *Journal of Applied Hermeneutics,* Article 3, <http://hdl.handle.net/10515/sy5qf8k16>

Laing, C. M., & Moules, N. J. (2014b). Children's cancer camps: A sense of community, a sense of family. *Journal of Family Nursing, 20*(2), 185–203. <https://doi.org/10.1177/1074840714520717>

Laing, C. M., & Moules, N. J. (2015). Children's cancer camps: A way to understand grief differently. *Omega: Journal of Death and Dying, 70*(4), 436–453. <https://doi.org/10.1177/0030222815572605>

Mathieu, F. (2011). *The compassion fatigue workbook: Creative tools for transforming compassion fatigue and vicarious traumatization*. Routledge, Taylor & Francis Group.

McCaffrey, G. (2012). *Nurse-patient relationship and Buddhist thought.* Unpublished doctoral thesis. University of Calgary. Calgary, AB, Canada.

McCaffrey, G., Raffin-Bouchal, S., & Moules, N. J. (2012). Buddhist thought and nursing : A hermeneutic exploration. *Nursing Philosophy, 13*, 87–97. <https://doi.org/10.1111/j.1466-769X.2011.00502.x>

Morck, A. (2009). *"Right There, in the Midst of it with Them": Impacts of the Therapeutic Relationship on Nurses*. Unpublished Master's thesis. University of Calgary, Calgary, AB, Canada.

Morck, A. (2014). *"Do You Think the Angels Will Speak Spanish?": Nurses' Experiences of Death in Pediatric Oncology*. Unpublished doctoral thesis. University of Calgary, Calgary, AB, Canada.

Moules, N. J. (2009a). Therapeutic letters in nursing: Examining the character and influence of the written word in clinical work with families experiencing illness. *Journal of Family Nursing, 15*(1), 31–49. <https://doi.org/10.1177/1074840709331638>

Moules, N. J. (2009b). The past and future of therapeutic letters: Family suffering and healing words. *Journal of Family Nursing, 15*(1), 102–111. <https://doi.org/10.1177/1074840709332238>

Moules, N. J. (2002). Nursing on paper: Therapeutic letters in nursing practice. *Nursing Inquiry, 9*(2), 104–113. <https://doi.org/10.1046/j.1440 1800.2002.00133.x>

Moules, N. J. (2003). Therapy on paper: Therapeutic letters and the tone of relationship. *Journal of Systemic Therapies, 22*(1), 33–49. <https://doi.org/10.1521/jsyt.22.1.33.24091>

Moules, N. J., Jardine, D. W., McCaffrey, G., & Brown, C. (2013). "Isn't all oncology hermeneutic?" *Journal of Applied Hermeneutics*. Article 3. <https://doi.org/10.11575/jah.v0i2.53221>

Moules, N. J., Laing, C. M., George, T., & Neimeyer, R. A. (2024). The public face of grief: Parental bereavement and social media. *Journal of Applied Hermeneutics*, Article 8, 1–25. <https://doi.org/10.55016/ojs/jah.v2024Y2024.79957>

Moules, N. J., Laing, C. M., McCaffrey, G., Tapp, D. M., & Strother, D. (2012). Grandparents' experiences of childhood cancer, Part one: Doubled and silenced. *Journal of Pediatric Oncology Nursing, 29*(3), 119–132. <https://doi.org/10.1177/1043454212439626>

Moules, N. J., McCaffrey, G., Laing, C. M., Tapp, D. M., & Strother, D. (2012). Grandparents' experiences of childhood cancer, Part two: The need for support. *Journal of Pediatric Oncology Nursing, 29*(3), 133–141. <https://doi.org/10.1177/1043454212439627>

Preserve. (n.d.). In *Merriam-Webster's online dictionary.* <http://www.merriam-webster.com/dictionary/preserve>

Rashotte, J. (2005). Dwelling with the stories that haunt us: Building a meaningful nursing practice. *Nursing Inquiry, 12*(1), 34–42. <https://doi.org/10.1111/j.1440-1800.2005.00248.x>

Risser, J. (1997). *Hermeneutics and the voice of the other.* SUNY.

White, M. (1993). Deconstruction and therapy. In S. Gilligan & R. Price (Eds.), *Therapeutic conversations* (pp. 22–61). W. W. Norton.

Williamson, W. J. (2012). Codes. *Canadian Journal of Disability Studies, North America, 1,* May. <http://cjds.uwaterloo.ca/index.php/cjds/article/view/47/50>.

Williamson, W. J. (2015). *The case of the disappearing/appearing slow learner: An interpretive mystery.* Unpublished doctoral thesis. University of Calgary, Calgary, AB, Canada

Williamson, W. J., & Field, J. C. (2014). The case of the disappearing/appearing slow learner: An interpretive mystery. *Journal of Applied Hermeneutics,* Article 4. <https://doi.org/10.11575/jah.v0i0.53227>

Williamson, W. J., & Paul, W. J. (2012a). The level playing field: Unconcealing diploma exam accommodation policy. *Journal of Applied Hermeneutics,* Article 13. <https://doi.org/10.11575/jah.v0i0.53205>

Williamson, J., & Paul. J. (2012b). The "slow learner" as a mediated construct. *Canadian Journal of Disability Studies, 1*(3), August. <http://cjds.uwaterloo.ca/index.php/cjds/article/view/59>

Wrathall, M. A. (Ed.). (2013). *The Cambridge companion to Heidegger's Being and Time.* Cambridge University Press.

Conducting Interviews in Hermeneutic Research

Data in hermeneutic studies are often (though not exclusively) gathered through interviews and cultivated in interpretive analysis. In this chapter, we discuss the conduct, complexity, and nuances of interviewing. Despite claims made by some that there is such a thing as a "hermeneutic interview" (Geanellos, 1999; Vandermause, 2011), we maintain that there is *not* a distinctively unique entity called a hermeneutic interview. Alternately, we claim that there are *good* interviews that generate *good* data, interviews that are conducted thoughtfully, openly, and deliberately to create space for understanding of the topic under inquiry. Conducting interviews in hermeneutic research is a skillful and practiced art, what Kvale and Brinkmann (2009) termed a "craft" that involves "intellectual craftsmanship." By this, they described craftsmanship as a "mastery of a form of production, which requires practical skills and personal insight acquired through training and extensive practice" (p. 86).

Interviews take on particular significance for hermeneutic research, based on the importance of language and conversation in the philosophical background. Heidegger regarded language as a house of being, a house that is big enough to hold many worlds, not just a house that includes some and excludes others. In this regard, we see data for human research as arising from a gathering and harvesting of experience. Heidegger (1975) further suggested that language or *legein*, is connected to the German word *legen*, which means to lay down and lay before:

> In *legen*, a "bringing together" prevails: the Latin *legere* understood as *lesen*, in the sense of collecting and bringing together. *Legein* properly means the laying-down and laying-before which gathers itself and others. (p. 60)

> To lay is to gather (*lesen*)...But gathering is more than mere amassing. To gathering belongs a collecting which brings shelter. Accommodation governs the sheltering; accommodation is in turn governed by safekeeping ... *legein* ... means just this, that whatever lies before us involves us and therefore concerns us. (pp. 61–62)

Gadamer emphasized the dialogic model of conversation, and his description of a genuine conversation is often conflated with the description of interviews in hermeneutic work with this widely cited quote:

> We say we "conduct" a conversation, but the more genuine a conversation is, the less its conduct lies within the will of either partner. Thus a genuine conversation is never the one we wanted to conduct. Rather it is more generally correct to say that we fall into conversation, or even that we become involved in it. The way one word follows another, with the conversation taking its own twists and reaching its own conclusion, may well be conducted in some way, but the partners conversing are far less the leaders of it than the led. No one knows in advance what will "come out" of a conversation. Understanding or its failure is like an event that happens to us. Thus we can say that something was a good conversation or that it was ill fated. All this shows that a conversation has a spirit of its own, and that language in which it is conducted bears its own truth with it—i.e., that it allows something to "emerge" which henceforth exists. (Gadamer, 1960/1997, p. 383)

Here, Gadamer was talking about the nature of genuine conversation; he was not describing a therapeutic conversation, which has its own intention, nor was he describing a research interview, which has its own purpose and focus as well. Therefore, we emphatically state that his quote about the conduct of a genuine conversation does not hold fully true for good research interviews. "The research interview is not a conversation between equal partners, because the researcher defines and controls the situation" (Kvale & Brinkmann, 2009, p. 3). Good research interviews *are* conducted and conducted well, even though there *is* an aspect of conversation involved that we discuss.

The Conversational Nature of Interviews

The word conversation comes from the Latin *conversa*, which means "turning around together" and the Latin *conversari* meaning "to dwell with; to keep company with, to wander together with" (Online Etymology Dictionary, n.d.). Research interviews are not of the same casual nature as those of phatic or social conversations. They have a structure of sorts, and more importantly, a purpose. This is not to imply that the interviewer enters with an immutable list of questions, but that the structure is defined by the topic and the interviewer attempts to keep the topic central in the conversation, while "turning around" with the participant. In this turning around, careful and mindful listening and skilled questioning are required.

In the more general qualitative research literature, Morse (1991) called these kinds of interviews "interactive" where the direction of conversation is reciprocal. There is an aspect, at times, of the participants having already interpreted what they are relating, but the research can help them move into a deeper interpretation. Kvale and Brinkmann (2009) identified 10 qualities of good interviewers: knowledgeable, structuring, clear, gentle, sensitive, open, steering, critical, remembering, and interpreting (pp. 166–167). To obtain good data, the research is highly dependent on the practiced skill of the interviewer, for the interviewer in this kind of work is the key research instrument. It requires discernment and instinct around choices of which direction to take the conversation, which leads to follow and which to divert, which statements to probe further, when to engage the participants in interpreting, and ultimately keeping the topic as the focus while respecting the participants' needs to tell their narratives of experience. Letting participants direct the interview is not always in the best service of the topic. It is not *just* about them telling their stories and recreating them or preserving them to explain human experience such as some phenomenological work does, but rather what in their stories and experience has something to say to, and about, the topic. "Yet, this restates Gadamer's problem: how to reconcile participation and critical distance" (Davey, 2013, p. 83). The act of participating while maintaining a distance is a crafted skill that is highly contingent on each circumstance.

The character of these kinds of interviews includes intense listening, finding a balance between allowing the person to finish and bringing attention to what seems most meaningful, avoiding invitations to counsel or teach, recognizing critical junctures, following leads, and curiosity as a means to remain engaged. Participation and conduct, engagement and distance, focus and flexibility are at constant play in the navigation of a good interview.

In 2021, Moules and Taylor published a paper in the *Journal of Applied Hermeneutics*, where there is a link to an interview between them. The interview occurred during a hermeneutic class where Moules was demonstrating how to conduct an interview. The class was held on Zoom and was recorded, and the two later decided to write about the interview experience from the perspective and intent of the interviewer and from the experience of the interviewee. A link to the video recording can be found in the article and here in this link (Moules & Taylor, 2021; <https://yuja.ucalgary.ca/V/Video?v=244868&a=130699778>)

Gathering Participants

Hermeneutics is deliberate in its selection of participants who can best speak to the topic under investigation. In this kind of research, the topic is not a storied account of the participants and therefore the writing is not a portrait of them (Moules, 2002). "Hermeneutic research is not validated by numbers, but by the completeness of examining the topic under study and the fullness and depth to which the interpretation extends understanding" (Moules, 2002, p. 14). "An adequate sample size in qualitative work is one that … results in … a new and richly textured understanding of experience" (Sandelowski, 1995, p. 182). In search of exemplar "cases" or the best participants, we are also faced with the realities and pragmatics of the research process. Ethical approval is often based on the provision that participants will volunteer, not be invited directly, or coerced in any conceivable way. As a result of this, those who volunteer are not necessary those sought or chosen and do not always offer the "best" data. It has to be considered, however, that those who volunteer do so for a reason and when one listens deeply enough, there is a truth that needs to be heard. This idea will be further discussed in a section included in this chapter.

The Pragmatics of the Interview

Unstructured interviews with guiding questions or areas of curiosity are generally employed in this kind of research. The questions generated before the interview do not have to be asked in all interviews if the direction of the conversation is led elsewhere, but they do help to orient the interviewer to the topic and the research team's curiosities and wonderings related to it. Though "unstructured" in content, the interview is structured in format with careful attention to context, settings, explanations, consents, audiotaping, engagement, process checking, and closure.

Context

The context and focus of the interview must be considered in any hermeneutic work. In fact, hermeneutics is about context and the recognition that phenomena cannot exist uncontextualized. For example, if one were studying children's cancer camps, one would need to attend them, to know them in some way, to have experience of what happens at them, to appreciate the atmosphere, process, and interactions. This is not the same as in ethnography where participant-observation or observation-only is an essential part of the research; it is more of an awareness of the topography of the topic, the *topos*. If one is interested in examining issues of mental health nurses, school principals, or disabilities in schools, one must become "schooled" about the topic. Unlike some other qualitative methods, then, the researcher immerses him or herself in the topic through extensive literature reviews, documents, lyric, novels, media, and anything else that has something to add to the context.

Setting

Typically, it is written in proposals and ethics applications that the interview will occur at place and time of the participant's choosing. This indeed is a very generous and open intent, however, not always pragmatically possible. The time and location have to be carefully negotiated to fit both schedules and be in a place that is conducive to the interview. Considerations of privacy, quality of audio recording (public places do not work well because of ambient noise), and convenience for the participants (finding an office at a university campus and parking costs can be deterrent) must be well thought out and negotiated.

Consents and Explanations

Consent forms are legal documents intended to provide full information to the participant regarding the nature of the study, risks and benefits, compensation, confidentiality, and rights of withdrawal. Prior to audio taping, the interviewer must be assured that the participants fully understand the nature of the study and any implications of their involvement in it. Offering an explanation, in addition to clarifying aspects of the consent, helps to focus the participants and the interviewer on the topic and offers a tether to which the interviewer can return throughout the interview process.

Audio Taping

Audio taping of interviews is a standard practice in hermeneutic research, as the interview content is the data and needs to be transcribed verbatim to capture the language of the research conversation, both verbal and non-verbal as much as possible. Hermeneutics is not concerned with a linguistic discourse analysis but there are linguistic and non-verbal aspects that are important to consider such as silences. In the transcription of the oral conversation to text, one attempts to capture these nuances as they may well factor into the interpretation. This will be discussed further in the next chapter.

Engagement

One of the first tasks of the interviewer is to engage the participants and create an atmosphere of comfort and trust where the participants feel safe to articulate their experiences. Some aspects of engagement are simply social courtesy: checking about the time constraints, thanking in advance the participants for taking part in the interview, ensuring that people have immediate needs taken care of such as refreshments or parking, and inquiring about any questions they may have regarding the study or their participation in it. Engagement might also take the form of crafting a genogram (family tree), or ecomap (a graphic representation of a person's or family's relationship with their environment). These tools offer a way to engage in meaningful conversation while eliciting important information about the participant's experience in a non-threatening way (Wright & Bell, 2021).

Process Checks and Unexpected Events

Engagement is an ongoing process that does not simply exist at the beginning of the interview. The interviewer must be conscious of maintaining engagement throughout, allowing for possible interruptions (phone calls, doorbells, children), and then re-engaging after such events. Process checks are done periodically throughout the interview, asking the participants if the time allotment is still fine, if the line of questioning is comfortable for them, and how their energy levels are. Depending on the focus of the study, some interviews can be very emotional, and the interviewer must have the skill to acknowledge strong emotion and be personally comfortable with it. An interviewer also needs to recognize that silences are important and to be able to sit through them without a pressured need to interject. Upon occasion, the interviewer might note incongruence between words and affect (outward manifestation of feelings) and make a decision about whether to comment on it openly and ask about it, or just to keep a record of it to add to the transcription as a side note. It is important to remember that the *point* of the interview is not therapeutic, but rather is research. This can be a difficult balance to maintain, yet important to keep in mind as a guiding approach to the interview. Where interviews are conducted with more than one person, for example two parents, there are further potential issues that might arise. Where there is disagreement or tension, it requires sophistication on the part of the interviewer to hold it without closing the conversation.

Closing the Interview

Interviews of this nature typically take between an hour to an hour and a half. At some point, either through time constraint or what appears to be a dwindling of any new information, the interviewer would start to "wind up" the conversation. This is often done by statements such as: "I just have one other thing I want to ask you about but before I do, is there anything you were hoping I would ask that I have not, or anything else you can think of that might be helpful to me?" In the end, the interviewer can also conclude by thanking the participants and assuring them that they have been very helpful. If there is something in particular that has stood out as a new learning for the interviewer, this can also be stated to the participants as evidence that they have contributed, and that the interviewer has learned from them. In our experience, participants are often quite concerned about whether they have said anything of value and are grateful when they hear that they have made a contribution.

Deep Listening, Openness, and Truth

Although we make a distinction between the "genuine conversation" and the research interview, there is an aspect of Gadamer's notion of the genuine conversation that *does a*pply to research interviewing. Gadamer maintained that "the possibility that the other person might be right is the soul of hermeneutics" (Gadamer, July 9, 1997, Heidelberg Colloquium, as cited in Grondin, 1994, p. 124). In the famous 1981 encounter between Gadamer and Derrida (Michelfelder & Palmer, 1989), which has been described by many as an "improbable debate," the debate never moved into the realm of conversation. Gadamer's genuine conversation is driven by attention to allowing the subject matter to conduct it, rather than to have either of the conversation partners conduct it. It is aimed at unraveling a truth regarding a particular subject. This may not involve consensus or agreement but involves a commitment on the part of the conversation partners to remain in the conversation with the aim of gaining insight and understanding, not simply to confirm what either already holds to be true. This does apply to research interviews as well, as the interviewer listens to what the participants hold to be true, whether the interviewer agrees or not.

In a similar way but from a very different discipline, Humberto Maturana, a Chilean neurobiologist, suggested that there are two ways we can listen to another. We can listen to see if the other person agrees with what we already know, or we can listen to find a truth in what the other person is saying. In the first instance, we are really only listening to ourselves; in the second, we are listening to the other (Maturana, 1988). "Anyone who listens is fundamentally open. Without openness, there is no genuine human relationship and no responsiveness to an … address" (Davey, 2013, p. 84).

Listening well is a fundamental skill for the hermeneutic researcher, and one that is often done poorly. Fiumara (1990) offered that we live in a culture that knows how to speak, but not to listen, and urges us to find balance by attending to the other side of language—listening. However, just as we have stressed the distinction between a therapeutic conversation and research interview, so too does there exist a distinction in the way one listens in a hermeneutic interview. It is not listening the way one might listen to a friend, or to someone engaged in therapy; it is more purposeful, or, said differently, it is with different intent. It is not done to empathize or sympathize (although that might happen anyway); it is done to explore, question further, and understand. When one listens deeply, there is a sense that the person is what one of the authors (Moules) has named being "right behind their eyes"—a presence of attentiveness that is apparent to the other in the conversation. Listening right behind your eyes requires watchfulness, openness, and searching to find a truth in what the other is saying.

Asking Good Questions

Heidegger (1996) suggested that posing a question is disclosure and provides the context of meaning in which a particular inquiry will move. Kvale (1996) offered two contrasting metaphors for interviewing: the first metaphor is seeing the interviewer as a miner who seeks to uncover buried knowledge without contamination; the second is the interviewer as a traveler who wanders with the participants in conversation on a journey that leads to a tale to be created together and then told upon the traveler's return home. It is the second metaphor which fits most closely with interviews in hermeneutic research; however, we would offer that the traveler is not simply "wandering" but striding very purposefully with the participants in an open conversation that is very much influenced by the posing of good questions.

The art of asking good questions must be honed and practiced because it is fundamentally important and leads to distinct qualitative differences in richness of the data obtained in the interview. Good questions are carefully crafted, timed well, and are ones that hold the most potential to invite the participants into deep reflection. Good questions cannot always be answered in the moment as they are invitations to reflection, and silence is less the sign of a bad question than indication of a phenomenological nod or pause—an experience of being caught in an immediate and often reflective experience of something.

Questioning Possibilities

Questions are tools used by researchers to invite data that are useful and directly related to the focus of understanding the topic being investigated. As stated, the art of knowing how to ask good questions is very much a skill, or as Kvale and Brinkmann (2009) suggested, a craft that can be learned, honed, and developed over time and through practice. There are several different types or categories of questions that are often employed in interviews.

Opening Questions

These are questions that lead to descriptions of experience or of the phenomenon under investigation. They generally are open-ended and invitational, designed in part to make the participant comfortable and also to move into the focus of the interview. Examples include: "Can you tell me about a time…?"; "Can you recall an occasion when…?"; or "Could you describe in as much detail as you can a situation when…?" Another opening question might be the invitation for the participants to recount their experiences, as in the example interview later in this chapter, where the parents are asked to tell the story of their daughter Molly's diagnosis and treatment of cancer.

Follow-up and Probing Questions

As a way of "turning around together" in conversation, the responses given by the participants invite a response from the interviewer. It is here where curiosity motivates the interviewer to "go deeper." Sometimes when we think we know, curiosity shuts down and questions and inquiry end so, therefore, remaining curious is the way to stay open to the newness that comes to meet us. These questions can be of a direct nature such as "That is really interesting. Can you tell me more about that?," or an indirect nature through non-verbals, such as nodding, saying "yes," or "hmmm" or even just saying "and?" to invite the participant to continue. An example of a probing question might be: "You mentioned that you were glad when the Public Health Nurse came to do a home visit, even when you did not expect to see her. What did that say to you that she continued to come? What did you say to yourself about why she did that?"

Interpretive Questions

These questions are used to invite the participant into some of their own interpretations of the story/event/experience they are describing. How the participant understands or makes sense of what is being told is often very useful in developing the interviewer and the research team's understanding. It is not about looking for explanations but understandings. Such a question may sound like this: "That is a really useful situation with the school principal that you have just told me about.

How do you make sense that you were able to form such a good relationship with her when you didn't with the last principal you worked with?"

Interjections of Structure

Though not necessarily a question, these are decisive moves that the interviewer makes that are intended to interrupt and to refocus the interview onto the topic of the inquiry, or to shift to another line of inquiry. It involves transparency, which makes the interruptions less intrusive and is respectful of the participant. An example might be: "I'm just going to do a little shift here if that's okay with you as there is another area I'm really interested in hearing about. Are you okay with that?" Another example might be to acknowledge the importance of something an interviewee has said and being transparent about setting priorities: "That sounds very important, and I would like to come back to that, but for now, could you say more about…"

Reflexive Questions

In 1988, family therapist Karl Tomm, under the influence of the Milan family therapy group, devised and named a cluster of questions that he then termed as interventive questions (Tomm, 1988). Wright and Leahey (1990, 1994, 2000, 2005, 2007, 2013) then incorporated these questions, identifying them as circular questions in family nursing literature. Though intended to be therapeutic in nature, we have learned that the structure of such questions has utility in bringing out important distinctions and a depth of response that is richer than what another style of questioning may elicit. These reflexive questions are unique in their ability to make distinctions, invite reflection, offer or speculate about the perspective of another, and make the connection between the effects of one person's behavior on others. The kinds of questions first offered by Tomm and refined by Wright and Leahey include *difference questions; behavioral effect questions; observer perspective questions; and hypothetical or future oriented questions.*

Difference questions pursue differences in beliefs, relationships, people, time, or behaviors and are useful for drawing distinctions. An example of a difference question might be: "Who of the two of you was most worried about the status of your relationship during that time?" The use of the word "most" is an invitation to reflection that takes the responder deeper than simply asking "Were either of you worried?" *Behavioral effect questions* inquire into the effect of one's behavior on another: "When your daughter would not share with you the news about the latest lab results, what effect did that have on you? What did you say to yourself about her choice to not do so?" An *observer perspective question* is aimed at trying to elicit a person's speculation about what another person might feel, experience, or think. "If your father were to be here right now and I could ask him what he needed from you at the time, what do you think he'd tell me?" Finally, *hypothetical or future-oriented questions*, allow the participant a chance to suspend beliefs and entertain other possibilities, inviting an insight into things that may not have previously been available to them. Wright et al. (1996) and Wright and Bell (2021) offered the example of a hypothetical belief question that is particularly useful in this endeavor. Such a question might be of the nature of: "If you were to believe that it was your mothering that gave your daughter the strength to go through her child's cancer experience in the way she has, and that her silence about the lab results are an effort to protect you in some ways, would you be able to understand the silence differently?" A future oriented question might be: "If you look ahead five years, what would you see that would indicate that things were going well for you?" While these questions may well have a therapeutic value for the participants, they are not used or intended for that purpose in research interviews but rather to increase the reflection necessary to offer deep, rich, and useful responses that bring understanding to the topic.

Crossing Boundaries

Hermes had the ability to cross boundaries.

> Like language … he can travel between realms freely—what he wants, he goes after. And it is in his playfulness, irreverence, and disdain for the rules, that his capacities for seeing things new, for invention, also reside … The power of Hermes is that of change. (Hirshfield, 1997, p. 186)

Interviewing in this kind of inquiry necessarily means stepping over the boundaries and conventions of social conversation. This is not, however, an easy maneuver, and it must be done with delicacy and tact. Kvale and Brinkmann (2009) wrote of the ethical nature of these kinds of interviews, which depends on the ability of the interviewer to create a condition where the participants are safe to talk about personal things and yet aware that what they are saying will be, in some form, made public. They referred to the work of Sennett (2004) who wrote:

> In-depth interviewing is a distinctive, often frustrating craft … the in-depth interviewer wants to probe the responses people give. To probe, the interviewer cannot be stonily impersonal; he or she has to give something of himself or herself in order to merit an open response. Yet the conversation lists in one direction; the point is not to talk the way friends do … The craft consists in calibrating social distances without making the subject feel like an insect under the microscope. (pp. 37–38)

Conventions of social conversation in some ways apply to research interviews, such as engagement, listening, and manners, but other rules and boundaries necessarily are broken. An example of this is interrupting to refocus the interview on the topic at hand. Another is asking questions of a personal nature. This is often one of the most challenging skills that new interviewers must develop, as there is a tendency to fall into practices of polite social conversation and, as a result, opportunities for a depth of data may be missed by the interviewer not being willing to refocus, interrupt, or to ask about areas that in another context would be seen as intrusive.

Reflexivity of Interviews

As mentioned, interviews in hermeneutic research are unpredictable, generative, and often very powerful experiences for the participants and the interviewer alike. The interviewer brings something to the interview, as does the participant, and it is unlikely that either will depart from the interview unchanged as a result. When the topic deals with human concerns and experiences, there is often emotion at play. There is also the factor that participants volunteer for reasons—for wanting to contribute, tell their stories, be heard, make changes, or to work things out for themselves—the reasons are varied and individual and therefore the effect of the interview cannot be known in advance or often even during it, as the reflective potential of questions linger. In this regard, ethics boards are rightfully careful and cautious about the sensitivity of such interviews, attending to their obligation to protect vulnerable populations and human rights. We would argue along with Corbin and Morse (2003), however, that people who volunteer for such studies do not suffer but rather stand to benefit from the sensitive interview. Years ago, one of the authors (Moules) was asked by an ethics board member around a study about grief: "Do you think it is ethical to make people revisit and talk about their grief?" Her response was "I think it's unethical not to." After all, people who volunteer to talk about their grief already know their own grief. Corbin and Morse wrote that "qualitative research using unstructured interviews poses no greater risk than everyday life and expedited reviews are sufficient" (p. 335).

An Interview Example

Here, we offer excerpts from a blinded transcription of an interview. The topic of this study was to understand the possible ways in which childhood cancer can affect the relationship between the parents of the child with cancer. The interviewer is an experienced researcher as well as having a background in family counseling. The interview transcript is in italics, interspersed with comments in regular font to explain the thinking behind particular questions or statements offered by the interviewer.

The interviewer starts by engaging the participants, in this case, a mother and father of a child who died of cancer. Interviewer = I. Mother = M. Father = F Deceased daughter = Molly (M). Son= Eric.

I: *First, I want to start by thanking you very much for contacting me and for being willing to speak about your experience. I believe that takes a lot of courage and it is a generous thing to do.*

F: *We want to do what we can to make her life worth something, to give back, you know.*

I: *To give back to other parents?*

F: *Yah (looks at wife who nods). We have talked about this a lot. If there is anything we can do to help other parents get through this experience, we are willing to tell them what we went through … are going through.*

I: *That is very generous and certainly a commemoration of Molly's life and I'm grateful to you as I believe other parents will be. I do need to mention here that I will keep your names out of the report and remove any identifying information but I cannot guarantee, given how small the community of childhood cancer is in this city, that someone might recognize you in the findings and the publications, so I can't promise that you will be anonymous.*

M: *That's okay. You can even use our names. We are okay with that.*

I: *Do you prefer I use your real names?*

M: *It doesn't matter. I just mean if someone figures out it's us, that's ok.*

I: *I appreciate your openness. If, however, you say something that you think later, you'd rather not have shared, I can take that out of the official transcript. I can't promise, of course, that I won't be influenced by it having heard it.*

F: *no problem*

I: *Okay, we'll get started here. As you know, the recorder has been on, and all of this will be transcribed to text and used as information for the study along with the other interviews I have done. We signed the consent prior to turning on the recorder but I just wanted to be sure that we were all clear on the issue of confidentiality. Are you still okay for the next hour or so to talk? Do you have any other commitments after this that I can honor by staying on time?*

The interviewer up to this point has been ensuring that the participants are fully informed and aware that, though confidentiality is attempted, complete anonymity cannot be guaranteed. This is explicit in the written consent but needs to be revisited in face-to-face conversation. The interviewer then starts by trying to map out the direction of the interview by revisiting the purpose of the study.

> I: *What I've found is most helpful to me is if we kind of walk through, you tell me a little bit about your cancer journey if you will or your narrative of what you've gone through with Molly right from beginning to end and then, cause I need to get sort of the context of where I want to ask you questions around your relationship. I need to try to hear and understand what you have gone through. And then we'll go back to it, but we'll do it through the lens of your relationship and ask you some of the questions that I'm interested in for this particular study. The premise of the study is that the experience of cancer in a family, and having a child diagnosed with cancer, treated with cancer and in your case, having lost your child can have huge effects on the family, we know of, it's a family with cancer, not just a child, right?*
> *(Both parents mumble yes)*
>
> I: *And it can have some effects on the parental relationship, sometimes good effects, sometimes not so good, sometimes just confusing, and so what we're trying to understand, at the end of the day, is for you to help me understand, how you, as a parent, as a couple, handled this and what we can we do to be more helpful to other parents. That's kind of what our biggest goal is. So, we'll get to that in a second, but do you mind talking a bit about Molly and that experience that you had with her having cancer?*
>
> M: *Not at all. (To husband). Since you're so good with memory, do you want to go through and if you miss anything, I'll tell you. If I remember it differently from you?*
>
> F: *I was gonna say the reverse. Why don't you start, and I'll chime in if I think you miss something?*
>
> M: *Okay. So, I just have to think about this. Molly was showing symptoms for a long time; we can now see in hindsight. I knew something wasn't right but our doctor just couldn't figure out why she was so tired all the time …*

Molly's mother proceeded to recap the medical narrative with her husband adding details or correcting inconsistencies. They walked through the diagnosis, treatment, and eventual death and aftermath of continuing grief. During this telling of the "story" of Molly's cancer experience, the interviewer injected only rarely, and that was to ask for more specifics around timing and clarity about the events that were punctuated in the recall. The interviewer's choice at the time, as mentioned, was that she needed context for their experience and also recognized that these kinds of stories are stories that need to be told and retold over time as a way for people to make sense and meaning of what they have undergone (Moules, 1998, 2009; Moules et al., 2004; Moules et al., 2007; Wright & Bell, 2021).

There were many moments where things were said that could have been portals for inquiry, trails that the interviewer may have chosen to pursue, and discernment and choice about what leads to follow were made, always guided by this question: "If I follow this line of inquiry, will it offer me a road to an understanding about the TOPIC at hand, or will it derail us and take us further from the topic?"

After a very tender discussion about Molly's death, the interviewer made a decisive shift in the conversation but only after carefully navigating the sensitivity of the conversation.

I: *So, when you said that she'd basically died in your arms, was that in taking her to the hospital? I'm sorry, (noticing his tears) I know this, it's hard to revisit this huh? Yeah.*
F: *Yeah (whisper). (Deep breath).*
(Silence of 10 seconds).
I: *How many years has that been now? That was 2004 you said?*
F: *(Tearfully) nine years yep.*
I: *Nine years. It's always …*
F: *(Sigh).*
I: *… in the work that I've done … because in my clinical work prior to when I was a professor, I was a bereavement counselor.*

The interviewer made a choice here to disclose something of herself. "To probe, the interviewer cannot be stonily impersonal; he or she has to give something of himself or herself in order to merit an open response" (Sennet, 2004, pp. 37–38). This was very intentional to offer that she knows something about the topic and to some extent appreciates and understands their reaction.

F: *Oh, okay.*
I: *It always strikes me that it doesn't matter if it's one year or nine years, or twenty years, that it's just as real as if it were today.*
M: *(Sniffling).*
F: *Yeah, when you talk about it right?*
I: *Yeah.*
F: *I mean you can certainly do your daily life, because we don't talk (emphasized) about it anymore. We don't talk this in-depth about …*

> *I: Yeah, is that a deliberate choice or are you …?*
> *F: I think it's because life continues on, and you can't talk about it every day, right?*
> *I: Yeah. Yeah. So maybe, thank you for telling me that. And as much as I've done a lot of, I've had a lot of conversations and had a lot of work, I've never had that experience of holding my child and having them die and so I, my heart goes out to you.*

Even though the death of a child is not the topic of this research, such a conversation and the depth of the emotion cannot go unacknowledged or unrecognized. To move on, it has to be acknowledged.

> *F: Yeah, thanks (tearfully).*
> *M: (Sniffling).*
> *(Silence of 5 seconds)*

The interviewer has delicately let the conversation rest temporarily on the grief that lives with this couple, the difficulty, messiness, pain, and angst that is a handmaiden that accompanies grief (Moules & Amundson, 1997). One could argue that this lingering on the pain of grief did not directly serve the topic, but the interviewer made a studied choice that, out of respect and honoring, out of an ethical imperative, the grief of having a child die had to be heard and acknowledged before the interview could move on. It is also about the context of the experience. This is a couple whose child did not live, and that outcome should be considered in examining the effects of childhood cancer on this family. The interviewer then makes a deliberate interruptive turn after the silence.

> *I: I wonder if we can kind of look back during that period of time and try as I had mentioned before, the focus of this study is on …*
> *M: (Blows nose).*
> *I: … maybe what kind of effect this might have had on the two of you and your relationship, both during the time that Molly was diagnosed and sick and treated and then since you've lost her as well. If you can, because I think relationships, marriages aren't easy at the best of times, and that sometimes when you go through something, this would be the worst thing you could go through, I'm guessing, that did you notice anything between the two of you during any of this time?*
> *M: Like when, after she was diagnosed, before she passed away? Is that the period?*
> *I: Yeah, well in the whole period, because I would consider this still part of the*

period so … So maybe at any point along the way, did the two of you struggle or did you feel really in sync around what you were facing?

M: *Well, I think just generally speaking there's a …*

F: *(Sniffling).*

M: *… (sigh) I don't know, sort of a, it's not a worry sort of mentality, but a mental approach that you'll have to do whatever is necessary to beat this.*

I: *Can you say more about that?*

M: *And what happens a lot (emphasized) is a lot of it's quite technical and clinical right?*

I: *Mmmhmm.*

F: *In terms of you have to be there at this time; this is what's going to be done; this is some of the repercussions; this is sort of the rescue approach you know when you're, if you have bowel problems or you're throwing up. All those sorts of tactical things or things that you just sort of execute almost on auto pilot …*

I: *Yeah.*

F: *… after a while, right? You get quite used to that. So, I think what happens a little bit is you, not that you suppress your emotions, but you only let them out at certain times. And I mean that could be difficult because you're, as the married couple, you're not necessarily in sync as to when those are right? And so if one of them is sort of "batten down the hatches" and, "we'll ride through the storm" and the other one wants to sort of talk about it and go through the mushy parts, I mean both parties have to be in sync for that conversation to really happen or have any value. And I know that that (sniffling) that's just at least the way I felt anyway, that was sometimes hard to get that synchronization of ideas and thoughts and willingness to do it I guess too.*

I: *Yeah. It, that's so true, because I've actually had a lot of parents say that to me that I'm beginning to believe that you can't ever be in sync with that.*

F: *Well, it's kind of what I was thinking is if you're, well sometimes it happens …*

I: *Yeah.*

F: *… you are in sync with it.*

I: *But not all the time.*

F: *But …*

M: *Mmm pretty rarely actually.*

F: *Yeah …*

M: *I think (chuckles).*

F: *… but and I think part of that is what keeps you going, right? Because if you were both in that all the time you're totally, emotions run everything and emotions, if you're running in emotions all the time, I don't think you're thinking clearly and you're not as productive and so …*

I: *But if you were of the belief that you had to be always in sync all the time, could that have caused trouble between you or? And did the two of you accept that you were just when one was up, one was down and or did you find that …*
M: *Well, I think we're inherently that way (laughing).*
I: *Oh, is that right?*
M: *I mean the two of us before we were married, albeit it wasn't a long time between the time we met and the time Eric arrived but there, it is a bit of a challenge to be in sync with kids and jobs and whatever else. I mean it's just …*
F: *(Sniffling).*
M: *… as you say it's, at the best of times marriage is a generally peaceful even keel, but there are little peaks and valleys that happen.*
I: *Sure, yeah.*
M: *So.*
I: *How long have you been married?*
M&F: *(in unison): 16 years.*
F: *Essentially.*
I: *And how long together?*
M: *Seven years before?*
F: *Almost 17.*
M: *17 years.*
F: *18 years, I guess. It'll be 18 years in March.*
M: *90 … (laughing)*
I: *18 years that you've been together?*
F: *Yep.*
M: *Since 96.*
I: *Yeah. And so, what you're saying is that there, two people can never always be in sync right in terms of …*

At this point, the interviewer is following a line of inquiry that is fueled by a core curiosity and beginning interpretive conjecture in this study: being in sync—what that means to people and how it plays out in this context of being parents of a child experiencing cancer.

M: *Well, I don't know if you'd want to be (laughing).*
I: *(Chucking).*
M: *Really, I mean. Yeah.*
F: *I mean I think for the hard decisions, we were in sync, which I think was important.*
I: *Yeah.*
F: *Taking her off treatment and what you do, the big decisions we would come together we didn't have, wouldn't have blow out fights about …*

I: *Mmmhmm.*

F: *... when we were in treatment there was a family there that was, I don't know if you'd, the Jehovah witness family there, the mom didn't want to do blood transfusions, and the dad did ...*

I: *Mmmhmm.*

F: *... for their daughter and they ended up in a great big legal custody. So, I think that for the big decisions we were there ...*

I: *Yeah.*

F: *... and for the tough decisions we came together whether it was emotionally like to tell Eric that, "your sister's ..." he was six, right?*

I: *Mmmhmm.*

F: *So how do you tell a six-year-old that your sister is dying? (tearful).*

I: *Even when the concept of death isn't quite formalized in their mind yet.*

F: *He didn't really get it.*

I: *Yeah.*

M: *And he's shut down emotionally I would think pretty much (sniffling). And I'm not big, I don't share a lot.*

I: *Mmm.*

M: *And probably through a lot of this we kept from him, he didn't see us cry a lot while Molly was sick. We tried to keep our house, in my mind we kept it, this is normal and I, Molly didn't remember life before cancer, so it was normal for her, going to the hospital was normal for Eric, he was always happy to go, he was always happy to go.*

I: *Mmmhmm.*

An area that the interviewer could have chosen to pursue is the idea of normalcy and "new normalcy" in the context of childhood cancer. This interviewer did not follow this line of inquiry, juggling the decision to pursue it with the other option of seeing where the participants were going to go in the interview.

M: *We, it was just a part of our life. And we're going to go to the hospital or we're going to go to clinic, and can we have friends there? She had friends there. So, I think in those kinds of decisions we were together.*

I: *Mmmhmm.*

M: *I think probably where we, what he is sort of referring to is that I'm, I don't go there as often probably as he would have liked me to. I think ...*

I: *Emotionally?*

F: *To the mushy part, yeah.*

I: *Okay. When you say the mushy part, you mean when you talk about the emotions yeah.*

M: *Well, I think the emotional, yeah. I'm, and I still run my life pretty much the*

same way, I don't go to the emotional as much. I'm more about, I'm a doer, right? So, I'm let's okay let's get the kids up, out the door, gotta make lunches ...
I: *So more pragmatic?*
M: *Yeah.*

At this point, the interviewer is going to bring her prejudices and knowledge into play—offering an idea, not with the intention of teaching or therapy but with the openness to the possibility that this way of talking about the difference in styles of grieving might further reflection and comment from the participants.

I: *And that's an interesting thing too around even some of the research that's been done around grieving is that they used to think there was a male and female way of grieving, but they don't think so anymore, they actually think now that there's different grieving styles ...*
F: *Right.*
I: *... and one of them is what they call more instrumental, which is to do things as a way to work through grief.*
I: *And the others the people that tend more to grieve intuitively, which is more emotionally ...*
M: *Mmm.*
I: *And neither one's right or wrong, or healthy or not healthy, but it's when sometimes when a couple have different styles of grieving that they almost perceive that the other person isn't grieving enough or is grieving too much. And that they run into some conflict around that.*
M: *Mmm.*
I: *Was that your experience at all? When you think about even after you lost Molly?*
F: *I would, I mean (sighing) (tearfully) I took, I don't know, six weeks off work or something after Molly died ...*
I: *Mmmhmm.*
F: *... and we went away. And I think we were both just raw (emphasized) at that point during that time (crying and sniffling).*
I: *Yeah.*
F: *So, and then one day we sort of looked at our house and looked at our son and he was doing everything in his little power to make us laugh or be happy ...*
I: *Mmmhmm.*
M: *... and it sort of at that point that I think that, you know I don't know if it's changing a grieving style but at first we were both just devastated and (sighing) but about that point, and we both sort of came to it I think about the same time*

and maybe it was because he was going back to work shortly, but sometime in September (clears throat) we sort of had a discussion that we need to pull it together. We can't be crying all the time because life still goes on, right?

I: *Mmmhmm.*

M: *So as devastated as we are, we have to do something because, poor Eric, our son was, and he didn't cry. He didn't cry; I didn't see him cry about Molly. I'm sure he did, but just that we didn't see until my, when he was in grade nine, he just said he was having some issues sleeping (sniffling) and didn't want to talk to me about it, and I said, "well do you want to go to a counselor?" I didn't know what the issues were …*

I: *Mmmhmm.*

F: *I still don't really know. But so, he went and saw somebody and, sorry, he did go to hospice sibling support group.*

I: *He did? Okay.*

F: *She was his sort of counselor …*

I: *Mmmhmm.*

F: *… at that point in time and I don't know if they had tears or not. I didn't, that was again a private session with him.*

I: *Mmmhmm.*

F: *Anyways, so Eric didn't cry about Molly until, that I know of, until he was like 13 or 14 years old or so*

I: *Do you think, was there any chance that you said that he was doing everything in his power to get you folks to laugh, was he, do you think he was protecting you from his tears?*

To the interviewer, at this point, the complexity and reflexivity of the research interview becomes apparent. This hypothetical question is quite sophisticated and holds the potential of being therapeutic, even though it was not intended as a therapeutic intervention.

F: *(Sigh) could be and maybe he was just doing that, so he didn't cry.*

I: *Mmm.*

M: *He was whatever. But so, I think, we had a discussion about it because it was just sitting here, and it was like death (emphasized) was just hanging in the room. And we needed to bring some life back to our …*

I: *So how did you do that?*

M: *I don't know, I mean we just started doing things with him that we like playing cards or …*

I: *Mmmhmm.*

F: *… going swimming again or doing things that were fun. We had a friend that gave us painting classes for Eric, so he had something because we just weren't even thinking about signing him up for anything and he still paints to this day, he doesn't sort of know, or maybe he does know that she gave him those lessons as I think a place for him to have a bit of an outlet.*

I: *Mmmhmm.*

M: *So, sorry I sort of sidetracked there a little bit but I would think that at that point in time we were grieving the same right?*

I: *Mmmhmm.*

F: *We were very much, and then probably but we agreed that we needed to sort of change our strategy a little bit. And we had brought some happiness back into the home because I would say that it wasn't a happy place for a long time. You know a long time we were sad right?*

I: *Yeah, of course.*

M: *But and then probably structure came back. He went back to work, we made a decision about that time, maybe even sooner that we would have another child.*

I: *I wondered if that was a deliberate decision that you, or was it something you struggled over? Did you both agree that you wanted to have another child? Because I know that some couples after they've had a child die that they, they're afraid to sometimes because they also know what they could lose, right?*

F: *Yeah, well I mean we did talk about it. I don't think we were, one of us had to talk the other one into it from what I remember.*

M: *Well and I think we had never really ruled out, we had never, we hadn't gotten to the point of saying, "we're not having any more kids."*

I: *Oh, I see.*

M: *Yeah. Even when Molly got sick, we said sometimes sort of talked about, "well maybe we should have a third," I guess before she got sick. We'd sort of I think we hadn't actually said, "ok we're not having three children."*

F: *Right.*

M: *… this is it.*

F: *Then she got sick and then …*

M: *And then that takes it out of the equation.*

F: *… all, yeah.*

I: *Yeah.*

M: *I did have friends that even when their son was on, or child was on treatment they went ahead and got pregnant and had another child during that process or but to me I didn't want to be, I didn't want to be pregnant and dealing with, and feel like I couldn't deal with her because, "oh I can't go into the room while you're having this because I'm pregnant."*

Different boundaries exist in these interviews and questions around territories that might be considered very private and personal may occur—but again only in the service of the topic. Questions cannot be based on an intrusive curiosity but rather a mindful and respectful curiosity that is driven by not "already knowing the answer." In this study, there might be questions about financial concerns or sexual and emotional intimacy, which are known to be relevant to a couple's relationship. The questions, though bold, must be offered sensitively and with an effort to normalize them as in the example below.

M: *And then I went on long-term disability for a year. And then Molly had been off treatment three or four months, things were good, they said, "do you want to come back to work now?" and I said, "no," so I quit (emphasized), basically on, end of March 2003. And then they said to me, "well you know we have this little part-time gig if you're looking for something at home."*

I: *Mmm.*

M: *And I said, "that would be great." So, then I started, I did some pre-work but officially I took that contract in July, so essentially, I didn't work for two years.*

I: *Was that a hardship financially for you?*

F: *Well, yeah when you have less money, but I don't think it really curtailed …*

M: *Well, essentially, I was …*

F: *… our activities a lot.*

M: *… essentially, I was making the same amount of money for the six months…*

I: *Mmm.*

M: *… short term disability was full pay and then long-term disability was 70 percent a year pay and …*

I: *The reason that I ask that is we actually know through some research that financial stresses on a marriage are really not easy to deal with either …*

F: *Yeah.*

I: *… and I just wondered if that factored in at all.*

F: *Well, I never felt that we changed our spending habits or saving habits … (incomprehensible) (laughing) … anyway.*

M: *Mmm, yeah. We pretty much have had the same style …*

I: *Okay.*

M: *… I would say ever since we've been together, right? That's sort of just been.*

I: *And did in terms of going back to your relationship too then, was during the time when Molly was sick and then after she died was your intimacy as a couple affected at all? And I don't mean intimacy as only sexual but emotional intimacy and affection and all those things. Did you see any changes in that area of your lives?*

M: I would say probably didn't start because of Molly being sick it probably started with having children.
I: (Chuckling).

This chuckle was a recognition of being a new mother and the interviewer knew it.

M: Right?
I: No, I think you're, every single couple has said this to me …
M: Yeah, just …
I: … that things change once you have kids.
M: You don't have, you're not, if you're sitting around on the couch or whatever, you've got a baby in your arms.
I: Yeah.
M: And we had Eric and Molly only 19 months apart so …
I: Mmmhmm. You were pretty busy.
M: Yeah, so essentially you had two, somebody said to me in the park one day, a little boy, he was like five, Molly was like brand new and Eric was basically just walking, well 19 months or whatever, and the little girl said to me, "wow you have two babies!" And I thought yes, what was I thinking? (Laughing) I have two babies."
I: (Laughing).
M: So, I think that changes your intimacy.

The couple then moved into a discussion that revealed their beliefs about different needs in relationships. For the most part, the interviewer deliberately allows them to talk without interjection. This choice was based on flow, rhythm, tone, and cadence of their conversation, a discernment in the moment to let it evolve without interruption.

M: … some people need physical touch, so it doesn't have to be sex or whatever it just needs, they just need to be …
I: Hugged or …
M: … hugged or whatever. Doing things together, quality time is one. So, it doesn't matter like whether someone is going skate shopping or …
F: (Laughing). She looks at me!
F: She wanted to come with me to shop for skates and I was sort of …
M: He's like, "really? So, you want to come with me?" I said, "yeah, just doing things with you, doesn't matter right?"
F: (Laughing).
M: And he's, so for me doing things together is important.
I: Mmmhmm.
M: For him, physical touch is important.

I: *Mmmhmm.*

M: *So, we recognize that about each other, but it's hard to, and I'm not a physical touch person.*

F: *Well, you don't recoil when I touch you!*

M: *Well, I don't recoil … no!*

I: *(Laughing).*

F: *But …*

M: *But it's not my way …*

I: *And would yours be more the quality time?*

M: *Yeah, doing things together or having people do things for me.*

F: *So, acts of service …*

I: *Were there ever any times that you thought your marriage was in jeopardy?*

F: *Yeah, last Tuesday (laughing).*

M: (Laughing).

F: *Nah, well, I mean overall I would say no. I think the reality is that as you started off with, marriage is an entity, the process itself is fraught with all kinds of challenges obviously and Molly getting sick was probably the biggest one we'll ever have. And I'm only speaking for myself, I mean sometimes you think is this what I want? Is this, not that I don't want it but …*

F: *… does this make sense? (Clears throat) we heard, I don't think read (emphasized), although maybe we did, that quite often couples who've got kids that have to go through cancer struggle from a marriage standpoint, and I think I remember somebody saying the divorce rate is much higher than for the normal population.*

M: *Someone told us that at the hospital … pissed me off. Told us that 87 percent of marriages end in divorce right and I was like, "so on top of it…" I remember very, I was really… … pissed off. I walked out of that room, and I said to him (husband), I said, "oh great, not only is our child going to struggle, we're probably going to end up divorced."*

I: *So, and can … I just say here that's actually not true anyways.*

N: *I know that after the fact, right?*

I: *You didn't find that comment useful?*

M: *No, it was devastating (emphasized) … because you're not only are you thinking, "oh God my child's going to die … now I'm going to be divorced, a single mom, a single dad"*

M: *… it was a total waste of time.*

I: *Say that that had been said to you in a different way. Like I'm just saying, say that you weren't offered a number, but say she had said that this can be quite stressful on a relationship so …*

M: *Well, then, I would have said …*

I: *... try to keep communication open. Try to talk to each other. Would that have been a useful comment to have been made?*

M: *Well, I think that it was self-evident to us that this wasn't going to be an easy battle. Regardless.*

I: *You didn't need someone to say that ...*

M: *No.*

I: *Because did anybody ever ask you, other than that comment, did anybody ever ask how things were going between the two of you? And well, this is a two-part question, did any health care professional ever ask that and if so, would it have been helpful if they would have or would you have found that intrusive?*

M: *we basically went through that whole program, and it wasn't until the end I joined the Parent Advisory Committee the last year Molly was alive, and I met a social worker in the department ...*

M: *And then, just discussions with her, because she became like a friend ...*

I: *Mmmhmm.*

M: *... that might have been, and I don't necessarily recall, and that would have been somebody that I opened up to.*

I: *Did she help you?*

M: *Yeah.*

I: *Yeah. So, it sounds like as though it would have been fine for someone to inquire but it would depend on who that person was and what was the nature of the relationship with them?*

M: *Yeah.*

I: *Is that fair to say?*

M: *Yep. I think so.*

F: *Well, I mean, I suppose. I mean they're sort of checking in with you to see if you're aware of some of these issues. Your child's sick and (deep breath) the odds may or may not be in your favor but that the odds aren't really, you don't get two thirds of a kid, you get one or you get zero. So, I don't know, I mean it's, I'm not sure what the value would be of any kind of advice or question that way.*

I: *Mmm. Okay.*

F: *Maybe there would be some, but I don't know.*

I: *I mean it's an interesting thing because, like I kind of agree with you, you don't get one third of a kid, like those stats have, when I worked in Hawaii, that's when I worked in pediatric oncology we had an oncologist who when the families would say, "well what are the chances?" he'd say, "I can give you numbers but there's only two numbers that matter to you, and it's zero or a hundred ... and we're working with the hundred." That made such sense to me.*

F: *Yeah.*

M: *But as a parent you still need to know that number because you need to know realistically …*

I: *To prepare?*

M: *Yeah. I mean I think we went into it with "Molly's going to survive." But we also knew, like we also knew when we were sitting next to, or maybe I did I don't know, the leukemia patient and Molly … you know what, chances are your, in three years' time you're done and your child's going off, chances are …*

I: *Mmm.*

M: *You know?*

I: *Yeah.*

M: *So, I think you need to know that.*

F: *And with the Internet being so … now prevalent, well even when Molly was diagnosed.*

I: *Everything's accessible.*

M: *There's not too much that's sort of secret anymore. Right?*

I: *Yeah.*

M: *So, unfortunately, we knew because we knew of someone else going through the same thing before.*

F: *Yeah.*

M: *And was horrified with that situation that they were facing. And then little did we know that within just a limited amount of time we'd had the same scenario.*

I: *Did your friend lose her child?*

F: *No.*

I: *Oh. That would be hard for you too.*

F: *Yeah.*

I: *I mean …*

I: *Have you stayed, well Eric's involved with the kids cancer camp, so have you folks stayed involved with the camp community at all?*

F: *We go to some of their events; they had a memorial event in September …*

M: *They do an ornament sort of tree ceremony at the hospital.*

I: *Is that through the grief group?*

M: *Yeah, that's a different group. Yeah.*

I: *I'm trying to think if there's anything else, how's our time? I don't want to keep you too long. Is there anything that you were thinking that would be helpful to me in this study that we haven't talked about?*

F: *I don't think so.*

I: *Any advice that you'd offer other couples facing the same thing?*

M: *I guess what I saw with family relations and family dynamics of all of our friends and the people that we knew that went through the cancer world, we're all together still right?*

I: *Mmmhmm.*

M: *So, I think personally, if you are struggling when your child gets cancer, you might not make it, right? But if you're doing good when your child gets cancer, you'll probably come out of it okay.*

I: *Yeah.*

M: *So, I mean that's not something you want to tell people, right? Because if they're looking at their husband thinking, "I'm thinking about leaving ya," well chances are having a child have cancer is not going to make that change right?*

I: *It's interesting though, I did interview one person who said that they were struggling prior to, and the cancer experience actually brought them …*

F: *United?*

I: *… it brought them together, but then when their child died, that was the end of the relationship.*

M: *Yeah. So maybe they were a unified front for that period …*

I: *Yeah.*

M: *… but then when that (emphasized) goes away all the stuff that was problems before …*

I: *Yeah. And that …*

M: *… are still there.*

I: *That's really fascinating to me that you say that because when I actually first conceptualized this study, which was a hypothesis in my mind is that maybe we're going to find that it's more the state of the relationship prior to that is a determinant.*

F: *Yeah.*

I: *Yeah.*

F: *And I think that that's the case. In my experience.*

I: *If you were to frame that in, like you say you can't really say that to someone to be useful, but what kinds of things could you tell another couple that, like if you were to give your best advice, say I was given 10,000 dollars and I could hire you to write an advice manual for parents going through what you went through, what would you advise?*

M: *I mean I think that we were in a lot of ways in a fortunate situation that I could quit my job … and I could be the full-time caregiver. Some families didn't have that option, right? So, there you'd see the grandma there and the mom was working and the dad you know like …*

I: *Mmmhmm.*

M: *… or the daughter, or the child was older, some of it depends on your child's age* *too, right? Maybe you don't need to quit, but when you have a two-year-old, I, we felt that I needed, and we were in agreement on that.*

F: *The idea of both of us continuing to work and just leave Molly, because I think 30 or 40 years ago, people might have done that. You just put your child in the hospital … and the parents weren't as involved right?*

I: *Yeah. And sometimes, well probably a bit longer than that but there was even just visiting hours. The parents were only allowed to come from two to four.*

M: *Yeah. So, times have changed, and I think part of the expectation was, I mean not that I was ever told that I had to be there 24/7 but I think the expectation was that I would be there 24/7. So, we were in a situation where we didn't see each other the first, well, five weeks, I don't think we slept in the same bed. Because either one of us was at the hospital with him.*

I: *You were tag teaming then?*

F: *Yeah. Tag teaming. So, we would see each other …*

M: *Well, I can remember when your mom was here and we had a little rendezvous because, I don't know exactly when that was but …*

I: *Did you think having the rendezvous was important to your relationship?*

F: *Not really. We just kept thinking about Molly and that we should be with her and not out having a holiday. I think the thing I'd tell other parents is that your relationship is gonna be put on hold during this time and it should be. All that should matter is your child. You just have to learn to tag team and trust that you'll get back together when it's all over. That's what is important.*

M: *He's right.*

Further discussion continued but even at this moment of the interview, the interviewer knew that something important had just been said in the service of the topic. This comment from the father would eventually develop into an interpretation of "relationships on hold tethered by trust."

I: *I'm aware that we have gone beyond the time we booked for this, and I apologize for that.*

F: *No problem; it's been good*

M: *Yeah*

I: *I'm just wondering if there is anything else that you would like to add or actually, let me ask you this: When you were thinking about me coming today was there one thing you were most hoping I would or would not ask you about?*

M&F: *(laughing at the last part of the question)*

M: *I don't think so. I think it was kind of what we expected.*

F: *nothing for me but I will be interested in seeing the report*

I: *Of course. And I'm wondering if there is something that comes up for you when you think about our conversation or something that comes up for me, is it okay if we stay in touch by email?*

M: *of course. For sure*

F: *Ya*

I: *Well, I'd like to end here by thanking you so much for your time, honesty, openness, and trusting me with your tears. You have made a real contribution to this study, and I believe what you have taught me WILL make a difference to the lives of other parents going through what you have and are still facing. So, I'm most grateful and I thank you.*

M: *You're welcome. And thank YOU for doing this.*

F: *Ya, it's really important.*

This portion of the interview does not reflect the entire experience, or the fullness of the many things offered and discussed but it does represent the powerful nature of these intense conversations of human experiences. In this case, the interviewer, having a wealth of interviewing experience from both research perspectives and therapy perspectives, did not enter it with any set guiding questions but rather with a clear focus on the topic, an unbridled curiosity, and immense respect for the strength and wisdom of the participants.

Summary

> Participation is a strange word ... participation is not taking parts, but in a way taking the whole. Everyone who participates in something does not take something away, so that others cannot have it. The opposite is true: by sharing, by our participating in the thing in which we are participating, we enrich them, they do not become smaller, but larger. (Gadamer, 1984, p. 64)

Participation in research interviews is not about taking something away but about creating something that adds to understanding, enriches our knowledge, and offers portals to interpretation. An act of *aletheia*, a good interviewer seeks to enliven, awaken, remember, and open up understanding about the topic at hand. These interviews cannot be prescriptively described but need to be learned through experience and practice so that, in time, the interviewer has a honed dexterity with language and relationship, tact, discretion, courage, and timing, enough that every condition is set for the arrival of good data.

In this chapter, we have discussed the character and conduct of research interviews in hermeneutic inquiry. We turn now to the heart of this work—interpretation as analysis in hermeneutic research.

References

Corbin, J., & Morse, J. M. (2003). The unstructured interactive interview: Issues of reciprocity and risks when dealing with sensitive topics. *Qualitative Inquiry* 9(3), 335–351. <https://doi.org/10.1177/1077800403009003001>

Davey, N. (2013). *Unfinished worlds: Hermeneutics, aesthetics and Gadamer.* Edinburgh University Press.

Fiumara, G. C. (1990). *The other side of language*. Routledge.

Gadamer, H.-G. (1960/1997). *Truth and method* (2nd rev. ed.; J. Weinsheimer & D. G. Marshall, Trans.). Continuum.

Gadamer, H.-G. (1984). The hermeneutics of suspicion. In G. Shapiro & A. Sica (Eds.), *Hermeneutics: Questions and prospects* (pp. 54–65). University of Massachusetts Press.

Geanellos, R. (1999). Hermeneutic interviewing: An example of its development and use as research method. *Contemporary Nurse, 8*(2), 39–45. <https://doi.org/10.5172/conu.1999.8.2.39>

Grondin, J. (1994). *Introduction to philosophical hermeneutics* (J. Weinsheimer, Trans.). Yale University

Heidegger, M. (1975). *Early Greek thinking* (D. Farrell Krell & F. A. Capuzzi, Trans.). Harper & Row.

Heidegger, M. (1927/1996). *Being and time* (J. Stambaugh, Trans.). SUNY.

Hirshfield, J. (1996). *Nine gates: Entering the mind of poetry*. HarperCollins.

Kvale, S., & Brinkmann, S. (2009). *InterViews: Learning the craft of qualitative research interviewing* (2nd ed.). SAGE.

Maturana, H. R. (1988). Reality: The search for objectivity or the quest for a compelling argument. *The Irish Journal of Psychology, 9*(1), 25–82. <https://doi.org/10.1080/03033910.1988.10557705>

Michelfelder, D. P., & Palmer, R. E. (1989). *Dialogue and deconstruction: The Gadamer-Derrida encounter.* SUNY.

Morse, J. M. (1991). Qualitative nursing research: A free-for-all? In J. M. Morse (Ed.), *Qualitative nursing research: A contemporary dialogue* (2nd ed.; pp. 14–22). Sage.

Moules, N. J. (1998). Legitimizing grief: Challenging beliefs that constrain. *Journal of Family Nursing, 4*(2), 142–166. <https://doi.org/10.1177/107484079800400203>

Moules, N. J. (2002). Hermeneutic inquiry: Paying heed to history and Hermes. An ancestral, substantive, and methodological tale. *International Journal of Qualitative Studies, 1*(3), 1–21. <https://doi.org/10.1177/160940690200100301>

Moules, N. J. (2009). A parent's worst nightmare: Grief, families and the death of a child. *Relational Child and Youth Care Practice, 21*(4), 63–70. <http://hdl.handle.net/1880/48643>

Moules, N. J., & Amundson, J. K. (1997). Grief—An invitation to inertia: A narrative approach to working with grief. *Journal of Family Nursing, 3*(4), 378–393. <https://doi.org/10.1177/107484079700300405>

Moules, N. J., Simonson, K., Fleiszer, A. R., Prins, M., & Glasgow, B. (2007). The soul of sorrow work: Grief and therapeutic interventions with families. *Journal of Family Nursing, 13*(1), 117–141. <https://doi.org/10.1177/1074840706297484>

Moules, N. J., Simonson, K., Prins, M., Angus, P., & Bell, J. M. (2004). Making room for grief: Walking backwards and living forward. *Nursing Inquiry, 11*(2), 99–107. <https://doi.org/10.1111/j.1440-1800.2004.00204.x>

Moules, N. J., & Taylor, L. M. (2021). Conducting interviews in hermeneutic research: An example. *Journal of Applied Hermeneutics*, Article 1. <https://doi.org/10.11575/jah.v2021i2021.71844>

Sandelowski, M. (1995). Focus on qualitative methods: Sample size in qualitative research. *Research in Nursing and Health, 18*, 179–183. <https://doi.org/10.1002/nur.4770180211>

Sennett, R. (2004). *Respect*. Penguin.

Tomm, K. (1988). Interventive interviewing: Part III. Intending to ask lineal, circular, strategic, or reflexive questions? *Family Process, 26*(6), 167–183. <https://doi.org/10.1111/j.1545-5300.1988.00001.x>

Vandermause, R. K., & Fleming, S. E. (2011). Philosophical hermeneutic interviewing. *International Journal of Qualitative Methods, 10*(4), 367–377. <https://doi.org/10.1177/160940691101000405>

Wright, L. M., & Bell, J. M. (2021). *Illness beliefs: The heart of healing with families and individuals* (3rd ed.). 4th Floor Press.

Wright, L. M., Watson, W. L., & Bell, J. M. (1996). *Beliefs: The heart of healing in families and illness*. Basic Books.

Wright, L. M., & Leahey, M. (1990, 1994, 2000, 2005, 2009, 2013). *Nurses and families: A guide to family assessment and intervention*. F. A. Davis.

Interpretation as Analysis

> *...though philosophical hermeneutics does not constitute a system or method, its critical procedures have a clear style and a discernible signature.*
> —DAVEY (2006, P. 18)

> Data analysis is another term that ought to carry a hermeneutic health warning, although it is no bad thing once more to draw attention to the tension between the generally given structures of research and the far more fluid interconnections of a hermeneutic study. (McCaffrey et al., 2012, p. 221)

Davey (2006) and McCaffrey et al. (2012) remind us that hermeneutic research has a focus on a particular topic in relation to how it is lived out in the world of practice, how it has evolved over time, how it relates to the surrounding culture, and what it means to the practitioners involved. Analysis requires a comportment toward the data on the part of the researcher which makes room for complexity and "the development of a practice, of a preparedness or skill in changing mental perspectives" (Davey, 2006, p. 37). Data analysis in hermeneutic research differs from other research approaches because it is divergent rather than convergent: it involves carefully opening up associations that strengthen understanding of the topic rather than focusing in on a single governing theme. Thus, for hermeneutics, analysis is synonymous with interpretation; analysis *is* interpretation. Interpretation occurs throughout the multifaceted engagement with a topic via literature and research interviews, transcribing the interviews to text and reading and re-reading them, developing interpretive conjectures and writing about them. It also requires, as Gadamer (2007) has stated, that there be "some kind of methodological consciousness at work. The interpreter not only possesses the art of exegesis (*Auslegung*), he or she knows how to justify his or her exegesis theoretically" (p. 45).

This approach to analysis contrasts with quantitative research, where analysis involves the adherence to a strict method and often the application of rigorous measurement tools. In some qualitative methods too, there is a clearly delineated method in approaching the data, such as in grounded theory and the use of procedures of category coding, or thematic analysis and line-by-line coding, or software searching for repetitive themes. In some forms of hermeneutic phenomenological inquiry, authors have offered procedural steps in approaching the data (see for e.g., Colaizzi, 1978; Fleming et al., 2003; Giorgi, 1985; Lindseth & Norberg, 2004; van Manen, 1984). In this chapter, we offer a less defined procedural approach to data analysis but rather describe the philosophical underpinnings that guide the intent and, therefore, focus the conduct of analysis. This is itself an interpretive enterprise, offering one way of applying aspects of Gadamer's philosophical hermeneutics to research in practice disciplines.

Interpretive analysis can be thought of as movement through the landscape of the topic, such that perspectives change with the varied points of view of interview participants and are informed by reference to disciplinary and other pertinent literature. Crucially, it is the researcher who finally commits to an interpretation of the material. Interpretation requires shaping and articulation so that insights are developed and honed and finally written up in a research report. At the early stage of analysis, the search for interpretive elements is a search for those aspects that catch our attention, have "grab," and call for a deconstruction of their meanings. Analysis involves careful reading, re-reading, and writing around significant interpretations that arise from the data. When working with a team, the initial individual interpretations of researchers are then raised to another level of interpretive analysis in the research team's conversations through in-depth, rigorous, reflexive, and communal attention to the data.

Identifying "significance" in this context is a matter of judgment that always depends on a plausible connection to the topic. Teamwork is one way of supplying rigor by testing out the worth of an emerging interpretation in dialogue with others. Madison (1988) described criteria of good interpretive work that can be taken as guides in research. He identified context, agreement, coherence, comprehensiveness, potential, and penetration as aspects of sound interpretation. We take up these criteria of rigor more fully in Chapter 9, but for now they can be treated as characteristics of analysis that usefully elaborate on the topic without losing touch with the topic.

Hoy (1998) reminded us of another essential feature:

> one central aspect of what makes an interpretation better will be whether it understands, not only its object and subject matter, but also itself. Interpretations that are methodologically more self-aware are therefore better if they bring to light unnoticed features, not only of the object of interpretation, but also of the conditions and procedures of interpretation… An interpretation presupposes a self-understanding, and bringing features of this implicit self-understanding to light will make the interpretation insightful. (p. 193)

In other words, good interpretive work should disclose something about the meaningful existence of the interpreter and the world.

Unlike some other qualitative methods, the practice of hermeneutics is not aimed at inducing themes, semantic codes, constructs, or theories, but rather seeks to deepen understanding of a topic in such a way that it can be seen differently and, ultimately, can be practiced differently. Although the goal is not to end up with themes, it can be helpful to identify what may appear as themes in transcript data to organize the material and relate statements from participants to emerging interpretations. The art of interpretation, which is often only learned through experience and is difficult to teach, involves the process of moving past the initial descriptive themes into the depth and richness of interpretation. Themes, therefore, are more of a tool along the way than the goal of analysis. While they may be useful in bringing some order into disparate material (see examples in Chapter 8), it is the differences between participants at least as much as the similarities that may be productive in elucidating the complexity of the topic. A movement beyond what presents as themes is what we refer to as the "deep dive" into what is presenting itself. Stated simply—in hermeneutics, one does not *end up* with themes but with interpretations.

Hermeneutic analysis is a very deliberate attempt to listen for particulars of experiences and thoughts that are not based on repetition to authenticate their authority to speak to the topic. Hermeneutic work, true to its phenomenological roots, encompasses a rich description of the phenomenon, but it must also complicate the description through highlighting exemplars, possible counter-exemplars, by exposing the phenomenon to contextual material, and by engaging in deconstruction, so that we are not simply imprisoned by our interpretations in our own standpoint. Interpretation in this work is a messy, difficult, complex, sophisticated endeavor that is honed and developed over time and through practice. It is both deconstructive and reconstructive, questioning how things, such as schools and hospitals, have come to be what they are, but also bringing to light new possibilities for better practice. In this chapter, we articulate ways to embark on deep interpretive practice, mindful of the intentions of it to enliven and deepen understanding of the subject matter.

Role of the Researcher in Interpretation

The role of researcher takes a particular place in hermeneutic work, based on views about objectivity and subjectivity in hermeneutic philosophy. Our strengths, as hermeneutic researchers, lie in a belief in the interpretability of the world and in a willingness to allow ourselves to be read back to us. Hermeneutics demands that we proceed delicately and yet wholeheartedly, and as a result of what we study, we carry ourselves differently, and we live differently. We are situated in the work, but the work is not an autoethnography or an autobiography. We are situated in a conversation with the topic. Smith (1991) reminded us that the writing is *by us*, but it is not *about us*, though in one sense all writing is autobiographical as it comes from us and involves self-understanding. The point is not to remove subjectivity from the work, which is impossible, but to acknowledge how it allows us into the interpretive process. We can then take it up with a sense of responsibility in recognizing how it translates into the way we listen to participants, what we hear, what stands out to us, and how we interpret it. Returning to some of the ideas discussed in Gadamer's philosophy in Chapter 3, it is possible to see how they inform the work of data analysis as interpretation.

Forestructures and Prejudices

Gadamer did not see objectivity and subjectivity as opposites, as an either/or proposition, but as dialectically related aspects of human understanding. We cannot see the world but from within the horizon of our own experience, and yet our experience is not fully our own, separate from the world. We share in histories, communities, and languages to the extent that, "(t)he self-awareness of the individual is only a flickering in the closed circuits of historical life" (Gadamer, 2004, p. 278). For the purposes of research, the significance of this insight is that subjectivity is a resource, to be handled carefully, but nonetheless available to the research process.

As mentioned in earlier chapters, one of the ways of describing the workings of the subjectivity/objectivity dialectic is through what Heidegger identified as forestructures, and Gadamer called prejudices. Heidegger (1996) asserted that our understanding proceeds from our preunderstandings and forestructures. Contained in this preunderstanding, lies what Gadamer (1960/1997) termed our "prejudices" or presuppositions, or our leanings toward what we are able to see. Gadamer described prejudices as prejudgments that exist or are rendered before all other situational elements are examined. Unlike the notion of bracketing, we do not hold our prejudices in abeyance but think *with* them and we situate them in our understandings. Our prejudices allow us to hear something we would not have heard otherwise, they determine what we can recognize, and they provide our access to the world. The criticism sometimes lobbied against hermeneutic work is that it is subjective and therefore something less than a removed, objective view. Davey offered the idea that "subjectivity is not a block to greater objectivity but rather a gateway to it" (Davey, 2006, pp. 18–19). In other words, we cannot know anything other than subjectively, and it is our prejudices that help in allowing us this particular view.

By the time the researcher arrives at data analysis, they should already have been working reflexively to consider "why this particular topic for this particular researcher," and should be able to articulate the angle of attention to the topic. For Laing studying cancer camps, for example, her discussion of her encounters with the camps as a student nurse outlines the way her "prejudices" actually enabled her to enter into her research in an informed and committed way. Prejudices mobilize the space of understanding between the researcher and the topic and are thus inherently contextual. It is important to bring them into data analysis, both in the initial stages and in the eventual writing of a finished report but this has a different emphasis to the kind of declarations of identity sometimes seen in interpretive work. When researchers simply declare which categories of age, ethnicity, gender, or occupation they belong to, it often reflects a commitment to an ideological position around the importance of identity politics. While that is one kind of statement of positioning, it forgets that prejudices and positions are there to be tested as well, to sort the good from the bad, as Gadamer would say. We argue that it is better hermeneutic practice to position oneself as an individual in relation to the topic, rather than as a representative of broad categories.

The Hermeneutic Circle

Interpretive data analysis demonstrates the hermeneutic circle as a metaphorical way of conceptualizing understanding and the process of interpretation in which we participate, and to which we belong, are situated in, and living through. It is not a method for uncovering meaning, but rather a description of how human understanding can be created from a stance of focused curiosity and reflexive attention to different standpoints and ways of seeing a topic. It also describes, after Heidegger, the relationship between self and other, between what is familiar and what is strange in experience, so it has an existential as well as conceptual aspect to it. The hermeneutic circle reminds us that all understanding is context dependent.

The hermeneutic circle is the generative recursion between the whole and the part. *Entering* the circle is accomplished by responding or listening to the call of the topic. *Staying in* the circle requires discipline and creativity, rigor and responsiveness. There is an inherent process of becoming immersed in and engaging in a dynamic and evolving interaction with the data as a whole (the topic) and the data in part (a particular instance), through extensive readings, re-readings, reflection, writing, and conversation. In this process, there is a focus on recognizing the particular, isolating understandings, dialoguing with others about interpretations, making explicit the possibilities for being and doing that are implicit in the data and, eventually finding the appropriate language to clearly describe the understanding of the topic generated in the process.

On Conserving Stories and "Representing" Participants

The dynamic play between part and whole has particular implications for research application. Abram, a phenomenologist and deep ecologist, used a lyrical description of a bowl to show how we perceive an object in a flow of changing perspectives, each of which is partial at a given moment:

> The clay bowl resting on the table in front of me meets my eyes with its curved and grainy surface. Yet, I can only see one side of that surface—the other side of the bowl is invisible, hidden by the side that faces me. In order to view that other side, I must pick up the bowl and turn it around in my hands, or else walk around the wooden table. Yet, having done so, I can no longer see the first side of the bowl. Surely I know that it still exists; I can even feel the presence of those aspects which the bowl now presents to the lamp on the far side of the table. Yet, I myself am simply unable to see the whole of this bowl all at once.

To take the bowl apart to learn more about it would be to lose the object as such:

> If I break it into pieces, in hopes of discovering these interior patterns or the delicate structure of its molecular dimensions, I will have destroyed its integrity as a bowl; far from coming to know it completely, I will simply have wrecked any possibility of coming to know it further, having traded the relation between myself and the bowl for a relation to a collection of fragments. (Abram, 1996, p. 51)

Data analysis as interpretation involves looking at the topic one aspect at a time, asking questions of it, being attentive to what the questions reveal, and yet it is not about breaking it apart or "cleaning the data," with the thought that any one story, statement, theme, or opinion is separable from the vital complexity of the topic. When we consider a "part," it is always with the knowledge that our attention is not on any other part, but that the larger world of the topic is implied in any particular aspect. Likewise, thinking of the "whole" in relation to the parts, does not mean a presumption of knowing everything there is to know about a topic, but rather generating an awareness that there is more to be said, and that topics need to have boundaries, for the moment at least, to come into view and be speakable, or able to be described.

The principle of part-whole interchange, expressed in the hermeneutic circle, applies to the treatment of participants' stories as data. Hermeneutics differs from other methodologies such as ethnography, grounded theory, or phenomenology that attempt to give an account of the participants, and whose researchers sometimes return to the participant for member checks to authenticate and substantiate how well they were represented (Smith, 1991). The purpose in hermeneutic research is to bring understanding around the topic; the participants in the study are not the topic but are chosen to bring their knowledge about, and to, the topic. Therefore, the goal is not to describe the participants fully, nor to simply conserve their stories and experiences intact, but rather to listen to what participants have to say and for that which will cast new light on the topic and expand our understanding of the phenomenon we are attending to in the conversation. Therefore, an interpretation made by a researcher does not need to be authenticated by the participant. Rather, its authentication comes from the fact that it has opened new possibilities for seeing and doing; it has "enlivened" practice. Allen (1995) suggested that "the strategy of returning to the subjects for validation is often based in a mirror epistemology in which the goal is to copy or reproduce the original meaning of the subjects' responses. This is questioned in hermeneutics" (p. 179). This is not to say that the researcher disregards the participant's perception, rather that the researcher is reliant on what has been said to reach strong interpretations, that is, new understanding of the topic. There are occasions where the researcher returns to the participants to clarify something that is questionable, or provocative, or to ask further questions that may have arisen from insights generated during the analysis, but this is very different in intent, process, and outcome than member checking. Hermeneutics does not report on meaning but creates it. Its intent is to generate new understanding, not simply affirm what is already known. Through careful attention to, selection, and crafting of participant contributions, which is the responsibility of the researcher, the topic is illuminated further and stands enriched beyond the initial horizons of either the researcher or the participants.

This does not mean to imply that participants' stories do not matter. They matter immensely, or rather their subject matter—how they address the topic and what they reveal matters—and, without them, the research could not occur. Embedded in their stories are invitations to understanding the topics, events of experience that *are* the topic. This work is not an autobiography of the researcher; it has a topic other than the researcher's life, and for this reason, it is also not a biography of the participants' life. Frequently, for this reason, individual participant quotes will not be named, as it matters less who it came from than what it has to say about the topic. Quotes then are often arranged around the interpretations rather than the persons. Participants know of their experiences intimately; they know something about the topic. However, our intent is not to re-create participants, psychoanalyze them, or "correctly" portray them, but to generate insight derived from their unique knowledge and contribution.

The Analysis-Interpretation Process

> ...the term data implies separated objects of knowledge with analysis as a distanced examination of them. The hermeneutic understanding of language as interpretive instead demands an attention to aesthetics and expressive fluidity ... Through this interpretive writing reflexivity once more emerges as one of the signatures of philosophical hermeneutics. Reflexivity is not the same as subjectivity—the researcher does not redraw the topic on a whim but rather commits to the play of the topic. (McCaffrey et al., 2012, p. 221)

Divergence, as a principle of interpretive work, makes particular demands on the researcher at the stage of data analysis. There is freedom that comes with opening up pathways of understanding and seeking out illuminating associations in relation to the transcript data. The risk of too much freedom, however, is a chaotic pursuit of connections that distract and lead away from the data and the topic. Hermeneutics owes a great deal to aesthetic understanding, which is a helpful way of thinking about the researcher's approach to data. Davey (2013) wrote that, "aesthetic attentiveness demonstrates that the receptiveness associated with aesthetic reception is not grounded in subjective preference but in subjects' participation in enabling cultural horizons that shape their being" (p. 66). There is rationality in aesthetic understanding, an ordering and meaning-making whereby the art object—or research interpretation—takes its place in the world. There is, in Gadamer's (2004) phrase, a "transformation into structure" (p. 110).

Preparing and Reading Transcripts

Interpretation is the dynamic of hermeneutic research, running throughout the course of a project (and even before and after in the historical life of a topic). Thus, interpretation is, in a sense, already going on during the interviews—in the selection of lines of inquiry, the wording of questions, and the decision of when to finish. The audio recording and written transcript of the interview, however, become the focus for sustained and repeated analysis. Transcription is time consuming but can bring closeness to the particulars of the material through careful moment-by-moment attention, listening not only to what was said but also to the pauses, hesitations, and silences.

In this kind of work, transcripts can be designed in a line-by-line numbering format with a wide right-hand margin for notes. The transcript becomes a working document, to be read and re-read, written on, marked and remarked, so that it becomes a concrete work of dialogue between researcher and text. Working with transcripts in this way generates possible future directions for interpretive lines of inquiry. The text is read not only sequentially, as the representation of the linear interview, but also in terms of parts and wholes, looking at similarities or dissonances within a single interview, or between multiple interviews and, most importantly, for that which makes a difference. Researchers read for ideas that stand out, raise questions, provoke curiosity, answer questions, catch our attention and, most importantly, call our present understanding into question.

Writing Interpretive Conjectures

Alongside listening to the recordings and reading and annotating the transcripts, interpretive writing can take the form of noting beginning ideas and conjectures of possible meanings in a style that may form future writing. Keeping notes serves the practical purpose of tracking ideas and being able to retrieve them later, both for the researcher's own use, as part of the unfolding story of doing the research that needs to be told and, importantly, as an audit trail to demonstrate rigor in the research. These beginning conjectures also support the practice of interpretive writing, and they provide a strategy for testing out emergent ideas, associations, and new ways of seeing things. At this early stage of writing, there is plenty of room for trial and error, to follow ideas to see where they lead. Writing, in turn, often leads to further reading, thinking, and searching back for an evocative quotation that suddenly finds a home, or looking for new material to support a fresh angle on the topic that is provoked by the data. Writing interpretive musings regularly throughout the data analysis is a practice that helps to generate possible interpretations. Over time, as a transformation into structure happens, there must be reasoned choices made and articulated about the most useful, fitting, and interesting interpretations that generate new understanding. The writing informs the choices made, but also retains the possibilities held in the conjectures that may not make it into the final report. There may be ideas, or parts of ideas, phrases, or references that can be incorporated into other contexts. Nothing is ever wasted at this stage of developing interpretations—it is often marked by a creative superfluity and excess which will leave traces in finished interpretive writing.

Developing Interpretations

Hermeneutic interpretation is pluralist because it entails attention to the particular instance, which retains its particularity even next to other similar instances.

Commitment to the idea of *Lebenswelt* has the effect that we are aware both of our unique, incommensurable experience of the world, and of our shared experience of a shared world. Thus, in working out interpretations from the data, there is recognition of similarity-in-difference and difference-in-similarity. There is no need for individual experiences to be subsumed into themes under the rubric of the same, but neither is any individual experience wholly separate from the fabric of understanding. Resistance to thematic reductionism as a goal of analysis is one of the hallmarks of hermeneutics. It flexibly allows for the recognition of extraordinary occurrences and exceptional views in the data while also seeking out points of affinity and relationship. This double movement can be seen in the exchange between part and whole in the hermeneutic circle, and in the tension between self and other that results in a kind of estrangement or distance from topic, necessary by Gadamer's account in *Truth and Method* for seeing the truth in the topic. The topic of research is the whole (in the sense of being a certain distinguishable aspect of the world, not as a discrete separate entity) to which data are related back through interpretation. There is a centrifugal and centripetal movement to interpretation (Davey, 2006): outwards by way of the unique insights afforded by each participant, and back inwards toward the topic, and toward the self, necessitating a transformation—"the transformation of structure that allows a subject to see its world differently and to become different to itself also sets the hermeneutic subject at a distance from itself" (Davey, 2006, p. 135). Thus, the imaginative, creative, associative forces in hermeneutics are balanced by the worldliness of the topic itself.

For example, while exploring a topic such as grief, bereaved people may often speak about guilt; they may not necessarily name it as guilt but the substance of what they are discussing may sound like the experience of guilt that can happen frequently in grief. Clinical work in the area of bereavement counseling bears this out (Moules & Amundson, 1997). The interpretive possibilities of the theme of guilt are revealed in the depth to which guilt then is unpacked and expressed as opposed to just a naming of it and a description of it. That is the distinction between arriving at a theme as part of a defining statement and using a theme as a jumping off point for interpretation. Within the theme in the latter sense, there may be many examples given from multiple participants who spoke of guilt and yet any of them could inflect the interpretive discussion by its difference or unique expression. Guilt would thus be taken up with suspicious curiosity, ready to question prevailing assumptions, or to make original connections that introduced new perspectives. Interpretation involves some degree of confidence trying out ideas, but also humility in relation to one's ideas, which will hopefully be illuminating and useful but never the last, final, or total word. In this example, guilt, as understood and interpreted, becomes a layer in the understanding of grief as an entire experience that is contextual, nuanced, and particular. A finer, different sense of one's own guilt and grief would emerge from the interpretation as well. Thus, it is that interpretation is always in relation to the topic, and in relation to the self, as a movement of the part-whole dialectic, and a movement on the part of the subjectivity of the researcher, who must be careful and aware of his or her prejudices to stay open to the potential interplay of multiple perspectives, and the development of self-understanding.

Interpretation does not have to emerge from some aspect of the topic that, as with guilt and grief, is already a recognized dimension. Sometimes a particular word or turn of phrase, in the context of an interview transcript, might be enough to suggest that there is potential for reflection, questioning, and elaboration. For an example of something that can catch one's attention, in the interview offered in the previous chapter, one might be struck by the comment made by one of the participants that "parents' relationships *should* be put on hold while a child has cancer and that there must be trust that they will endure." From this statement, one could begin to work out an interpretation of "being on hold" and what that means. How is being on hold experienced; what are its costs and requirements? How does one understand trust, and what does one trust? It is not just about describing what it means to be on hold or to trust, but to dig deeply, with hermeneutic sleuthing, into the complexity of this idea. These kinds of questions would then open a portal for the interpreter to enter and begin the process of taking these ideas to life in language.

The reflexivity of the research process means that interpretation might also be sparked by apparently incidental events that are not part of the data as such. One example of an interpretive conjecture that did not arise so much from the words spoken but from the process itself is as follows. A graduate student was examining the experiences of women who had suffered a serious depression and were currently living with the possibility of a return of the depression once they had been relieved of it. The student called the supervisor (Moules) in distress recounting that she had just completed one of her "best interviews yet." However, when the interview was over and she went to transcribe the interview, she realized her tape recorder had not worked and nothing was on tape. Moules asked her what happened in the interview, what was said, and why it was such a good interview. The student proceeded to explain that the participant was talking about her sense of being failed by the promise of medication, that she had held such hope that medication would cure her but instead it had immense and unlivable side effects. Her sense was that of having been let down by science and modern medicine's promise to cure or provide relief. After this recounting, Moules said to the student,

> *Then you write about that and about the failure of technology to live up to its promise and you write about the failure of your tape recorder as a mirror of technology's inability to always deliver as promised. And then you go to Heidegger, and you read his quote "Everywhere we remain unfree and chained to technology, whether we passionately affirm or deny it. But we are delivered over to it in the worst possible way when we regard it as something neutral" (Heidegger, 1977, p. 4). And that's where you begin your interpretation.*

Out of this beginning, the student developed a beautiful interpretation around Technology, Promises, Hopes, and Disappointments. It is clear from this example, too, that to get to the pathway of the interpretation, the researcher needed dialogue with someone else, in this case her supervisor, to see something, a connection, that she had not noticed in her preoccupation with the seemingly irrevocable loss of material.

Interpretation, as the example above shows, can be organized around an interruption of the anticipated narrative with its striking character of attention to the instance and the particular, rather than an effort to generalize or to smooth over that which presents as disruption (Moules, 2002). Thus, the process of interpretation engages in a deconstruction of data and a reconstruction of meaning. The idea of deconstruction, most often associated with Jacques Derrida, involves a process of questioning traditional assumptions and certainties, rather than accepting them as assumed truths.

> Far from being opposed to deconstruction, philosophical hermeneutics requires it. Without difference and without language's endless deferral of meaning, the achievement of new understanding would not be possible. Philosophical hermeneutics contends that the vitality of understanding actually depends on difference. (Davey, 2006, p. xii)

One of the consequences of this deconstructive movement is that interpretation need not rely on complete stories, or logical narratives as data. As with themes, there is no rule against narrative, but interpretation serves an understanding of the topic, not any particular narrative offered by a participant. Interpretation goes on with the sense of truth as *aletheia*—unconcealment. While the goal is to bring to life some aspect of the topic, to remember forgotten or neglected truths, and generate new possibilities for practice, it is always at the cost of letting go of other possibilities. Interpretation involves choice at every moment, requiring tact, ethical focus, and clear sense of purpose.

Interpretive Writing: Bringing the Topic to Life in Language

Experience is not really meaningful until it has found a home in language.
—Madison (1988, p. 165)

As mentioned, analysis in interpretive work has no beginning point, but rather is an ongoing experience. In the shaping of words on paper, something miraculous happens.

> Nothing is so purely the trace of the mind as is writing but nothing is so dependent on the understanding mind either. In deciphering and interpreting it, a miracle takes place: the transformation of something alien and dead into total contemporaneity and familiarity ... that is why the capacity to read, to understand what is written is like a secret art, even a magic that frees and binds us. (Gadamer, 1960/1997, p. 163)

Hermeneutics requires a "tragic, loving relationship with language" (Moules, 2002, p. 15), meaning that language is the thing that carries interpretation into being but language, as Gadamer (1960/1997) suggested, has a forgetfulness of itself. It expresses one thing while at the same time silences another thing, and it is unstable, constantly open to re-interpretation: "... understanding and the hermeneutic translation and transcendence it affords depend upon the vital instability of the 'word'" (Davey, 2006, p. xv). Writing also must reveal the vulnerability of the writer to not knowing, of being struck by something beyond words and understanding, of not fully understanding the topic, and of only partially and provisionally knowing what things mean. We are, after all, human beings on the move, caught up in things on the move. Phenomena are fluid, ever changing in time, as are we. Thus, we can never fully understand, and our awareness of this needs to show in our writing. This is not an easy thing to accomplish—to say things with confidence that does not also betray the provisional character of life itself.

Language holds something open in its possibilities; it clears a space around it and hands it on through articulation. Articulation, however, needs to be done well and in a way that allows the topic to stand against the articulation and not be consumed, constrained, or contained by it. Things should not be captured in the writing, not imprisoned by it, but set free within it. Yet, the tragedy lies in the notion that whenever words and meanings are given, other words and meanings are denied. This is the work of *aletheia*—to simultaneously reveal one thing while concealing another. *Aletheia*, in its enlivening, remembering, and unconcealment, is the goal of interpretive writing. Yet, writing itself inherently preserves some of the concealedness of the topic, respecting that all things cannot be fully known and there remains a privacy, mystery, and unknownness of all topics. Articulation should not flatten something out, but infuse it with vitality, energy, image, and imagination, in such a way that the articulation itself disappears, and the topic shows itself, perhaps even allowing it to be read in a more generous way than it reads itself.

> There is undoubtedly a question of style involved in philosophical hermeneutic writing, a valuing of creative expression that goes against the grain of contemporary belief that technical... language [necessarily] betokens substance. This is one of the challenges of

> hermeneutic research, both because it is not easy to do and because style cannot be allowed to run away with sense and purpose. (McCaffrey et al., 2012, p. 221)

Hermeneutic writing does have a "discernable signature" (Davey, 2006, p. 18). It is imaginative, creative, engaging, poignant, and stimulating. It can also be, perhaps should also be, disconcerting and tragic, "a condition of exposure in which one's conceptual resources have been blown away by what one has encountered. In this event, one finds oneself radically situated with no place to hide" (Bruns, 1992, p. 184).

Hermeneutic writing often has the character of exaggeration in strengthening what it wants to be heard (Smith, 1991). This does not mean that researchers invent things but instead highlights them. Exaggeration occurs deliberately, purposefully designed to disrupt, find, and cultivate the familiar. Hermeneutic work has to be more than just a good description; it has to be carefully crafted versions that will bear up clinical descriptions and exemplars and expand them into rich and full descriptions of the understandings generated and created within the study. For this reason, interpretations must be supported by data to allow the reader some recognition of how the interpreter arrived at the interpretations and to show that they are not just "made up" but came out of somewhere, something, or someone. Hermeneutics is the art of strengthening.

"Let the data speak for themselves these scientists say. The trouble with that argument is, of course, that data never do speak for themselves" (Keller, 1985, cited in Lenzo, 1995, p. 17). Steeves (2000) wrote of the dilemma of sending manuscripts to journals for review and receiving comments from reviewers with the criticism that he had "gone beyond his data." After his initial frustration with reviewers' lack of understanding, he came to realize that is exactly what he is supposed to do in hermeneutic research.

> It is the obligation of the researcher to go beyond his or her data, but not in the sense of reaching conclusions unrelated to the data or unjustified by the data. I am using *going beyond the data* to mean thinking what the data might mean in a broader way or using the data as a means of thinking about the broader world. What is the point of doing this work, investigating human experience, if thinking about this human condition in its largest sense is not allowed? (Steeves, 2000, pp. 97–98)

Steeves continued suggesting that one needs to "think *with* the data" (p. 98). Thinking with the data then means to be in the dialectic that interpretation requires, the back-and-forth of conversation, thought, questions and answers, possibilities, and puzzles. Davey (2013) offered the idea that interpretation is always X=X+; there is always something more to be interpreted and thinking with the data means going beyond it.

Jardine (2008) suggested that "(i)f one pursues a hermeneutic study … it is not enough to write about different things … I must also write *differently*, in a way that acknowledges, attends, and waits upon the agency of the world. Hermeneutics is therefore akin to the opening up of 'animating possibilities presented by each event' (Hillman 1982, p. 177)" (Jardine, 2008, p. 110). Writing differently is difficult. What is even more difficult is maintaining the creative and generative spirit of interpretive writing while remaining scholarly, citatious, deliberate, and mindful. This kind of writing does have a certain kind of flair and flavor, and done well, it also holds a keen sense of scholarship that is recognizable, and a keen sense of the limitations of the scholarship. If data analysis in the beginning is about looking to deconstruct the obvious, and unpack the assumed, it can be thought of as White (1993, p. 35) described as "exoticizing the domestic"—taking what is just a "given" and seeing it with a new lens. Once exoticized though, interpretations cannot be simply left there to dangle in an exotic display but must be brought back into the world where the topic is located; one could think of this as domesticating the exotic, "making what was once exotic to be recognizable and 'true'" (Moules, 2002, p. 3). Deconstruction is always in play with reconstruction.

Metaphors

Two senses of metaphor are at work in hermeneutics: one that signals our fundamental relationship with the world, and the other is that which is at work in language to make it possible to give expression to the nuanced character of experience. Often, in interpretive writing, metaphor is used as a linguistic device that can express the interplay of familiar and other. Well-placed metaphors draw the reader in, and an original metaphor suddenly throws open an unexpected insight. For that reason, metaphor is often found in hermeneutic writing, but we offer the caveat that metaphors, as a means to communicate meaning, can be overused. Writing that is rife with metaphor after metaphor may be engagingly picturesque but loses its hold on the topic, which disappears behind the metaphors rather than let the metaphor illuminate the interpretation. The word metaphor means to carry beyond, carry over, transfer or to bear (Hoad, 1986; Neufeldt & Guralnik, 1988); "Metaphor is the way language carried itself past its own powers to enter new realms" (Hirshfield, 1997, p. 111).

> Metaphors provide a view of something from a viewpoint of another thing and yet they work to make one feel "at home." "*Yes, that is right; that is what it is like; I recognize that.*" Paradoxically, a metaphor simultaneously serves to remove us, while at the same time offering us a home in language and understanding … Metaphors perhaps offer something to grasp, something that can be pictured and understood as a place to rest the mystery of the profound, wordless, faceless experience of suffering. (Moules et al., 2004, p. 105)

Metaphors have the ability to carry and bear things while providing meaning and understanding (Lakoff & Johnson, 2003). Used judiciously, they are rich and relatable ways of conveying interpretations. For example, in a hermeneutic study on grief cited in the quote above, Moules et al. (2004) used the metaphor of the "uninvited houseguest" to describe the arrival of grief after the death of a loved one. Since the publication of that study, Moules has received much feedback from bereaved people who can "relate" to this description and the metaphor has "grab" (Glaser, 1978, p. 95), serving to offer language and give meaning to an experience that is often indescribable.

The art of using metaphors relies on creativity, fit, and discernment about when and why to use them. As mentioned, the overuse of many metaphors, mixed metaphors, or metaphors that contradict each other can only serve to muddle the interpretations rather than to bring them clarity. When metaphors are overused, they become signifiers of implied shared values and points of view—fostering complacency rather than questioning. One such metaphor that has been overused in research (and elsewhere) is that of "the journey." This is not to say that it cannot be used but it should be substantiated, and presented and argued cogently so that it does manage to bear and carry the interpretation forward in such a way that the topic is illuminated richly. Another caution about the use of metaphors is that one can become so married to the metaphor that the data appears to be made to fit the metaphor rather than the metaphor serving to fit the data.

Etymological Tracings and Intoxications

As a part of deconstructing or unpacking topics, an often-used practice in hermeneutic work is to carefully dismantle the meanings of words and their etymological origins. This can be a useful exercise if, as in the case of metaphor, it is not overused so that the paper begins to read like a dictionary or playing with words for its own sake. Etymological tracings are a linguistic example of the importance of history for hermeneutics. Past meanings of words, and meanings of root words in other languages present layers of potential meaning within a word. There is no presumptive original or definitive meaning, but rather the presence of multiple meanings opens another way of entering into dialogue with tradition and finding a way of questioning contemporary taken-for-granted points of view (Nicholas Davey, personal communication, August 7, 2014). As mentioned though, there can be an overreliance of the use of etymology as an interpretive tool, what Gadamer referred to as "etymological intoxication" (2004, p. 409), and this can begin to disrupt or interrupt the fullness and flow of the interpretation with a constant return to the etymological tracing of the word. When this happens, it begins to appear as if the researcher is using word definitions and histories of words as the only means to reach an interpretation; in some cases, it even begins to resemble what could be called an etymological "trickery" in the sense that the play on words becomes an end in itself and a distraction from a lack of interpretive substance. It can begin to feel that the interpreter is looking up the words, rather than listening to them.

Tracing words back to their origins can be useful in the service of understanding the topic, if in fact it does bring understanding to the topic. For example, if one is trying to look at the topic of suffering and compassion, understanding the meanings and history of these words is vital. To suffer means to undergo, endure, tolerate, allow. It is connected to the word passion which is tied to the word patient. Compassion means to suffer with and suffering together. These tracings then make an argument for an interpretation that says something about what being compassionate is in the face of suffering, an understanding that has direct implications for practice (see for e.g., Moules, 1999, in her interpretive analysis of *Suffering Together: Whose Words Were They?*). Understanding the historical use and evolution of words as well as their multiple meanings is helpful when it serves the topic with substance and when the researcher can explain the purpose of an etymological exploration.

Summary

Hermeneutics involves answering questions that could be differently answered with different interpretations.

> All interpretation works under the promise of truth… When we opt for a given interpretation, we do not do so because we know it to be true … but because we *believe* it to the best, the one that offers the most promise and is the most likely to make the text intelligible and comprehensible for us. (Madison, 1988, p. 15)

In believing something, we also need to be convincing; interpretations must be well-grounded, justified, and articulated but not presented as incontrovertible.

Interpretation does not simply end; it offers a plausible and prudent response to something, but it does not offer a final answer. "What are perceived as the weaknesses of philosophical hermeneutics—its inability to arrive at a final interpretation …are indeed its strengths" (Davey, 2006, p. xv). The strength lies in the difficulty and vitality of the work. Davey (2006, p. xiv, citing Vattimo [2002]) reminded us of "the ever-present difficulty of residing within the 'quietness of a single interpretation.'" Interpretations are not quiet; they are bold, robust, assertive claims of something, but it has to be remembered that they can silence other claims if they are not made carefully, thoughtfully, and with enough room to allow an invitation to dialogue.

In spite of the boldness of interpretations, we do not want to protect any hermeneutic work from re-interpretation. Kvale and Brinkmann (2009) addressed the issue of the critique of hermeneutic analysis that different interpreters will find different meanings in the text, saying that this demand for objectivity premises on a belief that there can be only one correct interpretation. They countered this claim in acknowledging that it is the gift of hermeneutics to allow for pluralities of meanings and interpretations. There is an experience of needing to give the work up, of letting it move out of our hands into the hands of others, when we are finished the work to the best of our abilities, satisfied that the interpretations are fitting, and ring true of something; there is a handing over and that is exactly the right thing to do. In one way, it is as though the interpretation cannot settle and rest in one's own hands for, if it does, it stops growing; it stops being generative and fertile. It settles into a reified version of something without experiencing the life force and generativity of others and of the topic that it needs to sustain it. When interpretations go out of our hands and into the hands of others, they situate themselves exactly where they are supposed to be—in movement and play, and we cannot even save the work from our own re-interpretations. This is the curse and the gift of this kind of work.

In hermeneutic interpretation, we do not seek consensus or agreement; difference is not something to be overcome in hermeneutics. Interpretations are more about arriving at an understanding and "coming to an understanding certainly does not imply agreement [Übereinstimmung]. On the contrary, where people are already in agreement, they do not need to come to an understanding" (Gadamer, 2016, p. 179). We hope for the newness that comes with understanding, the invocation for different interpretations. We hope for responses, and that the writing evokes something in the reader, that the reader's interpretation might make it better. Caputo (1987) suggested that hermeneutics succeeds

> only if it brings to words what we have all along understood about ourselves but have thus far been more or less unable to say … it comes down to its ability to provoke in us the ultimate hermeneutic response: "*That* is what we are looking for. That puts into words what we have all along understood." (p. 81)

The measure then of the credibility of the interpretations lies in the ways it brings understanding to the topic.

> When you talk to me about my research, do not ask me what I have found; I found nothing. Ask me what I invented, what I made up from and out of my data … I am not confessing to telling any lies about the people or events in my stories … The proof for you is in the things I have made—how they look to your mind's eye, whether they satisfy your sense of style and craftsmanship, whether your believe them, and whether they appeal to your heart. (Sandelowski, 1994, p. 61)

We have not laid out a formula for analysis in interpretive work, as that would be antithetical to hermeneutics, however we offer guidelines, suggestions, philosophical groundings, and invocations to move into interpretive analysis and to take interpretations to writing. In the next chapter, we offer examples of interpretive writing—of "writing differently" while maintaining scholarship and integrity.

References

Abram, D. (1996). *The spell of the sensuous: Perception and language in a more than human world*. Vintage Books.

Allen, D. G. (1993). Hermeneutics: Philosophical traditions and nursing practice research. *Nursing Science Quarterly, 8*(4), 174–182. <https://doi.org/10.1177/089431849500800408>

Bruns, G. (1992). *Hermeneutics ancient and modern*. Yale University Press.

Caputo, J. D. (1987). *Radical hermeneutics: Repetition, deconstruction, and the hermeneutic project*. Indiana University Press.

Colaizzi, P. F. (1978). Psychological research as the phenomenologist views it. In R. S. Valle & M. King (Eds.), *Existential phenomenological alternatives for psychology* (pp. 48–71), Plenum.

Davey, N. (2006). *Unquiet understanding: Gadamer's philosophical hermeneutics*. SUNY.

Davey, N. (2013). *Unfinished worlds: Hermeneutics, aesthetics and Gadamer.* Edinburgh University Press.

Fleming, V., Gladys, U., & Robb, Y. (2003). Hermeneutic research in nursing: Developing a Gadamerian-based research method. *Nursing Inquiry, 10*(2), 113–120. <https://doi.org/10.1046/j.1440-1800.2003.00163.x>

Gadamer, H.-G. (1960/1997). *Truth and method* (2nd rev.ed.; J. Weinsheimer & D. G. Marshall, Trans.) Continuum.

Gadamer, H.-G. (1960/2004). *Truth and method* (2nd ed.; J. Weinsheimer & D. G. Marshall, Trans.) Continuum.

Gadamer, H.-G. (2007). *The Gadamer reader: A bouquet of later writings* (R. E. Palmer, Ed. & Trans.). Northwestern University Press.

Gadamer, H.-G. (2007). Hermeneutics on the trail. In P. Vandevelde & A. Iyer (Eds. & Trans.), *Hermeneutics between history and philosophy: The selected writings of Hans-Georg Gadamer, Vol. 1* (pp. 179–206). Bloomsbury Academic.

Giorgi, A. (1985). *Phenomenology and psychological research*. Duquesne University Press.

Glaser, B. (1978). *Theoretical sensitivity*. Sociology Press.

Heidegger, M. (1977). *The question concerning technology and other essays* (W. Lovitt, Trans.). Garland.

Hirshfield, J. (1996). *Nine gates: Entering the mind of poetry*. HarperCollins.

Hoad, T. F. (Ed.) (1986). *The concise Oxford dictionary of English etymology*. Oxford University Press.

Hoy, D. (1998). Heidegger and the hermeneutic turn. In C. Guignon (Ed.), *The Cambridge companion to Heidegger* (pp.170–190). Cambridge University Press.

Jardine, D. W. (2008). Because it shows us the way at night: On animism, writing, and the re-animation of Piagetian theory. In D. W. Jardine, S. Friesen, & P. Clifford, *Back to the basics of teaching and learning: Thinking the world together* (2nd ed., pp. 105–116). Routledge.

Keller, E. F. (1985) *Reflections on gender and science*. Yale University Press.

Kvale, S., & Brinkmann, S. (2009). *InterViews: Learning the craft of qualitative research interviewing* (2nd ed.). SAGE.

Lakoff, G., & Johnson, M. (2003). *Metaphors we live by*. University of Chicago Press.

Lenzo, K. (1995). Validity and self-reflexivity meet poststructuralism: Scientific ethos and the transgressive self. *Educational Researcher, 24*(4), 17–24. <https://doi.org/10.3102/0013189X024004017>

Lindseth, A., & Norberg, A. (2004). A phenomenological hermeneutical method for researching lived experience. *Journal of Caring Sciences, 18*, 145–157. <https://doi.org/10.1111/j.1471-6712.2004.00258.x>

Madison, G. B. (1988). *The hermeneutics of postmodernity: Figures and themes*. Indiana University Press.

McCaffrey, G., Raffin-Bouchal, S., & Moules, N. J. (2012). Hermeneutics as a research approach: A reappraisal. *International Journal of Qualitative Methods, 11*(3), 213–229. <https://doi.org/10.1177/160940691201100303>

Moules, N. J. (1999). Guest Editorial. Suffering together: Whose words were they? *Journal of Family Nursing, 5*(3), 251–258. <https://doi.org/10.1177/107484079900500301>

Moules, N. J. (2002). Hermeneutic inquiry: Paying heed to history and Hermes. An ancestral, substantive, and methodological tale. *International Journal of Qualitative Methods, 1*(3), 1–21. <https://doi.org/10.1177/160940690200100301>

Moules, N. J., & Amundson, J. K. (1997). Grief—An invitation to inertia: A narrative approach to working with grief. *Journal of Family Nursing, 3*(4), 378–393. <https://doi.org/10.1177/107484079700300405>

Moules, N. J., Simonson, K., Prins, M., Angus, P., & Bell, J. M. (2004). Making room for grief: Walking backwards and living forward. *Nursing Inquiry, 11*(2), 99–107. <https://doi.org/10.1111/j.1440-1800.2004.00204.x>

Neufeldt, V., & Guralnik, D. B. (Eds.). (1988). *Webster's new world dictionary of American English: Third college edition*. W. W. Norton.

Smith, D. G. (1991). Hermeneutic inquiry: The hermeneutic imagination and the pedagogic text. In E. Short (Ed.), *Forms of curriculum inquiry* (pp. 187–209). SUNY.

Steeves, R. H. (2000). Writing the results. In M. Zichi Cohen, D. L. Kahn, & R. H. Steeves (Eds.). *Hermeneutic phenomenological research: A practical guide for nurse researchers* (pp. 93–99). Sage

van Manen, M. (1984). Practicing phenomenological writing. *Phenomenology + Pedagogy, 2*(1), 36–69. <https://doi.org/10.29173/pandp14931>

White, M. (1993). Deconstruction and therapy. In S. Gilligan & R. Price (Eds.), *Therapeutic conversations* (pp. 22–61). W. W. Norton.

Interpretation as Writing

Interpretive writing is at the heart of hermeneutic research, and it is a learned and practiced art that is often difficult to discern and develop for beginning researchers. Sometimes the most helpful way to understand how to conduct hermeneutic research or explain interpretive writing is to look at work that has already been done. In fact, our experiences with those new to the hermeneutic tradition, have shown that hermeneutics often "explains itself" when one is able to read a published manuscript or dissertation of a hermeneutic study.

In this chapter, we offer three examples (with several excerpts in each) of recently completed and, in some cases, published hermeneutic research. These examples are not the only way in which one can write hermeneutically, however they offer ideas of how the address, being "on the trail", conducting interviews, and interpretive analysis might look as an end product, as something available for public consumption.

Example 1: Listening to the "Voices" of Children With Serious Illness: Art, Metaphor, and Silence (Wong, 2025)

This study was the doctoral research done by Katherine Wong (supervised by Moules). Wong came to this research with an extensive clinical background in pediatric palliative care, having noted that there was a paucity of research that included children's perspectives in the pediatric palliative care literature. One barrier to involving children in this type of research is the perceived communication challenges of children with serious illness (Liben et al., 2014; Rahimzadeh et al., 2015). Wong was addressed by a drawing created by a bereaved sibling that expressed their feelings of grief and hope in ways that they were unable to articulate with words alone. Wong considered how art is used to help children express themselves in art therapy, and how art could be utilized in research interviews with children to assist with communication. Philosophical hermeneutics places a special emphasis on the communicative power of art and its ability to reveal truths about our lives (Gadamer, 1960/2004; 1986); hermeneutic research was a methodological fit for the interpretation of children's art as data. The research question was: How might we understand experiences of children with serious illness through their artistic forms of expression? Wong interviewed six children with serious life-threatening and life-shortening illnesses who created art during their interviews. From this study, four interpretations were generated and excerpts from three interpretive chapters are presented below.

Excerpt 1: From the Chapter "The 'Voices' of Children: Art, Metaphor, and Silence"

During data collection, Wong noted that, while the artwork that children created during their interviews added to understanding children's experiences of serious illness differently, art was not the only form of expression the participants used. The participants offered detailed descriptions or striking metaphors to describe their illness experiences. There were also moments where they were unable to summon the language to speak to an experience. During the analysis, it became apparent that, while the artwork was a meaningful addition to the data, the participants did not need to create artwork to say something of their experiences. The original inquiry became secondary to the primacy of children's voices in shaping understanding. Moules encouraged Wong to reconsider what was exposed in the analysis and the ways in which children conveyed their experiences. A new research question, that both encapsulated the original topic while broadening the analysis in a meaningful way, was proposed: how might we understand the "voices" of children who are seriously ill? With this revised question came the need to clarify how voice might be interpreted, given that children expressed themselves through a variety of ways that could be interpreted hermeneutically. The first interpretive chapter described how children's "voices," including art, metaphor, and silence, might be understood.

Children's Voices

The ways in which voices and children are conceptualized have implications for how children's voices are interpreted in hermeneutic research. Voice can be simply defined as a sound produced by human beings, the faculty of utterance, or the right of expression (Merriam-Webster, n.d.). Voice can also be defined as a "construct that operationalizes access to a person's perspective" (Singh et al.,

2020, p. 400). Spyrou (2016) argued that, for the last three decades, the field of Childhood Studies has taken up this definition of voice as the "all-too-easy and unproblematic desire to render children and their words comprehensible and transparent through a surface reading of their utterances" (p. 106). Carnevale (2020) described such approaches as "thin conceptions" (p. 2) of voice, which regard statements made by children, or a person of any age, as a direct representation of their independent preferences, desires, or perspectives. It is important to consider the possibilities for how voice might be interpreted within and beyond what children "say" in trying to understand how children experience serious illness. I have come to understand "children's voices" for this research as the unity of testimonial justice, agency, and recognition.

Importantly, children's voices in the context of research involve encounters between adults (i.e., the researcher) and children (i.e., as participants or as subjects of observation). Miranda Fricker's (2007) work on epistemic injustice highlights what is at stake in the interactions between children and adults, namely "the sharing of meaning" (Risser, 2012, p. 92). Epistemic injustice arises when someone is "wronged specifically in their capacity as a knower" (Fricker, 2007, p. 1), which Fricker further categorized as testimonial injustice and hermeneutical injustice. Testimonial injustice occurs when prejudice (in a negative sense) causes a listener to assign a reduced level of credibility to a speaker's word, usually due to their social identity.

Burroughs and Tollefson (2016) argued that children, as a social identity, are subject to testimonial injustice due to being categorized as irrational, suggestible, and unreliable. This results in children receiving less testimonial credibility than they deserve without having to utter a single word. This perceived lack of credibility also contributes to a paucity of research in which children are participants, as children's accounts of their experiences are deemed less reliable or credible than those of their adult counterparts (Docherty & Sandelowski, 1999). Voice might be partially defined as testimony, with the caveat that the testimony of the speaker is deemed reliable regardless of their social identity. However, testimonial justice for children in research is unlikely to be achieved by acknowledging the credibility of what children have to say alone, particularly if their interpretive frameworks, their ability to assign meaning to something, is also in question. By itself, testimony might run the risk of being too close to "thin conceptions" of children's voices (Carnevale, 2020, p. 2) if presented simply as the recitation of what children said.

The work of bioethicist Franco Carnevale, who applied Charles Taylor's philosophy to construct a framework for children's agency, is helpful in considering how voice might be understood as agency. Taylor (1985) presented two conceptions of agential persons. First, "the ordinary notion of a person, defined by certain capacities: a person is an agent who has a sense of self, of [their] own life, who can evaluate it, and who can make choices about it" (Taylor, 1985, p. 103). In this view, what makes an agent a person, is the power to plan and act on those plans. This is problematic for children, as they are often seen as lacking certain capacities, such as the ability to make informed decisions, perform critical reflection, and speak or act on their behalf (Carnevale, 2021). Taylor's (1985) second conception of a person posits that

> [A]gents are beings for whom things matter, who are subjects of significance. This gives them a point of view on the world. But what distinguishes persons from other agents is not strategic power, that is, the capacity to deal with the same matter of concern more effectively. Once one focusses on the significance of things for agents, then what springs to view is that persons have qualitatively different concerns. (p. 104)

In this view, a person's valuation of matters of significance will inform their actions and decisions, which are always contextualized in the agent's situatedness in the world (Carnevale, 2021; Taylor, 1985). Using Taylor's conception of a person as someone for whom things matter, Carnevale (2021) emphasized that children's voices must be recognized and interpreted as agential expressions of meaning. With testimony and agency, children's voices can be acknowledged as credible statements about matters of meaning for children. One additional concept, hermeneutical recognition, will further clarify that children's voices also reveal possibilities for understanding differently.

Voice, from the Latin root *vocem*, can be translated as "sound, utterance, cry, speech, language, or word," but it can also mean a "call" (Online Etymology Dictionary, n.d.). A call carries with it an attempt to reach someone, as well as the demand for a response. As George (2020) showed, in working through Gadamer's moral gradations of our recognition of the Other, such a response can come in different forms. First, a response to the call of the Other may be diminished to generalization, where rather than recognizing others as having their own voice, we look for what is predictable about them as a means to our own ends. James (2007) warned that the conception of "children's voices" risks ignoring the diversity of children's individual lives and experiences by "uncritically clump[ing] children together as members of a category" (p. 262). The second level of recognition positions the Other as a "person with an independent voice, but instead of allowing them to say something of their own, we demand that they confirm the validity of what we have to say" (George, 2020, p. 108).

The third moral gradation recognizes the Other as having a voice of their own, and, importantly, listening for the possibility of validity in what the Other has to say (Gadamer, 1960/2004; George, 2020). This does not mean that the listener should blindly accept the Other's claim, but that the listener is willing to place their own beliefs and understandings aside when considering the call of the Other. This kind of open listening requires interpretation and is enacted through a back-and-forth of question and answer (Risser, 2012), in a call and its open response. Listening to children's voices is the recognition that when they speak about their experiences, their voices carry testimonial credibility, agential expressions of meaning, and the possibility that we might learn something from them and come to understand differently. In this research, the participant's "voices" came in different forms. Often, their experiences of serious illness were relayed through narration and storytelling. However, they also conveyed their experiences through other kinds of "voices": artworks, metaphors, and silences. These voices also carry with them testimony, meaning, and possibility.

The Voice of Art

Philosophical hermeneutics places a special emphasis on the revelatory function of art. In the case of children's artwork, the viewer may not pay close attention to what an image "says" insofar as children's artwork is regularly regarded as decorative, rather than a work to contemplate (Matthews & Mullen, 2020). Considered hermeneutically, children's artwork might reveal possibilities for understanding their experiences of the world. Gadamer's notion that a picture is a "speechless language" (1986, p. 83), rather than a thing created for pleasure and considered for its mere beauty, suggests that it has something to say. Once made, the work of art stands and speaks for itself (Gadamer, 1986): it has a voice. In standing and speaking for itself, a work of art is absolute; it is "there" completely, and ready to be encountered by those who view it (Gadamer, 1986, 1992/2006). I do not think Gadamer was referring to children's artwork when he developed his philosophy of hermeneutical aesthetics. However, hermeneutics has interpretive implications for how children's artwork is viewed and engaged.

The participants in this study used artwork as a voice to say something about their illness experiences and present their matters of concern. Nate (Figure 1) and Maddie (Figure 2) chose to draw the things that were important to them after being diagnosed with cancer. These drawings helped them to expand on why the things and people depicted in these images were significant to them. For Nate, his family, his dogs, his healthcare providers, decorative aspects of the hospital, and the remaining free of infection were matters of significance. Even the addition of a ponytail on his mother's head was meaningful to him. As George (2020) wrote, "the arts and humanities … aim at nothing else than making things that matter to us visible" (p. 143).

Nate: *She used to have a ponytail so I'm just gonna add that ... Yeah, see I'm grown my hair after I cut it, my brother already grown his hair, and my dad is, but she's still doesn't have her hair [i.e., his mother kept her hair short].*
KW: *No? Did you shave your head at one point?*
Nate: *Yeah, because of my chemo that I've been doing.*
KW: *So, did everyone shave their head?*
Nate: *Yeah ... to make me feel like I'm not the only one with a shaved head.*

The addition of a drawing of Nate's pet was significant because he did not have access to his dog, who was an important source of comfort, while admitted at the hospital.

Nate: *... the brown dog, he's my dog. He's really attracted to me, and he loves to play, and he protects me too ... he comforts me because he's so soft, so I just hold him, and he just sits there. He doesn't care how I hold him; he will just fall asleep on me.*

In one image, Nate's world and the things that matter to him are presented in a unifying way.

Figure 1. (Nate)

Figure 2. (Maddie)

Maddie also drew her dog, who was a supportive presence in her life after she was diagnosed with cancer. Her dog was present during our interview, and the bell on her collar can be heard jingling throughout the audio recording.

> *Maddie: Well, my dog has always been really important to me. She helps me take meds. All I have to say is "Spot [pseudonym] meds!" and she comes up and lets me hold her paw and my mom gives me the medicine.*

The aim of hermeneutic research is not to represent the participants, but to interpret what they can speak to about the topic, such that the topic is expanded in new ways (Moules et al., 2015). Thus, the point would not be to say that children with serious illness should always have their dogs with them, but to recognize that children have matters of concern that can appear and be given shape in their artwork. Important aspects of their illness experiences, such as comfort, solidarity, anxiety, and friendship, are presented in art "with a unity, a structure, and thus an intelligibility that experience itself lacks" (Schmidt, 2015, p. 347). Through such a creation, experiences are transformed into something immediately perceptible with an abundance of possible meanings (Gadamer, 2004; George, 2020; Schmidt, 2015). In pictures of dogs, friends, and a mother's ponytail, children's voices appear and demand a response.

Excerpt 2: From the Chapter "Nope, I'm Outta Here!": Children's Experiences of Clinical Environments"

> *The ethos of hospitality is never guaranteed. It is always shadowed by its twin: hostility.*
> *—Kearney (2015, p. 173)*

In this chapter, Wong was unsettled by a participant quote that described the hospital as "*a hostile environment.*" While she was not surprised to hear that the participants disliked going to the hospital, Wong felt that "*hostile*" was a strong word to describe a children's hospital that was designed to feel welcoming to children and their families. As Moules et al. (2015) offered, the tracing of etymological roots can be a productive exercise, allowing the researcher to explore the past meanings of words or how language shifts over time in ways that reinvigorate the contemporary sense of a word or phrase. Wong found that hostile shares the same Latin roots, *hostis* and *hospes*, with the origins of hospital, hospice, and hospitality. Wong used these etymological tracings to understand how children experienced their clinical environments as both hospitable and hostile. Wong then built an interpretation around children's experiences of place and how place can provide a structure for experience in a similar manner to Heidegger's (1927/1962) idea of temporality and Gadamer's (1960/2004) idea of history and tradition.

Wong explored participants' comments about the hostilities of the hospital, including the place itself and the things inside. Being taken to the hospital was often their first indication that something was wrong, and one participant described it as being "*the place where I've been told the worst things*." The hospice environment was experienced differently than the hospital, and participants noted the home-like feeling of the place, while acknowledging that it was not like *their* home. Despite the hostility or unfamiliarity of the children's clinical environments, many participants noted that the hospitality of their healthcare providers helped to mitigate their negative experiences of the places in which they received care.

Children's Experiences of the Hospital

The Alberta Children's Hospital (ACH) has been available to children and their families since 1922 (ACH Foundation, n.d.), albeit in different buildings and locations over the years. In his TEDxCalgary (2023) talk, Architect Bill Chomik explained that he designed the "new" Children's Hospital, established in 2006, with its primary patrons in mind (ACH Foundation, n.d.; TEDxCalgary, 2023). A panel of children advised that the exterior of the building should look like Lego blocks (TEDxCalgary, 2023) and the font in the sign above the main entrance mimics a child's handwriting. The hospital's address is on Oki Drive; "oki" means "welcome" in Blackfoot, one of the languages of the Indigenous Peoples of Alberta. The threshold of the building features pictures of smiling children and adolescents, and there is an impressive aquarium in the lobby full of clown fish and blue tangs, the favorite sea creatures of children since the release of the Disney film *Finding Nemo*. The interior decorations were chosen to promote healing and assist with children's wayfinding (TEDxCalgary, 2023). I have been told that extensive research went into the selection of periwinkle blue, the color that best encouraged a sense of serenity, for the walls of the spiritual space. Each child has their own room, outfitted with parent beds, private bathrooms, and large windows, some of which overlook the Rocky Mountains west of the city.

According to Adams and Theodore (2002), following World War II, children's hospitals shifted to focus more on medical and research innovations, transitioning away from their roots as centers for the custodial care of marginalized children. The architecture of the hospitals during this time openly conveyed the emphasis on medicine and science, with modern layouts and technology on display, and their exteriors appeared no different from adult hospitals or office towers. However, as conceptions of childhood became increasingly whimsical and playful, so too did the architecture and design of children's hospitals (James & Curtis, 2012; Lomax, 1996; Mahnke, 2000). By the 1980s, children's hospitals began to include references to children's popular culture and entertaining features, such as the large statues of flying animals seen in the atrium of Sick Kids (Adams & Theodore, 2002).

The design of these spaces took cues from psychology, where new research suggested that children needed to be distracted when ill (Adams & Theodore, 2002). One can now expect children's hospitals to be brightly colored, imaginative, and lively spaces.

It may also be the case that children's hospitals and their design took cues from the prioritization of patient experience in adult health centers. Practices from the hospitality industry are gradually influencing the services and design of hospitals, with the goal of providing exceptional experiences for patients who are treated as customers or guests, rather than the recipients of healthcare (Ocak et al., 2024). For patients, the technical aspects of care delivery may be concealed by the "actions of the employees, the layout of the hospital rooms, and the atmosphere of the service" (Ocak et al., 2024, p. 1). It is not surprising that modern hospitals have adopted practices from the hospitality sector. The word hospital stems from a group of words sharing similar etymological roots and histories as hospitality (Benveniste, 1973; Derrida, 2023; Online Etymology Dictionary, n.d.). Children's hospitals are often built and designed to be hospitable to children, amenable to their unique needs and distinct tastes. However, there is one more word that shares its etymological and historical roots with hospitality: hostility.

In his work on Indo-European languages, Benveniste (1973) noted the expansive history of the concept of hospitality. From the Latin root *hospes* or *hostis*, hospitality has linguistic ties with the words guest and stranger. According to Benveniste, through developments that are partially understood but related to relational shifts from smaller communities or clans to nations, *hostis*, as stranger, assumed a hostile connotation and subsequently only pertained to the enemy. A strange guest entering one's home is as likely to be a friend as they are to be a foe (Kearney, 2015). As Kearney (2015) noted, hospitality is never guaranteed, "it is always a challenge and a choice" (p. 178). An offer of hospitality simultaneously introduces the possibility of hostility.

Hospitality, at first glance, may seem implicit in the care of patients in the hospital, particularly in countries with universal health care. There are, however, conditions to meet on the part of the patient as a guest in the hospital. Patients must abide by hospital policies, demonstrate respect to staff and other patients, and are expected to follow the advice of their healthcare professionals. While receiving the hospitality of the healthcare team, patients may undergo treatments that might be experienced as hostile, such as chemotherapy. Importantly, most patients in the hospital do not want to be there, and any hospitality offered by nurses may be received begrudgingly. Most of the literature about hospitality in hospitals is related to introducing concepts from the hospitality industry or the "unconditional hospitality," a concept from Derrida, that patients should receive. Hostility has been researched in the context of horizontal violence and patient-to-nurse abuse.

The participants in this study did not describe hostilities arising from interactions with people; they experienced the hospital itself, and the things inside it, as hostile.

> Vinnie: *I actually get real bad anxiety knowing I have to go to the hospital. I need to be told at least a day before and know what is going to be happening but even then, once I get there, I feel the worst. The hospital just feels like I'm in a hostile environment. I always feel like something bad is going to happen to me emotionally or just getting tests like MRIs and being poked. It just doesn't feel good. It's just a place where I've been told the worst things, so continuously being here just scares me.*
>
> Nate: *I had to do my chemo, and it was really long, and I didn't feel so happy, and I got sad quite a bit. I was away from home, and I didn't feel so happy being there.*

For many of the children in this study, illness arrived with abrupt changes to their body and their environment. Going to the hospital was often the first indication that something was wrong, and for many of the participants, the hospital was the place where their illness experience originated.

> Sam: *My first memory [of having ITP] was going to the hospital and getting an IV [intravenous line] … I'm like "nope! I'm out of here!" I can't stand this anymore.*

Often, children with serious illness spend many days or months in the hospital, sometimes with little indication of when their stay will end. Maddie drew the hospital (partial image from Figure 2) among her most important things, because it was a place where she could be made to feel better but acknowledged that it was also a place she wished to escape from.

Partial Image from Figure 2 (Maddie)

Maddie: *When I was in the hostable [hospital], I was always trying to figure out a plan to break out. I even tried like to make something out of pipe cleaners to, like, drill a hole in the wall. I was so close, I even tried digging my way out with a plastic spoon. I covered it over with like a piece of paper, but instead of making a giant hole, I just kept on making little dents on the wall. Yeah, I wanted out. Gonna draw me trying to escape, "let me outta here!"*

Much like art and text, place may be interpreted with an abundance of possible meanings. Place not only stands as something to be interpreted, but as central to hermeneutic understanding itself, as interpretation stands in relation to the world, and the world appears "in and through a certain happening of place" (Malpas, 2015, p. 360).

> Even if the point is sometimes obscured, the essential insight of hermeneutic thinking is that knowledge and understanding are grounded in human situatedness—in the being of the human in place—and on this basis hermeneutics can be seen to consist precisely in the attempt to elucidate this fundamental situatedness. (Malpas, 2015, p. 356)

However, place is often reduced to ideas of our position or location within a physical space or obscured by its familiarity and proximity to us (Kearney,

2015; Malpas, 2018), and through my familiarity with the hospital, I had taken for granted how others might experience the hospital as a place that structures their experiences. As Malpas (2018) noted, the relationship between place and experience is not that "place is properly something only encountered 'in' experience, but rather that place *is integral to the very structure and possibility of experience*" (p. 31, italics in original). The participants' experience of their clinical environments has prompted me to consider how place, in its exteriority and objectivity, might be interpreted and structure understanding, rather than one's situatedness in other hermeneutic ideas, such as time, history, or tradition.

Excerpt 3: From the Chapter "The 'Good,' the 'Bad,' and Everything In Between: Apprehension in Serious Illness"

In this chapter, Wong described the participants' experiences of feeling "*stuck*" in between health and illness, feeling "*normal*" despite a new diagnosis of a serious illness, the challenges of the limitations associated with a terminal illness, and the anxiety of the possibility of life after the successful treatment of a serious illness. One common thread was that the children were hyper-aware of their limitations and what they needed to avoid to maintain a state of wellness despite their serious illness. They were also more aware of their bodies during the times when they felt unwell, which aligned with Gadamer's writings in *The Enigma of Health* (1993/1996). In deciding on a word to describe how the participants talked about their bodies, health, and illness experiences, Wong felt that apprehension seemed appropriate. Apprehension can mean to detect, discern, or comprehend something (Merriam-Webster, n.d.). Apprehension can also mean the fear of a future evil, a sense of foreboding, or indicate anxiety about something (Merriam-Webster, n.d.). Serious illness allowed the participants to apprehend aspects of life that are often taken for granted by healthy individuals, but also served to increase their anxiety regarding their health and the future. The following excerpt explored the participants' apprehension of the limitations associated with serious illness, while acknowledging that illness was also something that made other experiences possible.

"Everyone Else Gets to Move On": Being Unable-to-Be

A distinctive feature of Heidegger's (1927/1962) idea of Dasein is its ability-to-be (*Seinkönnen*), the "capacity to inhabit a particular range of possibilities" (Large, 2021, para. 1; Heidegger, 1927/1962). As Dasien is constantly projecting itself into the future, our present actions have meaning by virtue of a possible future where we imagine ourselves as being able to do or be a particular thing (Carel,

2018; Large, 2021; Heidegger, 1927/1962). This characterization of human existence allows us the freedom to become what we want, and to "transcend our present self with a future self that is more developed, more able" (Carel, 2018, p. 84). Carel (2018) suggested that Heidegger's notion of the ability-to-be omitted important aspects of Being: that of the decline, the disability or inability, and the failure to be. Aging and illness are two disclosive periods of life characterized by our becoming gradually unable to act, where our possibilities are truncated (Carel, 2018; Svenaeus, 2000). Being unable-to-be, according to Carel, must be recognized as a way of Being.

The idea of projection is especially significant for children, as so much of how childhood is understood in western society is related to children's preparation for adulthood and the expectation that children have a future to grow into (Wong, 2023). Additionally, children are limited in ways that adults are not: they are still growing physically and cognitively and are not permitted the same agency and autonomy that adults are. For children who live with serious illness or children who are dying, the inability-to-be or the impossibility of a future, coupled with their present limitations and the normative expectation that they should become increasingly able-to-be, can be remarkably difficult. Nate and Vinnie both died following their interviews, and their quotes highlight the challenges associated with the limitations of serious illness.

> *Nate: Um, sometimes well—me being sick, because I don't like to feel sick, it really bothers me and it's not comfortable. And also, it would make me sad, as well, whenever I see something I can't do.*

The inability-to-be is more pronounced when children with serious illness are contrasted against their healthy peers. Vinnie stated, "*I feel like I'm stuck re-reading a chapter while everyone else gets to move on*" and noted that her younger sister was now a grade ahead of her in school, as she had "*kind of just stopped doing school because the chemo was affecting me really bad.*" At the time she was diagnosed, Vinnie was experiencing other changes brought on by the pandemic and a new living situation. Reflecting on that time, she said, "*my whole life just paused.*"

As Vinnie's tumor made verbal communication very difficult, she spent the interview typing out her answers and agreed to complete her artwork after. She had her canvas and paints for some time and eventually let me know that she was unable to finish her artwork due to her evolving illness. When I went to see her and pick up her painting, I asked her if there was any wisdom that she gained from her experience that she wanted to share.

Vinnie: *You can do so much if you just have the want to do it ... Do whatever you want, there's never a better time than when you're motivated to do it.*

When I received her painting, Vinnie's tumor had grown through her cheek, into her mouth, and was beginning to block her airway; she died a month after that encounter. Reflecting on her comment, I often wonder if there were things that Vinnie was unable to do because of her illness that she wished she could have done, had she been given more time or a less cumbersome diagnosis. Conversely, I wonder if there are things that Vinnie did precisely because she was seriously ill, that she may not have been motivated to do otherwise.

While Carel's (2018) idea of Being-unable-to-be and its relation to the experience of serious illness is intriguing, I wish to point out that by virtue of some possibilities being concealed, others are simultaneously revealed. For some participants, while being seriously ill created limitations on some of their possibilities for being, it also disclosed others. Illness made what was truly important for them apprehensible, as well as revealing a kind of wisdom that they may not have gained if it were not for their illness.

Vinnie: *I think the biggest change I've seen in myself is how much I've learned not to care what others think about me.*
KW: *What advice do you have for other kids who get sick, as a kid who has gone through it?*
Nate: *Well, tell them not to worry and feel happy about it. Don't get sad and know that have a positive attitude and believe in yourself ... To know that they're loved by people.*
Sam: *When you have ITP, sometimes it's a whole new discovery in life and sometimes it's just something that gets in the way ... like, there's way more things that can happen.*

In hermeneutic work, a limit rarely signifies a dead end or closure, it is always related to possibilities (T. George, personal communication, August 12, 2024). Despite the limitations that illness created for him, Sam shared that life with his illness was "*more exciting*" and that "*if I didn't have ITP, [my life] would be wwwwaaaayyyyy more boring.*" Put another way, living with illness is also a life of possibility.

Closing Remarks Despite the Provocation of Possibilities

Children with serious illness navigate some of the most complex and humbling experiences all at once: the threat of death, growing up, coping with limitations, imagining other possibilities for existence, and significant loss. Children's voices elucidate how we might understand these experiences differently. The children in this study helped me to understand the significance of hostile places and relational spaces, the challenges of living in between health and illness, the possibilities for understanding in the absence of speech, and the unspeakable character of death. As a result of these interpretations and in coming to understand differently, as Rilke (1995) proclaimed, I must change my life. Perhaps one of the most difficult things for me, in writing this thesis, is its conclusion. Having engaged with this topic for several years, I know that, while I must arrive at some kind of understanding in response to my research question, that I must proceed "tentatively, openly, and with the hermeneutic humility that recognizes that no one question can be answered definitely once and for all" (Moules et al., 2015, p. 191). The task of understanding is never over (Gadamer, 1960/2004), and this thesis work presents one of many possibilities for understanding the experiences of children with serious illness. Put differently, the voices of children presented in this thesis work do not have the last word.

Example 2: Emerging Horizons: Crafting Meaning and Cultivating Understanding Through Digital Storytelling (Lang, 2021)

This study was the doctoral work of Michael Lang (supervised by Laing) whose research pertained to understanding the experiences of adolescent and young adult (AYA) cancer survivors as they participated in a digital storytelling (DST) workshop. DST is a genre of media where a trained facilitator supports lay people to craft their own short film, called a digital story, about important moments in their life (Lang et al., 2019). While the therapeutic benefits of DST are well documented (Laing et al., 2017a; Laing et al., 2017b; Laing et al., 2019; Laing et al., 2020), the specific aim of this project was to gain a deeper understanding of the DST process and potential outcomes for AYAs throughout their participation.

Lang's background as a documentary filmmaker and health researcher allowed for a unique form of data collection in this study, namely, the creation of a documentary film called *Emerging Horizons*[2], from which the primary interpretations were drawn. Using the hermeneutic conceptualization of data, a phenomenon might be best understood not only through the words captured in a recorded interview, but also through the facial expression, body language, and voice tone

2 The film "Emerging Horizons" can be viewed here: <https://youtu.be/GZw2zwNR6nY>

of participants, as well as the other spontaneous story events that can be captured on film. As the excerpts below show, deep understanding was cultivated through both the finished documentary film and the 30 hours of footage that was collected over the course of the DST workshop.

The data collected in this study lead to seven interpretive chapters, all of which were serialized in the 2022 edition of *the Journal of Applied Hermeneutics*. Excerpts from several chapters are included below.

Excerpt 1: From the Chapter "Amanda's Story"[3]

The excerpt below relates to a central metaphor of Lang's thesis: relaying the emotional experiences of DST through the image of physical trauma. In this chapter, a parallel is drawn between broken bones, which exist under the surface but are apparent through their symptoms, and the experience of a storyteller being "in the midst of the trauma" that they wish turn into a digital story. This metaphor is built upon by equating open wounds, which are visible to the eye, to the visible emotional expression of the storyteller as they participate in a DST workshop. Finally, the excerpt below discusses how to care for storyteller wellbeing in a DST workshop when emotional broken bones or open wounds are apparent.

Wound Care: Safeguarding Participant Wellbeing

Mike: Just let us know if you'd like to chat with someone, and yeah, I can connect you with that person if you want.
Amanda: No, I'm good, but thank you.

There is a lot of exposing and palpating that occurs during a DST experience. Kelsey highlighted this during lunch on the second day of the weekend workshop as she described her experience so far, "*You know, you keep relistening and relistening to it [cancer story]. Like, it kind of reopens the wound, or like, keeps picking at it.*" With this description, it could be suggested that the DST process may not be the best form of psychosocial support for certain AYA cancer survivors. In particular, if a chaos narrative and unstoried emotion are apparent, a decision needs to be made that safeguards storyteller wellbeing.

---

3 This chapter has been published in the *Journal of Applied Hermeneutic Research* (see Lang & Laing, 2022a)

The word "safeguard" comes from the old French *salve* or *sauve* (safe) and *garde* (a keeping; Online Etymology Dictionary, n.d.). The term *salve* in English also signifies a healing ointment applied to a wound (Online Etymology Dictionary, n.d.) and consequently, one interpretation of the word safeguard could be "wound keeping." If we are all wounded storytellers (Frank, 2013), it could be said that our wounds need to be kept safe until and during their storying. Specifically, a wounded digital storyteller may not need to be fully healed, but perhaps the bone needs to be set and immobilized, the wound salved and bandaged, and the acute emotional pain subsided before a DST process can be a meaningful "brick in the pathway to healing" (Laing et al., 2017a, p. 276). A chaos narrative with unstoried emotion is a raw, complex open fracture of the psyche, and the salve of time, or in some cases professional psychotherapy, may be necessary to cultivate the reflective distance and emotional understanding necessary to craft it into a digital story. If a chaos narrative is still being lived and the emotions remain unstoried, it follows that the response to an open complex fracture being exposed and "picked at" through the DST process is intense and uncontrollable emotional pain.

Amanda's DST experience demonstrates that the complexity and severity of the psychosocial wounds of a cancer experience may not be apparent until the DST process is underway. As she said in her opening line from the film, "Is it going to, you know, be exhausting? Is it going to be too much to handle? You just never know." If it is apparent in the early phases of a DST experience that an AYA is attempting to story a broken bone or open wound, the ethical imperative is to have safeguards in place.

Excerpt 2: From the Chapter "Kenzie's Story"[4]

This excerpt begins with a conversation that Lang had with Kenzie about her story circle experience. The story circle is a portion of the DST workshop where participants read aloud the voiceover that they have written for their digital story and receive affirmation, thoughts, and creative feedback from the group. The goal is to harness the collective creativity of the group to enhance the story that the participant wishes to tell. The excerpt below provides an example of incorporating personal experiences and hermeneutic philosophy into interpretive writing.

4 This chapter has been published in the *Journal of Applied Hermeneutic Research* (see Lang & Laing, 2022b)

Bubbling Up: The Reflective Power of the Story Circle

Mike: *You didn't actually have anything written down, but as you were sharing all of a sudden, those two themes came out.*

Kenzie: *Yeah, it kind of all fell into place as I was talking about it. I guess I knew what I wanted to say!*

Mike: *Yeah, and everyone else did too! … There was a clear theme or message that started to develop as you were sharing it with us.*

As a 23-year-old, I spent five weeks hitchhiking and traveling around the Tibetan plateau. I was warmly welcomed into every monastery, village, and encampment I visited, often staying for a few days and participating in the daily activities of life. Stepping through those doors felt like traveling back in time, except for one piece of modern looking equipment that most monks, townspeople, and nomads possessed. It was a large parabolic dish of polished metal with a steel tripod in the middle. One calm, sunny afternoon, I summoned the courage to pantomime a question about the purpose of the apparatus to a young monk, who proceeded to place a large metal teakettle full of water on the tripod. I immediately understood that the dish was meant to heat the water in the kettle but was shocked when we returned to the courtyard 30 minutes later to find the kettle steaming and bubbling over. In the rarefied atmosphere 4,500 meters above sea level, a mirror could boil water faster than a yak dung cooking fire. One of the many lessons I learned from my time in Tibet is that focused reflection can be powerful.

Across many health contexts and functions (e.g., disability advocacy, aging research, sexual health education, etc.) the DST process has been highlighted as an effective tool to help participants disrupt dominant cultural narratives of illness by enabling focused reflection on their own lived experiences, but also, and perhaps more importantly, as their story is reflected back to them in the story circle (de Jager et al., 2017; Fiddian-Green et al., 2019; Gubrium, 2009; Lambert, 2013; Rice et al., 2018; Rice & Mundel, 2018). After facilitating many story circle conversations over the past eight years, I am continually amazed by how the focused reflection of a group can bring the tepid water of everyday experience to a rolling boil. However, I have struggled to find the words to adequately convey the uniquely emotional, emergent, and co-creative nature of this process. Fortunately, Kenzie's story circle experience in *Emerging Horizons* and Gadamer's account of genuine conversations have provided a mirror to focus and reflect these story circle experiences.

In real time, the story circle depicted in *Emerging Horizons* lasted just over one hour and each story led to engaged discussion as exemplified by the three and a half minutes that were included in the film. Through the story circle, potential metaphors were clarified (Harmony), images suggested (Kelsey), controlling ideas affirmed (Derek and Bethany), and for Kenzie, meaningful language uncovered. According to Gadamer (1960/2004), each person in a conversation comes with their own unique horizon or "vantage point" (p. 313), and through genunine conversation a fusion of horizons occurs and new understanding emerges. Building on this metaphor, it could be said that the multiple participant horizons represented in a story circle increases the "surface area" of lived experience, reflecting the story back to the storyteller and leading to an intensification of understanding.

In *Emerging Horizons* each AYA in the story circle was a mirror for the others, and as Kenzie gazed at her experience through the reflected language of "moving on versus moving forward," "healing versus curing," and "living with uncertainty," a fusion of horizons occurred that allowed new understanding to bubble up in her consciousness. Kenzie's story had always been there, embedded in her experience, but the fact that all the phrases provided by the other AYAs in the story circle were integral to her completed digital story, demonstrated that a fusion of horizons had occurred. The combined reflective surface of six horizons was powerful enough to boil away the superfluous content of Kenzie's cancer story and cultivate a moment of truth that she apprehended in her digital story (Lang et al., 2020). Kenzie's digital story itself is a demonstration of how the reflective focus of a group of peers in genuine conversation can lead to the intensification of meaning and transform vague tepid ideas into a roiling caldron of understanding.

However, the potential understanding cultivated in and through the story circle experience can only be achieved if the conditions of a genuine conversation are achieved. Gadamer (1960/2004) provided a clear description of how the story circle experience portrayed in *Emerging Horizons* could be considered a genuine conversation:

> The way one word follows another, with the conversation taking its own twists and reaching its own conclusion, may well be conducted in some way, but the partners conversing are far less the leaders of it than the led. No one knows in advance what will "come out" of a conversation. Understanding or its failure is like an event that happens to us. (p. 383)

There was no knowing in advance what would "come out" of the story circle in *Emerging Horizons*, only that there would be stories about cancer. Moreover, although the story circle was "conducted in some way," by me encouraging participants to share and prompting discussion with a single question ("what resonated with you in the story?"), the conversation took its own twists and came to its own conclusions that revealed or clarified something for each storyteller. It was clear that in the story circle both the AYAs and I were "far less the leaders of it than the led" and that it was through the focused reflection of the group that understanding struck like lightning, like an event that happened to us all.

If truth is an event (Gadamer, 1960/2004), then Kenzie's experience in *Emerging Horizons* demonstrates how DST can create the opportunity for truth events to occur by placing a topic on the tripod, focusing the beam, and watching to see what bubbles up. By being aware of the conditions of a genuine conversation and purposely cultivating its generative possibilities through the story circle, a deeper truth—or perhaps a new truth—emerged from Kenzie's cancer story. In this way, DST could help AYAs like Kenzie address the enigma of endings, shed ill-fitting, culturally accepted narratives, and find a new, more meaningful story through genuine conversation with their peers. That Kenzie accomplished her goal was apparent during the voiceover recording of her story in *Emerging Horizons*:

Mike: Cool ... that's a good ending!
Kenzie: [Nodding head emphatically] Yeah, I like the way that ends.

Excerpt 3: From the Chapter "Lessons Learned"[5]

This final excerpt is from the interpretive chapter that draws understanding from the entirety of the DST workshop experience portrayed in the film. It focuses on the "lessons learned" from an AYA cancer survivor perspective. This excerpt begins with a quote that Lang shared in the film at the ending of the friends and family screening where participants invited three to four people to come watch and discuss the finished stories as a group. This quote provides an example of how interpretive writing can effectively cultivate new understandings because this type of writing is not constrained to one specific data source or one narrow field of academic inquiry. Indeed, it is precisely because interpretive writing can draw ideas from the vastness of human experience, that it can keep topics "in play" while also generating profound understanding that contributes to the knowledge of the topic.

For AYA Cancer Survivors: An Artist of Our Days

Each of us is an artist of our days; the greater our integrity and awareness, the more original and creative our time will become.
—O'Donahue (2008, p. 191)

There were many didactic elements of the DST workshop not depicted or explored in either the film or the previous interpretations in this thesis. One of these

5 This chapter has been published in the *Journal of Applied Hermeneutic Research* (see Lang & Laing, 2022c)

elements was the quote above that I shared at the friends and family screening immediately before the "one-word" exercise and standing ovation that closed the film. I believe this quote encapsulates some of the lessons for AYA cancer survivors embedded in *Emerging Horizons* beyond what was contained in the digital stories themselves.

First, through a DST experience AYA cancer survivors can literally and figuratively become "an artist of our days" (O'Donahue, 2008, p. 191). In a literal sense, the AYAs closer to their cancer treatments (i.e., Amanda, Harmony, Kelsey) were able to externalize (Angus & Greenberg, 2011), or *story,* elements of their cancer experience for the first time, while those further from their experience (i.e., Derek, Kenzie, Bethany), were able to *re-story* it as their horizon of understanding changed over time (White & Epston, 1990). Specifically, the opening session helped Amanda understand that she was still "in the midst of" her story (despite acute cancer treatments ending a year prior), while both Harmony and Kelsey stated that the DST workshop revealed to them that they had a story worth sharing (storying/authoring cancer experience; White & Epston, 1990). Harmony and Kelsey's post-workshop interviews confirmed that, for them, cancer was no longer a random, pre-narrative experience (Ricoeur, 1975/1990), but a compelling story, full of wisdom and meaning. Alternatively, Kenzie and Bethany were able to craft an entirely new cancer storyline that fit with their current horizon of understanding, while Derek was able to share a significant moment of his cancer story in a more meaningful way (re-storying/re-authoring cancer experience; White & Epston, 1990). Their final interviews indicated an increased awareness that life stories can be told differently, and that stopping and sitting with their cancer experiences in the reflective intensity of a DST workshop enabled this re-storying process to occur.

Regardless of whether the primary aim was storying or re-storying, all the AYA participants literally became "an artist of their [cancer] days" in the DST workshop, actively cultivating a deeper understanding of their own cancer experience and crafting meaning from it, thus the subtitle of this thesis. Interestingly, in this process of creating an artistic expression of their experiences, it became easier for the AYAs to grasp the figurative implications of being the artist of our days; they could not choose what happened to them, but they could choose how to tell the story. In their final interviews, all the AYAs indicated a new, or renewed, awareness that, although they could not control the conflicts encountered in life, like cancer, they could control how they interpreted and responded to them, an abstract concept that was made concrete in the praxis of DST.

The process of reframing life conflicts in this way was intentionally initiated in the first evening Introduction to DST session when I introduced the Law of Conflict; "nothing moves forward in a story except through conflict" (McKee,

1997, p. 210), and was further entrenched when I explained my fundamental orientation to all participants as a DST facilitator:

> *I am viewing you from a place of strength, not weakness. I am not pitying you for what you have been through. I think because of what we [AYA cancer survivors] have been through, our stories have a lot to offer the world.*

Through this explanation, the DST process portrayed in *Emerging Horizons* explicitly reframed conflict as a valuable and indispensable element of all life stories, and by doing so, placed the AYA participants in a perpetually agentic position: it is *because* of the life conflicts they experience (like cancer), that their stories hold wisdom for themselves and others. The "artist of our days" mindset cultivated through the DST workshop could help reframe the default response to life conflicts from *"why me?"* to *"what is the story and what can I learn from it?"* The opportunity to approach a life conflict with a sense of curiosity and actively practice the reframing process is perhaps one of the most profound, lasting, and life-altering possibilities of DST with AYA cancer survivors. Not only could DST help AYAs reclaim a sense of agency that is often lost during a cancer experience, but it could also help foster a more resilient attitude toward future life challenges.

Finally, O'Donahue's (2008) words emphasize that AYAs have the capacity to share their experiences in an aesthetically powerful way, like an artist, if given the opportunity. From the increasingly nuanced decisions made during the creation of their digital stories, and the stimulating discussions with each other and their friends and family, it was apparent that the AYA survivors in *Emerging Horizons* had become artists, capable of tapping into the deep aquifers of culturally embedded meaning that fuel our understanding of the world (Davey, 2013). This is a significant outcome considering Kelsey and Harmony did not feel they had a story, Kenzie had trouble writing hers, and Derek's motivation for participation was his inability to meaningfully convey his story. Of the group, only Bethany felt confident in her artistic capabilities and yet, all the stories were profound and insightful in their own way. This suggests that when AYAs are encouraged to cast off the culturally acceptable, hand-me-down cancer narratives, their stories can unmask the experience of AYA cancer and cultivate *phronesis* for themselves, other AYAs, their friends and family, and even the healthcare providers who care for them (Christiansen, 2011; Laing et al., 2017b). Ultimately, DST is only one of many possible interventions that could encourage AYA cancer survivors to (re)discover a sense of agency and (re)story their cancer experiences, but it is my hope that those who watch *Emerging Horizons* will understand that they have a story and that it matters.

Example 3: "Friendship ... or Whatever It Is": Understanding Nurse-Parent Relational Complexity in Pediatric Oncology Contexts (Webber, 2024)

In this final example, the doctoral research done by Katherine Webber (supervised by Moules) is shown. In discussions with Moules about potential doctoral research topics, an iteration of "what really brought me to graduate school was...." Moules' response was emphatic, "*This* is what you must study." The story that Webber recalled was a particular moment from her practice as a pediatric oncology nurse that she had, in all honesty, forgotten. As is the work of *aletheia*, though, when determining with Moules what research topic might be a fit for a study guided by hermeneutics, this memory of relational complexity in pediatric oncology nursing practice resurfaced. Webber had been assigned to care for a palliative patient, who Webber had worked with countless times over the years of this patient's treatment. On one of the patient's final days, Webber spent much of her shift in the patient's room with her and her family, orientating them to a new but emotionally challenging reality, one defined by finality. Due to the patient's disease progression, she was severely nauseated and despite the healthcare team's best attempts to control her nausea, the patient vomited, mostly all over her mother. While the patient's mother held her young daughter in her arms, cleaned her, and settled her, Webber leaned down to wipe the vomit off the mother's shoes. In trying to make light of the situation, Webber looked up at the mother, who was also a nurse, smiled, and in jest said, "I am being such a good ..." As Webber started to say "nurse," the mother interrupted her. At the exact moment Webber said "nurse," the mother said "friend."

Webber's research, guided by hermeneutics, sought to deepen understanding about nurse-parent relational complexity in pediatric oncology contexts. In the winter of 2021, Webber interviewed six pediatric oncology nurses and six parents of children with cancer. From this study, four interpretive chapters were produced, with each chapter delving into an aspect of relational complexity that surfaced during the interpretive analysis. Excerpts from two of the four interpretive chapters are provided below.

Excerpt 1: From the Chapter "Seeing Red": Anger, Conflict, and Openness

In this chapter, Webber sought to understand how frustration, anger, and conflict contribute to the relational complexity that nurses and parents experience in their relationships with one another. In pediatric oncology, the color gold is often used to represent, and raise awareness about childhood cancer. "Gold is a precious metal. Children are our most precious treasure ... gold goes through a process by fire to become stronger and tougher" (International Childhood Cancer Day, n.d., "The search for a universal symbol"). In many ways, the color gold is a fitting choice to represent the challenges and successes that are associated with childhood cancer. Considering the topic of nurse-parent relational complexity, the gold of nurse-parent relationships could be understood as the meaningfulness and closeness that often results from nurses and parents sharing emotionally intense experiences, while co-caring for children with cancer. While the gold, or the meaningful relationships formed through the difficulty of co-caring for children with cancer, is one part or one color, of the relational complexity that nurses and parents experience in their relationships with one another, it is not the only color worth considering in the pediatric oncology spectrum of colors.

When developing interpretations about how frustration, anger, and conflict contribute to relational complexity in nurse-parent relationships, Webber used a quote from a parent about another color that seemed to aptly represent when parents and nurses experience frustration, anger, and conflict in their relationships with one another—the color red. When a parent was asked about any relationships with nurses that might be considered challenging or difficult, they recalled feeling "so angry [that they were] seeing red."

> *Parent: There was one time when there was a nurse who was trying to access him [his central line] ... and she kept missing, and I really liked her, I really liked her a lot, but I was so angry I was seeing red.*

Throughout the chapter, Webber expanded on the "redness" of nurse-parent relationships. The first interpretation, which is the excerpt provided here, is how Webber interpreted the difficult language that nurses and parents sometimes use about one another as the "red language" in nurse-parent relationships.

"Sergeant" Nurses

> *Parent: It was just a sergeant nurse ... it could have been absolutely just in my head that I was just seeing her as an adversary that she was preventing me from going home, but I didn't feel the kindness or compassion to sort of say, "oh yeah, there's a lot."*

When discussing a situation that involved conflict between themself and a nurse, who they perceived to be preventing them from being discharged, one parent described a nurse as a "sergeant nurse." This parent did not feel the compassion that they had hoped to receive, particularly after a difficult week in which the child had been diagnosed with cancer. Without going into too much detail about the structure of an army, sergeants rank somewhere in the middle of the army leadership hierarchy. While it is certainly possible that parents might perceive nurses as sergeants, what is worth considering is why nurses might act, at times, like sergeants. It is worth noting that, despite significant strides to de-emphasize hierarchy and focus more on collaboration, in healthcare contexts, there are still those that write the orders, and those who carry them out.

Parent: *The doctors are telling the parents and the nurses what to do, but they're not the ones … I think all of us know that the nurses are the ones that do it, like they're doing everything.*

Parent: *Nurses are usually caught in the middle … I felt bad for the nurse, because it's not her fault but she's getting the back blow because of something with the doctor's orders and things like that. Yeah, so I feel bad for the nurses sometimes.*

Nurse: *Sometimes even our physicians have different ideas than what the rules are … something as simple as kids being on isolation because often, there're rules at the hospital, like the hospital policy that you have to follow based on … their symptoms, or this or that. But then the physicians go in there and say, "we'll just take you off isolation."*

As alluded to in the previous quote, there are also system-level structures that put nurses in a difficult middle position.

Parent: *There were times during his treatment that we were frustrated, but it wasn't the nurses, it's just the hospital, the system, you know?*

Nurse: *There was this one family in particular … they wanted to bring a different patient, who was in the clinic to come over and sit with their kid and I had to say, "no." They knew that wasn't allowed. They're never allowed patients in the same room together … mainly for infection prevention…[the] mom was livid. She was so mad. She had already planned all this. She was basically crying to me in the hallway, telling me that I was ruining her day, ruining her daughter's day … I just explained to her and said, "no, it's not allowed, there are these risks involved … if I start letting you guys do this then everyone's going to want to. It's just not fair."*

Being in the middle can be a difficult position to be in. One of the challenges of interpreting the data has been navigating the inherent power imbalance of the nurse-parent relationship. It would be fair to question, then, how highlighting the inherent hierarchies in armies and hospitals could be productive in understanding relational complexity, as this might appear to point even more acutely at power imbalances. However, what I suggest might be more productive is less about power, and more about authority.

Arendt (1958/1961) argued that "authority has vanished from the modern world" (p. 91). For Arendt, "since authority always demands obedience, it is commonly mistaken for some form of power or violence" (pp. 92–93). In this way, Arendt defended the role of hierarchy, in relation to authority. An unavoidable aspect of the modern world is almost immediate access to information. This access to immediate access to information has significantly affected relationships in healthcare. As one nurse with over 30 years of nursing experience reflected:

> Nurse: *When I first started nursing, we all went for break together and we would laugh and talk. There was a lot more interpersonal communication … I'm not saying your phones are bad … but I just really notice that difference about breaks now is that nobody really talks anymore, or not as much.*

It has also disrupted, in some ways, how authority is viewed in healthcare relationships, including nurse-parent relationships. Authority, in the ways in which I am speaking about here is in line with Arendt (1958/1961), in that it is less about power and control and more about earned legitimacy. Another nurse said:

> Nurse *I will also say that the families are different now. So, how I describe it to everyone is that I used to feel that I worked with the families, and now I feel like I work for the families.…All those old families … we worked with them, we were a team, versus now, and maybe we've had a slew of families that the respect or the trust or whatever isn't there, but I said to one mom, who was super rude, "I don't work for you, I work with you."*

Access to information has shifted nurses' relationships with other nurses, and nurses' relationships with parents. Access to information can be disruptive, in both productive and unproductive ways. For example, productively, access to information can help a parent better understand their child's diagnosis from more perspectives than just what is available at the hospital where they live. Sometimes, though, without a full understanding of the information being provided, access to information can also be unproductive, potentially leading to mistrust of their healthcare providers. Regardless, borrowing from Heidegger (1954/1977), access to information through technology should not be "regard[ed] as something neutral" (p. 4). Returning to the discussion about the authority of sergeant nurses, it is important to consider how access to information has shifted parents' recognition of nurses' authority. As Arendt (1958/1961) suggested, nurses' authority is less about power over parents, but more about earned legitimacy from parents, contributing to a more productive understanding of authority in nurse-parent relationships.

Over the 10 years of my clinical practice as a pediatric oncology nurse, I also felt a significant shift from being seen as an authority, in the legitimate and helpful sense, to being mistrusted, questioned, and challenged. Being a sergeant is not always easy. Sergeants have authority, but they are not the ultimate authority. Sergeants are not protected from being wounded. However, being a sergeant nurse might sometimes be necessary, for example, because upholding policies that are meant to uphold infection prevention is maybe the more difficult, but greater good.

In closing this section, what was interesting about the nurse's story about saying "no" to having a visitor from the clinic come to see the child admitted to the unit is what the mother said to the nurse afterwards. The nurse recalled worrying that the mother would "hate" her for saying no, for maintaining the hospital policy, even though it was disappointing for the patients and parents involved. Two days after the hallway tears and ruined days, the mother took the nurse aside and said:

> *Parent: I actually really appreciated that you just told me how it was ... and you just did what you were supposed to do, and in a sense, I appreciate that ... I appreciate that you felt comfortable enough to stand your ground and say that to me.*

Perhaps authority, in the legitimate and earned sense, rather than the power-lording sense, is sometimes needed, even if it is not always easy, enjoyable, or comfortable. Returning to the interpretation of the "red language" that nurses and parents use to describe one another by reconsidering how authority is recognized in nurse-parent relationships is a reminder that, when earned, nurses' capacity and legitimacy to care well for children with cancer and their parents, is bold, strong, and worth acknowledging, much like the color red.

"Manipulative" Parents

> *Nurse: I find sometimes the most difficult families to deal with are not necessarily the ones who are rude, or who treat you poorly, sometimes those ones are easier to deal with because you can just brush it off a bit, or you just—you're not worried about, I don't know, you maybe don't have the connection with those families as much, so it's just easier to [say], "Ok, whatever, they're just*

not coping." But it's the families you build these relationships [with] and then they're kind of, a little bit manipulative, and they kind of abuse—they use your relationship to get what they want.

In hermeneutics, there is certainly a case to be made for the power of the particular (Moules et al., 2015). One participant might offer something that can speak to the topic as richly, even with more depth than if every participant in the study had said it. What is interesting about the following particularity is that there was one term, in particular, that was repeated several times across four different nurse interviews to describe a complexity of closeness with parents—manipulation. While it is not necessary to count or demonstrate repeatability in hermeneutics, it is interesting to note that there was a particular word, *manipulative*, that was used to describe "difficult" parents 18 times throughout the interviews.

Nurse: Anyway, he was just one of those really manipulative people and he would threaten the nurses.

Nurse: Everyone just loved her, she just had such a great personality, but she can be kind of, I don't know if this is the right word to use, but a bit manipulative in what she wanted.

Nurse: I also realized how, not passive aggressive, what's the word, manipulative, that some families are when they do that. And they were a little bit manipulative.

The term, manipulate, at least in the way that the nurses used it to describe some parents, has a negative connotation: "to control or play upon by artful, unfair, or insidious means especially to one's own advantage" (Merriam-Webster, n.d.). Another definition of manipulate, though, is "to manage or utilize skillfully" (Merriam-Webster, n.d.). It is difficult to deny, particularly because it was said by four of the six nurse participants that parents, at times, might be perceived to be manipulating a situation to have a favorable outcome for themselves. What is worth considering, though, is that perhaps parents are only trying to skillfully, rather than insidiously, navigate the emotionally taxing experience of having a child with cancer and an often-inflexible healthcare system.

Sergeants and Manipulators: Protective Factors

Nurse: I'm probably the one that's closest with that parent because I mean everyone's like, "they're so mean, and they're so scary." …Their kid has been admitted for how long. They're actually just terrified.

There are many ways in which nurses and parents might feel the need to protect themselves, given the emotional labor involved in caring for children with cancer. In a scoping review of parents' perspectives of conflict in pediatric healthcare contexts, Parsons and Darlington (2021) found that there was a lack of research that focused specifically on conflict. Despite the lack of focused research on conflict, Parsons and Darlington found a significant number of studies in which discussions about conflict arose without prompting. Conflict between healthcare providers is complex (Parsons & Darlington, 2021). What Parsons and Darlington determined was that healthcare providers need to pay closer attention to the "strength of parental advocacy and expertise for their child" (p. 5). Put differently, parents might use manipulation, seen from the perspective of managing skillfully, to advocate for and provide their expertise about their child (Parsons & Darlington, 2021). Furthermore, manipulation could also be viewed as a way of protecting parents, and their children, from harm. In this way, nurses need to have an awareness of how parents might express their advocacy in diverse ways, but that most often, remembering their shared goal, of providing the best care for the child with cancer (Parsons & Darlington, 2021). This awareness, of the motive behind the manipulation, could be instrumental in helping nurses navigate conflict with parents effectively. When recounting working with a difficult family, one nurse said:

> *Nurse:* *Of course, you are particular about these things. It's been such a long, shitty road for you. Of course, I get it. It doesn't bother me when you question me, or when you question things. I get it. If I were on the other side, I would be grilling every single nurse.*

Just as parents might manipulate to advocate and protect themselves and their children, nurses also might become sergeant-like to be advocating for and protecting themselves, not necessarily from parents, but from their work. Working in pediatric oncology as a nurse can be stressful and emotionally burdensome (Boyle & Bush, 2018; Moody et al., 2013). According to Rushton et al. (2015), nurses who work in high-intensity settings, such as pediatric oncology, report high levels of emotional exhaustion. Boyle and Bush (2018) argued that the emotional distress associated with pediatric oncology nursing is due to challenging nursing competencies, difficult family scenarios, blurred boundaries, and coping issues related to the feelings of helplessness while caring for patients who are suffering. Emotional labor is a term that Boyle and Bush used to "describe the dissonance between the external display of emotion and the internal affective experience" (p. 65). According to Boyle and Bush, for nurses, emotional labor involves a "portrayal of steadfastness and competence while a visceral milieu of anguish and sadness prevails" (p. 65). In other words, what is felt on the inside is markedly different than what might be portrayed on the outside. A sergeant might feel differently about the orders that they are giving versus what they might portray when giving the orders. Similarly, what nurses might portray externally, might be vastly different than how they feel. There are certainly imperfections associated with being seen as sergeant-like or as manipulative. Perhaps, though, being sergeant-like or being manipulative are ways in which nurses and parents protect themselves from the difficulties that are associated with caring for children with cancer.

Excerpt 2: From the Chapter "Finding Language That Works: Articulating Closeness and Meaningfulness"

In Webber's final interpretive chapter, she returned to the complexity of nurse-parent relationships of naming what can make them close and particularly meaningful for both nurses and parents. The following excerpt addresses the difficulty of finding language that aptly responds to the complexity, depth, and significance of nurse-parent relationships.

(The Difficulty of) Finding Language That Works

> How often have you had an experience, especially one that is deeply profound, after which you exclaimed, "it so moved me there are no words to say what it means?" Words have failed to take hold of the meaning of the experience, and yet, presumably, you do want to speak about it, you do want to bring it to its understanding, if not to yourself, then to another. (Risser, 2019, p. 1)

There is an inexplicableness when trying to describe the closeness that nurses and parents sometimes experience in their relationships with one another. These experiences can feel ungraspable, particular, and even unknowable if you have not had an experience like it before. These encounters, as Gadamer (1970/2007) argued, might "leave us speechless" (p. 93), almost as though language has deserted us.

> *Parent:* *Oncology nurses are just a different breed, and you just care differently … It's just, I don't know, and I'm sorry that I don't have a better qualifier for it, but it just feels … different.*

While it certainly is simpler to leave understanding friendship in nurse-parent relationships as "friendship, or whatever it is," it feels as though there is still an opportunity to "find language that works" (Moules et al., 2015, p. 202). As Gadamer (1970/2007) also reminded us, "language deserts us … precisely because what enlightens is standing so strongly before our ever more encompassing gaze that words would not be adequate to grasp it" (p. 93). Before going further, I want to be clear that it is not my intention to contradict myself from the previous section, in which there was some room left for the ambiguity of "not *not* friendship" and "friendship, or whatever it is." Rather, my intention in this section is to say, "yes, and…"; to continue to work to give language to the relational significance that nurses and parents experience in their relationships with one another. As Risser (2019) argued, in the quote that opens this section, I do want to speak about it and I do want to bring it to understanding, not only for myself but for others, especially for those who might be influential in improving relational care supports for both nurses and parents in pediatric oncology contexts.

Risser (2019) provided two examples of experiences that involve the feeling of being at a loss for words. The first example comes from Kant, and it is an experience of what we would call the sublime (Risser, 2019). According to Risser, what is taking place in these profound, seemingly language-less experiences is wonder:

> [A] deeper phenomenon that draws us into the strange and challenging. The experience of wonder signals a certain placelessness with respect to what we are experiencing… [and] to be left almost speechless in wonder, one can say, is to be at the opening of thinking and speaking. (p. 2)

The second example that Risser (2019) provided, in which one might feel "*almost* speechless" (p. 2) happens "in those deeply personal experiences that range from the traumatic to the blissful, but also in the awkward situation of speaking in the face of death" (p. 2). In nurse-parent relationships, there is something to relate to in both of Risser's examples. There are certainly sublime moments of wonder and even joy, for example celebrating a child's last chemotherapy, and moments of deep sorrow—speechlessly and tearfully holding a parent as they sob over the death of their child. How might one even begin to give language to the relational significance of these moments between nurses and parents? As Gadamer (1970/2007) suggested, though, "the breakdown of language actually testifies to one's capacity to search out an expression for everything … In actuality, speaking has not come to an end but to a beginning" (p. 93). However, as Risser argued, simply giving names to objects, or in the case of this research, calling relational significance between nurses and parents friendship, is not language in its most full sense. In fact, once identified, something like friendship can become contained; "drained of its particularity when translated into words, which, ultimately, as the work of concepts, can only convey the general" (Risser, 2019, p. 3). Yet, despite the potential shortcomings of language, there is still the important work of trying to "find language that works" (Moules et al., 2015, p. 202).

There are several points Risser (2019) made that feel important to my project of finding a way to express the inexplicableness of relational significance in nurse-parent relationships. First, that language is speculative (Risser, 2019). What Risser meant by this is that "the subject matter is 'mirrored' in it but not just in a simple way; think of it more like a hall of mirrors" (p. 7). Put another way, naming something complex echoes the complexity of that which it is naming. Second, Risser argued that just because understanding must be worked out, there may not be success in finding the words for what one is trying to say. As Risser noted, "there are indeed limits to the communication of meaning" (p. 7). Risser then even admitted, "what has been said in words is always less than what is meant, as those deeply personal experiences often attest to" (p. 7). However, the third point that Risser made is that, even despite the seemingly impossible challenge of the limits of language to describe meaning, there is still, quoting Gadamer (1985/2000), "an unstilled desire for the appropriate word" (p. 17). For Risser, this pursuit of the better word "constitutes the true life and essence of language" (p. 7).

The difficulty that I have experienced is that it is challenging to come up with the right word, if not friendship, to describe nurse-parent relational significance. However, after engaging with the data, two words have resonated that I will propose. The first is a German word. Before continuing further, I want to be clear that I do not speak German. However, I do appreciate that, particularly in hermeneutic philosophy, the influence of the German language is important. So, there is a word in German that Carson (2002) argued is untranslatable into English. The word is *das Zwischenmenschliche* or *Zwischenmenschlichkeit*. Carson described this word to mean:

> [S]omething that happens between people when they are "in sync,' taking each other seriously and holding each other in mutual regard, Martin Buber wrote, "In a real conversation ... what is essential does not take place in each of the participants or in a neutral world which includes the two and all other things; but it takes place between them in the most precise sense, as if it were a dimension which is accessible only to them." (p.179)

Carson goes on to argue that, for Buber, this does not just happen in the "great thundering moments of life" (p. 179). This way of connecting also happens in ordinary experiences (Carson, 2002). Nurses and parents sometimes experience an "in syncness" that involves taking one another seriously and holding each other in mutual regard (Carson, 2002). It is a precise experience and the inexplicableness of the relational significance that they sometimes experience can feel as though it is in a dimension only accessible to them (Carson, 2002). As the parent quotes have previously suggested, sometimes relational significance is difficult to describe.

Parent: *Oncology nurses are just a different breed, and you just care differently ... It's just, I don't know, and I'm sorry that I don't have a better qualifier for it, but it just feels ... different.*
Parent: *Whether its friendship, or whatever it is, I don't know.*

The result, though, of relational significance, often involves an abundance, or as Carson called it, a surplus, of meaning. Dealing with surpluses is not our forte in healthcare. So often, the focus is on streamlining, cost saving, and making do with less. In many ways, we do not even know what to effectively do with surpluses.

There are not many tangible benefits of caring for children with cancer. What I mean by this is that nurses do not get paid any extra money for doing this work and parents certainly do not receive any tangible rewards for parenting a child with cancer. It is hard, emotional, and sometimes devastating work to care for children with cancer. What there does seem to be an abundance of is meaning. Caring for children with cancer changes your life. Whether as a parent, or as a nurse, the surplus of meaning that results from this experience alters the way you move forward. It is impossible to be unchanged by the experience. Importantly, the meaningfulness is multifaceted. By this, I mean that it is not necessarily meaningful in the positive sense. Sometimes the meaningfulness that comes from caring for children with cancer involves devastating loss. The experience, as a whole, matters significantly. Considering the surplus of meaning that I suggest nurses and parents experience in their relationships with one another as a result of caring for children with cancer, it might be difficult to know what to do with it. As examples, a nurse who is so moved by a relationship with a parent of a child with cancer or a parent who feels that nurses feel more like their family than their biological family. As Carson (2002) noted, though, we "take note of it, take it in, reinvest it in the relationship, and pass it on" (p. 180).

The second word that I suggest could be used to describe the significance of nurse-parent relationships is companionship. This interpretation of the closeness, connection, and relational significance of nurse-parent relationships is one that Dr. Moules suggested to me early in my graduate work, but one that I had left simmering for quite some time while I puzzled through friendship. The term companionship might help to elevate and increase understanding. As Risser (2019) wrote "the right word is the word that comes as an increase to meaning" (p. 9). Etymologically, from the late Latin *companionem*, companion literally means "bread fellow, messmate" (Online Etymology Dictionary, n.d.). Nurses and parents are often messmates, not in the sense that they are sharing meals, but quite literally, that they are in the messes together.

> Nurse: *I think the reason I became a nurse is because I wanted to actually be there, and I think a doctor is there so briefly that they never, as much as they get to know them, they don't really get to know them, versus we spend so much time with them, which is what I've always liked about nursing is that you don't kind of just blow in, this is what happened, this is the plan, call me if you guys need anything. You are actually in the room doing the things with the patients and the families and I think that probably makes the relationship a bit closer than with the doctors, because your patient puked all over you, I'm helping change, I'm helping clean up, your patient's bleeding, like I'm the one in there actually doing the things, which I think obviously makes you close with people.*

Companion is also defined as "one that accompanies another" and "one that keeps company with another" (Merriam-Webster, n.d.).

> Nurse: *I think parents see us more as on a level playing field with them, than a physician … I find that the questions happen during the family meeting to the physician, for sure, but the reiteration of the answers happens with the nurse, or the breaking down of the feelings, I feel like happens with a nurse.*

While it is possible to have friends as companions, it is not a requirement of companionship to be friends. Also, companions may or may not be equals. For example, companions can be employed to serve another (Merriam-Webster, n.d.). There is also a sense of temporality associated with companionship, in the sense that one is a companion for a period of time, for a particular experience. A companion goes alongside another, offering support and care, and sometimes even provides information or advice about a particular subject (Merriam-Webster, n.d.).

Moules et al. (2016) also wrote about two other words that are related to the word companion, connected by their origins in 1600s biblical translation. The first word is *helpmeet*, which literally means "a helper like himself [sic]" (Online Etymology Dictionary, n.d.) and the other word is *playmate*, which means a "companion or playfellow" (Online Etymology Dictionary, n.d.). According to Moules et al. (2016) "if a companion is a 'helper like himself [sic],' then professionals in pediatric oncology are eminently suitable companions" (p. 574). Moules et al. also pointed out the inescapability of the idea that companionship might be related to playfulness. For Moules et al., playfulness is not about trivializing the experience of nurse-parent relationships. Rather, it is a way to recognize that playfulness "is a state of wonder and openness that is both deeply existential and a pragmatic recognition of contingency" (p. 574). Put differently, for Moules et al. companionship is the solid ground from which parents might be supported in the unfamiliar and terrifying context of having a child with cancer. Companionship also offers a "soft landing" (Moules et al., 2016, p. 574) for when having a child with cancer tests parents in ways in which they had never expected. In addition to Moules et al.'s insights about how playfulness connects to companionship, sometimes, to walk through darkness, we require some light. For many nurses and parents, levity through humor offers a way to navigate the difficulty and often painful experience of caring for children with cancer.

Parent: There were days when it was horrible and there were days when it was fun, the nurses were always doing goofy things, if you needed it. They have a really good read on it.

Parent: She had an anaphylactic reaction, which is actually a huge deal, but we can all laugh about it afterwards because she had enormous lips and things like that. It's ridiculous and not funny at all, but at some point, there becomes some sick sense of humor about it.

Parent: Some days it's just them sitting there listening to you vent, if you need to vent. Some days you can laugh about the things that aren't funny, but you have to somehow make it funny, or you'll go crazy.

Parents and nurses recognize that humor and playfulness are a necessary aspect of childhood cancer. Of course, having a "good read" on the situation, as one parent reflected in the quote above, is part of a nurses' ability to discern what is needed in each particular moment, with each particular parent. However, it would be untrue to say that there is never laughter or playfulness involved in nurse-parent relationships. Arguably, this playfulness is a significant contributor to the companionship that nurses and parents experience in their relationships with one another.

Returning to the project of finding language that works and considering the accompaniment, helpfulness, and playfulness that nurses offer parents of children with cancer, companionship, might be a more fulsome way to recognize the relational significance of nurse-parent relationships. As a way to understand nurse-parent relational complexity, considering and acknowledging the companionship that nurses and parents experience in their relationships with one another might allow for both an enlargement and intensification of understanding (Risser, 2019).

Summary

Hermeneutics begins when we realize something is going on, something is happening. It is interested in things that happen to us—not only in what they might *mean*, but also of what they might be true. It is through the transcription process, reading and re-reading of the transcripts, reviewing of field notes, reflection on the interviews, and the generation of interpretations, that data will be interpreted. The process of how one goes from a transcribed interview to an interpretation that brings value, furthers understanding of the topic, and is *true of something* is challenging to explain in some respects, given that hermeneutics does not offer a defined method of conducting research or analyzing data. Some of what constitutes life is not measurable or analyzable by empirical means, and to make a topic conform to the likes of a technical method makes the topic technical in nature. In order to understand and bring forth meaningful interpretations from the data collected, the concepts of fusion of horizons and the hermeneutic circle are of assistance. The fusion of horizons, or the coming together of two or more understandings of the topic, coupled with the genuine curiosity of the researcher and desire to understand the topic in a new way will help to further the understanding of the topic. The hermeneutic circle—the metaphorical representation of looking at the whole and the parts—invites the researcher to consider the particulars of the topic in the context of the familiar, and similarly, the familiar in the context of the particulars (Gadamer, 1960/1997; Moules et al., 2013). This movement in and out of the data allows for consideration of that which might not have been initially visible and enhances the understanding of the topic. In the three examples offered in this chapter, we see the scholarship, beauty, art, and poetics of writing interpretively along with the careful attention to be citatious, rigorous, and meaningful.

In the next chapter, we address these important components of "good" interpretive research: rigor, integrity, validity, veracity, trustworthiness, and ethical conduct.

References

Adams, A., & Theodore, D. (2002). Designing for "the little convalescents": Children's hospitals in Toronto and Montreal, 1875–2006. *Canadian Journal of Health History*, *19*(1), 201–243. <https://doi.org/10.3138/cbmh.19.1.201>

Alberta Children's Hospital Foundation. (n.d.). Then + now. <https://www.childrenshospital.ab.ca/about-us/100-years-of-hope-healing/then-now/>

Angus, L. E., & Greenberg, L. S. (2011). *Working with narrative in emotion-focused therapy: Changing stories, healing lives*. American Psychological Association.

Arendt, H. (1961). *Between past and future: Six exercises in political thought.* Viking Press. (Original work published 1958)

Benveniste, E. (1973). *Indo-European language and society.* University of Miami Press.

Boyle, D. A., & Bush, N. J. (2018). Reflections on the emotional hazards of pediatric oncology nursing: Four decades of perspectives and potential. *Journal of Pediatric Nursing, 29*(2), 63–73. <https://doi.org/10.1016/j.pedn.2018.03.007>

Burroughs, M. D., & Tollefsen, D. (2016). Learning to listen: Epistemic injustice and the child. *Episteme, 13*(3), 359–377. <https://doi.org/10.1017/epi.2015.64>

Carel, H. (2018). *Illness: The cry of the flesh* (3rd ed.). Taylor and Francis.

Carnevale, F. A. (2020). A "thick" conception of children's voices: A hermeneutical framework for childhood research. *International Journal of Qualitative Methods, 19,* 1–9. <https://doi.org/10.1177/1609406920933767>

Carnevale, F. A. (2021). Recognizing children as agents: Taylor's hermeneutical ontology and the philosophy of childhood. *International Journal of Philosophical Studies, 29*(5), 791–808. <https://doi.org/10.1080/09672559.2021.1998188>

Carson, R. A. (2002). The hyphenated space: Liminality in the doctor-patient relationship. In R. Charon & M. Montello (Eds.), *Stories matter: The role of narrative in medical ethics* (pp. 171–182). Routledge.

Christiansen, A. (2011). Storytelling and professional learning: A phenomenographic study of students' experience of patient digital stories in nurse education. *Nurse Education Today, 31*(3), 289–293. <https://doi.org/10.1016/j.nedt.2010.10.006>

Davey, N. (2013). *Unfinished worlds: Hermeneutics, aesthetics, and Gadamer.* Edinburgh University.

de Jager, A., Fogarty, A., Tewson, A., Lenette, C., & Boydell, K. M. (2017). Digital storytelling in research: A systematic review. *The Qualitative Report, 22*(10), 2548–2582. <https://nsuworks.nova.edu/tqr/vol22/iss10/3>

Derrida, J. (2023). *Hospitality, volume I* (E. S. Burt, P.-A. Brault, & P. Kamuf, Eds. 1st ed.). University of Chicago Press.

Docherty, S., & Sandelowski, M. (1999). Focus on qualitative methods: Interviewing children. *Research in Nursing and Health, 22*(2), 177–185. <https://doi.org/https://doi.org/10.1002/(SICI)1098-240X(199904)22:2<177::AID-NUR9>3.0.CO;2-H>

Fiddian-Green, A., Kim, S., Gubrium, A. C., Larkey, L. K., & Peterson, J. C. (2019). Restor(y)ing health: A conceptual model of the effects of digital storytelling. *Health Promotion Practice, 20*(4), 502–512. <https://doi.org/10.1177/1524839918825130>

Frank, A. (2013). *The wounded storyteller.* University of Chicago.

Fricker, M. (2007). *Epistemic injustice: Power and the ethics of knowing.* Oxford University Press.

Gadamer, H.-G. (1986). *The relevance of the beautiful and other essays* (N. Walker, Trans.). Cambridge University Press.

Gadamer, H.-G. (1996). *The enigma of health*. Stanford University Press. (Original work published in 1993)

Gadamer, H.-G. (2000). Boundaries of language (L. K. Schmidt, Trans.). In L. K. Schmidt (Ed.), *Language and linguisticality in Gadamer's hermeneutics* (pp. 9–17). Lexington Books. (Original work published 1985)

Gadamer, H.-G. (2004). *Truth and method* (J. Weinsheimer & D. G. Marshal, Trans.). Continuum. (Original work published in 1960)

Gadamer, H.-G. (2006). Artworks in word and image: "So true, so full of being!" (Goethe) *Theory, Culture & Society, 23*(1), 57–83. <https://doi.org/10.1177/0263276406063229> (Original work published in 1992)

Gadamer, H.-G. (2007). Language and understanding (R. E. Palmer, Trans. & Ed.). In *The Gadamer reader: A bouquet of the later writings* (pp. 89–107). Northwestern University Press. (Original work published 1970)

George, T. (2020). *The responsibility to understand: Hermeneutical contours of ethical life*. Edinburgh University Press.

Gubrium, A. (2009). Digital storytelling: An emergent method for health promotion research and practice. *Health Promotion Practice, 10*(2), 186–191. <https://doi.org/10.1177/1524839909332600>

Heidegger, M. (1962). *Being and time* (J. Macquarrie & E. Robinson, Trans.). Harper and Row. (Original work published in 1927)

Heidegger, M. (1977). *The question concerning technology and other essays* (W. Lovitt, Trans.). Garland Publishing. (Original work published 1954)

International Childhood Cancer Day. (n.d.). *The gold ribbon*. <https://internationalchildhoodcancerday.org/>

James, A. (2007). Giving voice to children's voices: Practices and problems, pitfalls and potentials. *American Anthropologist, 109*(2), 261–272. <https://doi.org/https://doi.org/10.1525/aa.2007.109.2.261>

James, A., & Curtis, P. (2012). Constructing the sick child: The cultural politics of children's hospitals. *The Sociological Review (Keele), 60*(4), 754–772. <https://doi.org/10.1111/j.1467-954X.2012.02132.x>

Kearney, R. (2015). Hospitality: Possible or impossible. *Hospitality and Society, 5*(2). <https://doi.org/10.1386/hosp.5.2-3.173_1>

Laing, C. M., Moules, N. J., Estefan, A., & Lang, M. (2017a). Stories that heal: Understanding the effects of creating digital stories with pediatric and adolescent/young adult oncology patients. *Journal of Pediatric Oncology Nursing, 34*(4), 272–282. <https://doi.org/10.1177/1043454216688639>

Laing, C. M., Moules, N. J., Estefan, A., & Lang, M. (2017b). "*Stories take your role away from you*": Understanding the impact on healthcare professionals of viewing digital stories of pediatric and adolescent/young adult oncology patients. *Journal of Pediatric Oncology Nursing, 34*(4), 261–271. <https://doi.org/10.1177/1043454217697023>

Laing, C. M., Moules, N. J., Sinclair, S., & Estefan, A. (2019). Digital storytelling as a psychosocial tool with adult oncology patients and survivors. *Oncology Nursing Forum, 46*(2), 147–154. <https://doi.org/10.1188/19.ONF.147–154>

Laing, C. M., Moules, N. J., Sinclair, S., & Estefan, A. (2020). Understanding the impact on healthcare professionals of viewing digital stories of adults with cancer: A hermeneutic study. *Journal of Applied Hermeneutics, Article 1*, 1–11. <https://doi.org/10.11575/jah.vi0.69756>

Lambert, J. (2013). *Digital storytelling: Capturing lives, creating community* (4th ed.). Routledge.

Lang, M. J. (2021). *Emerging Horizons: Crafting Meaning and Cultivating Understanding Through Digital Storytelling* (Doctoral thesis, University of Calgary, Calgary, Canada). Retrieved from <http://hdl.handle.net/1880/114093>

Lang, M. J., & Laing, C. M. (2022a). Emerging horizons, part one: Amanda's story: Wound care. *Journal of Applied Hermeneutics, Article 2*, 1–9. <https://doi.org/10.11575/jah.v2022i2022.74856>

Lang, M. J., & Laing, C. M. (2022b). Emerging horizons, part five: Kenzie's story: Periods and ellipses. *Journal of Applied Hermeneutics, Article 8*, 1–12. <https://doi.org/10.11575/jah.v2022i2022.75370>

Lang, M., & Laing, C. M. (2022c). Emerging horizons, part seven: Mike's story: Lessons learned. *Journal of Applied Hermeneutics, Article 17*, 1–12. <https://10.11575/jah.v2022i2022.76467>

Lang, M., Laing, C., Ewashen, C., & Moules, N. J. (2020). Digital stories as data: An etymological and philosophical exploration of cocreated data in philosophical hermeneutic health research. *International Journal of Qualitative Methods, 19*(1), 1–9. <https://doi.org/10.1177/1609406920913673>

Lang, M. J., Laing, C. M., Moules, N. J., & Estefan, A. (2019). Words, camera, music, action: A methodology of digital storytelling in a healthcare setting. *International Journal of Qualitative Method, 18*(1–10). <https://doi.org/10.1177/2F1609406919863241>

Large, W. (2021). Ability-to-be (Seinkonnen). In M. A. Wrathall (Ed.), *The Cambridge Heidegger lexicon*. Cambridge University Press. <https://doi.org/https://doi-org.10.1017/9780511843778.003>

Liben, S., Langner, R., & Bluebond-Langner, M. (2014). Pediatric palliative care in 2014: Much accomplished, much yet to be done. *Journal of Palliative Care, 30*(4), 311–316. <https://doi.org/10.1177/082585971403000414>

Lomax, E. M. R. (1996). *Small and special: The development of hospitals for children in Victorian Britain.* Wellcome Insitute for the History of Medicine. <https://pmc-ncbi-nlm-nih-ov.ezproxy.lib.ucalgary.ca/articles/PMC2530979/pdf/medhistsuppl00031-0007.pdf>

Mahnke, C. B. (2000). The growth and development of a specialty: The history of pediatrics. *Clinical Pediatrics, 39*(12), 705–714. <https://doi.org/10.1177/000992280003901204>

Malpas, J. (2015). Place and situation. In J. Malpas & H.-H. Gander (Eds.), *The Routledge companion to hermeneutics* (pp. 354–366). Routledge.

Malpas, J. (2018). *Place and experience: A philosophical topography* (2nd ed.). Routledge. <https://doi.org/10.4324/9781315265445>

Matthews, G., & Mullin, A. (2020). The philosophy of childhood. In E. N. Zalta (Ed.), *The Stanford encyclopedia of philsophy* (Fall 2020 ed.). https://plato.stanford.edu/archives/fall2020/entries/childhood/>

McKee, R. (1997). *Story: Substance, structure, style and the principles of screenwriting.* Harper Collins.

Merriam-Webster. (n.d.). Apprehension. In *Merriam-Webster.com dictionary.* Retrieved July 16, 2024, from <https://www.merriam-webster.com/dictionary/apprehension>

Merriam-Webster. (n.d.). Companion. In *Merriam-Webster.com dictionary.* <https://www.merriam-webster.com/dictionary/companion>

Merriam-Webster. (n.d.). Manipulate. In *Merriam-Webster.com* dictionary. <https://www.merriam-webster.com/dictionary/manipulate>

Merriam-Webster. (n.d.). Voice. In *Merriam-Webster.com dictionary.* <https://www.merriam-webster.com/dictionary/voice>

Moody, K., Kramer, D., Santizo, R. O., Magro, L., Wyshogrod, D., Ambrosio, J., Castillo, C., Lieberman, R., & Stein, J. (2013). Helping the helpers: Mindfulness training for burnout in pediatric oncology—A pilot program. *Journal of Pediatric Oncology Nursing, 30*(5), 275–284. <https://doi.org/10.1177/1043454213504497>

Moules, N. J., Estefan, A., McCaffrey, G., Tapp, D. M., & Strother, D. (2016). Examining the effects of childhood cancer on the parental subsystem: Implications for parents and healthcare professionals. Part three. *Journal of Family Nursing, 22*(4), 559–578. <https://doi.org/10.1177/1074840716675986>

Moules, N. J., Jardine, D. W., McCaffrey, G., & Brown, C. (2013). "Isn't all oncology hermeneutic?" *Journal of Applied Hermeneutics, Article 3.* <http://hdl.handle.net/10515/sy5w95141>

Moules, N. J., McCaffrey, G., Field, J. C., & Laing, C. M. (2015). *Conducting hermeneutic research: From philosophy to practice*. Peter Lang.

Ocak, S., Arici, H. E., & Köseoglu, M. A. (2024). Evolution of hospitality research in hospital scholarship: A bibliometric analysis. *International Journal of Healthcare Management*, *17*, 1–16. <https://doi.org/10.1080/20479700.2024.2362025>

O'Donahue, J. (2008). *To bless the space between us: A book of blessings*. Convergent.

Online Etymology Dictionary. (n.d.). Companion. In *Etymonline.com*. Retrieved November 23, 2023, from <https://www.etymonline.com/search?q=companion>

Online Etymology Dictionary. (n.d.). Hospital. In *Etymonline.com dictionary*. Retrieved July 3, 2024, from <https://www.etymonline.com/search?q=hospital>

Online Etymology Dictionary. (n.d.). Hostile. In *Etymonline.com* dictionary. Retrieved July 3, 2024, from <https://www.etymonline.com/search?q=hostile>

Online Etymology Dictionary. (n.d.). Safeguard. In *Online etymology dictionary*. Retrieved October 12, 2020, from <https://www.etymonline.com/word/safeguard>

Online Etymology Dictionary. (n.d.). Salve. In *Online etymology dictionary*. Retrieved October 12, 2020, from <https://www.etymonline.com/word/salve>

Online Etymology Dictionary. (n.d.). Voice. *In Etymonline.com* dictionary. Retrieved April 25, 2024, from <https://www.etymonline.com/word/voice#etymonline_v_7867>

Parsons, E., & Darlington, A. S. (2021). Parents' perspectives on conflict in paediatric healthcare: A scoping review. *Archives of Disease in Childhood*, 1–6. <https://doi.org/10.1136/archdischild-2020-320975>

Rahimzadeh, V., Bartlett, G., Longo, C., Crimi, L., Macdonald, M. E., Jabado, N., & Ells, C. (2015). Promoting an ethic of engagement in pediatric palliative care research. *BMC Palliative Care*, *14*(50), 1–7. <https://doi.org/10.1186/s12904-015-0048-5>

Rice, C., LaMarre, A., Changfoot, N., & Douglas, P. (2018). Making spaces: Multimedia storytelling as reflexive, creative praxis. *Qualitative Research in Psychology*, *17*(2), 222–239. <https://doi.org/10.1080/14780887.2018.1442694>

Rice, C., & Mundel, I. (2018). Story-making as methodology: Disrupting dominant stories through multimedia storytelling. *Canadian Review of Sociology*, *55*(2), 211–231. <https://doi.org/10.1111/cars.12190>

Rilke, R. M. (1995). *Ahead of all parting: The selected poetry and prose of Rainer Maria Rilke* (S. Mitchell, Trans.). The Modern Library.

Ricoeur, P. (1990). *Time and narrative: Volume 1, 2, 3* (K. McLaughlin & D. Pellauer Trans.). University of Chicago Press. (Original work published 1975)

Risser, J. (2012). *The life of understanding: A contemporary hermeneutics*. Indiana University Press.

Risser, J. (2019). When words fail: On the power of language in human experience. *Journal of Applied Hermeneutics, Article 6*. <https://journalhosting.ucalgary.ca/index.php/jah/index>

Rushton, C. H., Batcheller, J., Schroeder, K., & Donohue, P. (2015). Burnout and resilience among nurses practicing in high-intensity settings. *American Journal of Critical Care, 24*(5), 412–420. <https://doi:10.4037/ajcc2015291>

Schmidt, D. J. (2015). Text and translation. In J. Malpas & H.-H. Gander (Eds.), *The Routledge companion to hermeneutics* (pp. 345–353). Routledge.

Singh, H. K., Macdonald, M. E., & Carnevale, F. A. (2020). Considering medical assistance in dying for minors: the complexities of children's voices. *Journal of Medical Ethics, 46*(6), 399. <https://doi.org/10.1136/medethics-2019-105762>

Spyrou, S. (2016). Troubling children's voices in research. In F. Esser, M. S. Baader, T. Betz, & B. Hungerland (Eds.), *Reconceptualising agency in childhood* (pp. 105–118). Routledge.

Svenaeus, F. (2000). *The hermeneutics of medicine and the phenomenology of health: Steps towards a philosophy of medical practice*. Kluwer Academic Publishers.

TEDxCalgary. (2023). Bill Chomik: The power of architecture [Video]. YouTube. <https://www.youtube.com/watch?v=sgv0UFlb1Nw>

Taylor, C. (1985). *Human agency and language: Philosophy papers*. Cambridge University Press.

Webber, K. M. (2024). *"Friendship … or Whatever it is": Understanding Nurse-Parent Relational Complexity in Pediatric Oncology Contexts* [Doctoral dissertation, University of Calgary]. University of Calgary PRISM Repository. <https://doi.org/10.11575/PRISM/43578>

White, M., & Epston, D. (1990). *Narrative means to therapeutic ends*. W. W. Norton.

Wong, K. (2023, May). *Death of the (little) other: Reflections on childhood, death, and grief in pediatric palliataive care [Paper presentation]*. Canadian Hermeneutic Institute 2023, Calgary, Canada.

Wong, K. L. (2024). *Listening to the voices of dying children: Art, metaphor, and silence*. [Doctoral thesis, University of Calgary]. Retrieved from <https://prism.ucalgary.ca> Open Thesis and Dissertations. <https://hdl.handle.net/1880/120285>

The Rigor and Integrity of Hermeneutic Research

Sandelowski (1993) suggested that "rigor is less about adherence to the letter of rules and procedures than it is about fidelity to the spirt of the work" (p. 2). We work from the premise that hermeneutic research is difficult, sophisticated, rigorous, and, most importantly, credible and relevant. Hermeneutics, like many qualitative research methods, is frequently asked to live up to the ways, means, and methods of the natural sciences and is evaluated by the same criteria (Moules et al., 2017) This application of criteria of acceptability and soundness is flawed in that the value, legitimacy, and integrity of hermeneutic research must be re-conceptualized and discerned by different regards than is natural scientific inquiry. In this chapter, we examine the difficulty, importance, and obligation of speaking to, and demonstrating, rigor in hermeneutic research.

As stated many times in this book, hermeneutics is about understanding. George (2020) offered that hermeneutics has an ethical responsibility to understand. He wrote that there is an urgency in our "factical questions about who we are, about who we believe we need to be in response to the demands of individual situations, and about how to develop our abilities to live and to act well" (p. viii). It is this very responsibility that demands that we respond to the obligations of this work with attentiveness, rigor, and integrity.

The word rigor is defined in Webster's dictionary as a strictness or inflexibility; exactness in precision or accuracy; or rigidity. In this consideration of the word, it cannot be applied to hermeneutic work, for hermeneutics is quite the opposite of strict, inflexible, precise, exact, or rigid. However, like many words, there are different definitions that apply. Another definition of rigor is the "quality of being careful" (Merriam-Webster online, n.d.). Rigor in hermeneutics is the careful attention to the treatment of topics such that the work engenders trustworthiness and believability. Rigor in this context does not show itself in a strict adherence to an inflexible method, or in absolute and precise findings that can be replicated to authenticate them, but rather in attention to a cohesive, comprehensive, cogent, and expansive contribution to understanding of the topic. Within criteria of rigor in research, the words validity, reliability, and veracity also arise.

Validity in Hermeneutic Work

Applied to interpretive work, the term validity has to be taken up differently from its conventional, technical meaning in quantitative research. First and foremost, validity is regarded as a form of social construction that affirms a legitimization of knowledge claims. What is deemed to be valid and therefore meaningful comes from a community of acceptability. Webster's offers a first definition of validity as applying to that which cannot be objected to because it conforms to law, logic, or facts, and is therefore free of error. The word, though, is also defined as strong, powerful, well-grounded, cogent, convincing, robust, healthy, and telling. Hermeneutic work, when done well, *is* strong, powerful, well-grounded, cogent, convincing, robust, healthy, and telling, and these are qualities that a hermeneutic researcher strives for in interpretations. Hermeneutics is not about explanation but understanding, and understanding can only be shared when it is put forward in a convincing, understandable, and telling way.

To make something valid, in the traditional scientific sense, is to make it repeatable. In hermeneutics, however, to reproduce more of the same does not make it more real. Rather, we think of *re-production* as a form of discovery, recovery, and legitimization, a freeing of something from encased and enclosed truths of the past, to recover possibilities and free the topic for new conversation as well as to discover something new. "Validity is an experience of application; it does not arise out of the past but from the future, becoming something only in the way it is lived out" (Moules, 2002, p. 17).

Gadamer (1984) offered us two approaches to achieving validity—*rhetorica* and *critica*:

> Rhetorica is obviously based on common sense, on the probably of arguments insofar as they are well received and assured by appearances. On the other hand, the critical attitude stands against appearances, on the side of the new physics with its insistence on method. (p. 55)

Rhetoric is the ancient Greek art of persuasion, the art of an argument well presented, the tradition of persuasive presentation that invites the listener or reader to participate. It is another term that Gadamer revitalized by reading it against its contemporary conventional implication of hollow language. Gadamer (1984) recognized an inherent persuasiveness in language and suggested that rhetoric has a "deep inner convergence" with hermeneutics in that one needs rhetorical tradition to not only "give a good talk but also in order to *read* and understand extended argumentation" (p. 55). Persuasion, however, does not mean to convince someone of an unbending truth, such that other truths are given up, but to convince that what is being presented is credible and believable, that it makes "sense" and has echoes of recognizability.

Writing about qualitative research as such, Angen (2000) preferred to speak of validation rather than validity, and described it as intersubjective agreement within communities and researchers that the findings are productive; in other words, they can be "lived out" (Moules, 2002, p. 17). This production or re-production is, as stated, something of both discovery and recovery. Within validation, Angen named processes of ethical validation and substantive validation. One measure of ethical validation is the appraisal of whether the research findings inform and transform our practices and assist us in doing things differently. Substantive validation is grounded in the ways that the research accounts for prior research and theory, self-reflexivity, and popular, political, and personal understandings—all of which have informed the research.

To borrow Angen's (2000) proposal of validation, then the validity of the work lies in the extent to which it is received, validated where it matters most. For example, a hermeneutic study on the impact of the death of a child on pediatric oncology nurses is validated and finds its validity by the community of nurses who work in this area. This is not always strictly the case, however, because it is not always the population studied that needs to offer validation of the findings. There may be others who are affected by this, for example, managers of pediatric nurses, physicians, or those who work in children's hospices. There are many instances where the findings might not hold as much interest to the participants as it does to other groups of end users. An example of this might be studying the work of bereavement therapists and interviewing clients who have been through this type of therapy to find out from them what was most useful and meaningful to them in their therapeutic encounters. These participants might offer validation of the findings but in many ways, it is the target population of bereavement therapists who might be in a position of validation.

Kvale and Brinkmann (2009) suggested the there are some studies where the validity is forefront in the product, executed through its strength and power of presentation.

> Ideally, the quality of the craftsmanship results in products with knowledge claims that are so powerful and convincing in their own right that they, so to say, carry the

> validation with them, like a strong piece of art. In such cases, the research procedures would be transparent and the results evident, and the conclusions of a study intrinsically convincing as true, beautiful, and good. Valid research would in this sense be research that makes questions of validity superfluous. (p. 260)

Hermeneutics does not aim for this kind of completion or for the product and interpretations to leave no question in the mind of the reader. Alternatively, Lather (1993) saw validity as the "incitement to discourse" (p. 674) and proposed "the conditions of possibility for validity are also its conditions of impossibility" (p. 687). The best hermeneutic work raises questions rather than just convinces, but on the other hand there must be *something* convincing enough in the presentation to incite discourse, and often in this kind of work it is not only in the presentation but also in its application.

Veracity: A Return to Truth

The veracity of hermeneutic work, or in other words, its truth value and credibility, depends upon the power of interpretations to offer faithful and recognizable descriptions of the topic that ring "true" to others. "Everything comes down to our capacity to recognize ourselves in the finished account, in the 'story' of human existence which is recounted there" (Caputo, 1987, p. 80). Hermeneutics recognizes that human experience is always storied and "good hermeneutical research shows an ability to read those stories from the inside out and the outside in" (Smith, 1991, p. 201). We argue that it is not just the act of recognizing "ourselves in the finished account"—we may not recognize ourselves at all but still recognize the "truth" in the account. To see that the work is true of something does not mean that we have had to experience it, but that it is presented so compellingly and persuasively, that it is possible to see how it helps us understand. As stated previously, to recognize something as true *of something* does not mean that it closes off other truths but that it offers a possibility of understanding that is generative and open. If one were to read a research study about a topic area unknown to the reader, it ought to be clear how the interpretations are linked to the data and how they help the reader to arrive at an understanding of the topic.

Madison (1988) suggested that a more useful question than asking if an interpretation is true or not, is to consider the acceptability of the interpretation. One interpretation may be accepted over another because it is more:

> fruitful, more promising ... it seems to make more and better sense ... it opens up greater horizons of meaning ... all interpretation works under the promise of truth ...

> when we opt for a given interpretation, we do not do so because we *know* it to be true ... but because we *believe* it to be the best ... (p. 15)

All interpretations are competing in one sense and can be falsified, so the argumentation is for a relative and defensible credibility of the work. Rather than finding or claiming truth, we attempt to remain true *to* something (the topic) and to interpret in such a way that it is true *of* something (within the topic). We are true to our work when:

> in our rewritings and retellings we are able to preserve and to take up, in a more meaning-giving way, with greater subtlety of narrative, the "truth" of our past, i.e., all the data that we have already made use of and their interpretations ... We are in the truth when we are able to ... maintain the openness of the conversation and keep it going. (Madison, 1988, p. 169)

Credibility in this work is shown and sometimes enacted differently than in other methods of research. As for reasons explored in Chapter 7, in hermeneutics as we practice it, it does not involve member checking or consulting the participants to have them validate the interpretations.

The process of generalizability is one that is often questioned in many qualitative research methods, a question of whether or not the findings of a study can be readily applied to other contexts. Kvale and Brinkmann (2009) made a distinction between forms of generalizing, ranging from formal and explicit statistical generalization to naturalistic generalization, which is personal and tacit, to analytical generalization which "involves a reasoned judgment about the extent to which the findings of one study can be used as a guide to what might occur in another situation" (p. 262).

Generalizability in any case is not where we believe that truth lies in hermeneutic work. We are not seeking an exactly replicable application of findings across any and all domains, so therefore the idea of transferability sometimes has a better fit with hermeneutics. This occurs when the findings of the research can "fit into contexts outside of the study situation and when its audience views its findings as meaningful and applicable in terms of their own experiences" (Sandelowski, 1986, p. 27).

However, even more than the ideas of generalizability or transferability, Madison (1988) offered that more meaningful criteria of good hermeneutic work are those of suggestiveness and potential. They describe the extent to which the research raises more questions than are closed off, thereby demonstrating its capacity for extension of understanding. He proposed other criteria: coherence, comprehensiveness, penetration, thoroughness, appropriateness, contextuality, and agreement. According to Madison, *coherence* is the presentation of a picture of something without glaring contradictions. We understand this to mean that, although there might well be differences or seemingly opposite points of consideration or paradox present, the writing itself shows an awareness of these and makes coherent sense of the contradictions. *Comprehensiveness* is a search for adequacy in the work—does it speak to the topic enough that it extends understanding or does it fall short of digging deeply enough into it? *Penetration* refers to the capacity of the work to make an impact on the reader, to "sink in" and make sense, to be heard. *Thoroughness*, similar to comprehensiveness, is the evidence that the work addresses significant problems and questions that show up within the topic. "The real power of hermeneutical consciousness is our ability to see what is questionable" (Gadamer, 1977, p. 13). *Contextuality* is recognition that topics do not happen outside of context, nor should the work be written or read outside of an awareness of the context from which it arises and emerges. *Agreement* does not imply consensus, but rather that there is agreement within the work to make it coherent and harmonious. Madison wrote of *suggestiveness* in regard to the way that the work is fertile and fecund and "raises questions that stimulate further research and interpretation" (p. 30). Lastly, in *potential*, he argued that the "ultimate 'validation' of a true interpretation lies in the future" (p. 30). Madison was not, in presenting these terms, attempting to create rules for the conduct of hermeneutic research, but rather to articulate guidelines for conduct of hermeneutic research and criteria for appraisal of the rigor of the work.

> There can be no *science* of interpretation. This, however, does not mean that interpretation cannot be a rigorous (if not an exact) discipline, an art in the proper sense of the term, and that one cannot rationally *evaluate* interpretations. (Madison, 1988, p. 31)

Rigor in Ethical Conduct of Hermeneutic Research

Hermeneutic research happens within the same structures of ethical standards as any other kind of research involving humans. Researchers have the same obligations to treat participants with respect, do their best to ensure informed consent, confidentiality and privacy and so on. Hermeneutic philosophy does, however, have an ethical slant that lends an additional perspective for thinking about the ethical conduct of research.

Ethics boards are necessarily concerned with the management of research according to established ethical principles, and they work with researchers to anticipate potential threats to the ethical integrity of research. What they cannot do is be present during the conduct of research, in the face of shifting, nuanced, multifaceted circumstances. This is another instance where hermeneutics emphasizes the contingencies of practice under the aegis of methodological structures of anticipation. There is a general point here about research ethics, although types of research that involve less formally determined interviews are likely to be more open to the dynamics of human relationships.

Stewart and Amundson (1995) suggested that it is not enough to acknowledge and follow the steps of ethical decision-making for we must realize that ethical dilemmas are personal dilemmas, composed of competing values, and capable of addressing us in ways that challenge our own beliefs and commitments. The ethical call is for us, as researchers, to make the best decisions we can. Ethical dilemmas will greet us in all research, from the moment of the address of the question, through the interviews, in the analysis, and dissemination of the work. Researchers are met with situations of asking delicate questions in interviews, deciding what is appropriate to ask and what might be potentially hurtful to the participant; deciding what information to include from the transcripts; discerning how to protect confidentiality and minimize the recognition of participants in the final reports; and deciding how to disseminate research that can easily be located in particular contexts. There is an ethical dimension to making decisions at all points in the research process so that they must be constantly negotiated with awareness and sensitivity.

From this view, ethical conduct in research is an example of phronesis, the practical judgment discussed in Chapter 3. Elements of phronesis appear in the nursing literature around relational ethics, which is another way of conceptualizing ethical practice. Although primarily concerned with clinical nurse-patient relationships, insights from this literature are also applicable to researchers. Gadow (2009) postulated a shift from universal and rational ethics toward a more engaged, relational version of ethics. In the latter case, "the situated self encompasses not only rationality but emotion, imagination, memory, language, the body, and even other selves. Individuals are intrinsically relational; existential subjectivity is intersubjectivity" (p. 575). This description fleshes out (pun intended) Aristotle's suggestion that practical judgment does make use of reason, but not only reason. This makes sense in the context of researcher-participant relationships in which there is an intermingling of proximity and professionalism, intimacy and distance. Engagement as a researcher is "personal responsiveness to the particular other" (Gadow, 2009, p. 575). Bergum and Dossetor (2005) similarly mapped out the ethical dimension of practice in the open, contingent and uncertain relational space of nurses' work with patients. It is important to remember that this way of understanding practice is not arbitrary or merely relativistic. Relational ethics do not arise regardless of institutional structures of professional standards, policies and codes of ethics. For the most part, good relational practice ought concretely to manifest those very structures. Relational ethics, however, is open to the possibility of the exception and the demands of the particular. Since relational ethics responds to the address of the particular situation, that response might also include an answering-back to, or a questioning of institutional structures. It implies a dynamic response to the conditions of practice, as well as to the specific moment of practice.

George (2020) argued that we are in an urgency or responsiveness to the demands of individual situations and the need to "develop our abilities to live and act well" (p. viii) and we do this by embracing a responsibility to understand. In this responsibility, it is acknowledged that understanding is not a "light encounter or a fleeting event; it is an act of deep attention, reverence, and care" (Moules, 2020, p. 2). Life, George argued, requires thoughtful and reasonable decisions, and striving to do the right thing in specific situations. What is the right thing cannot be decided in advance with a template of what is good and bad but rather, our responsibility involves "what the good means—right here and now" (p. 2).

Caputo described one of the consequences of acknowledging ethical responsibility amidst contingency:

> The "ghost" of undecidability hovers over the decision, before, during, and after the decision. It haunts it, lingering like a spectre, even after the decision. We do not dispel the ghost by deciding. We do the best we can to be just, here and now, under the law, but we must live with the consequences. (Caputo, 1993, p. 104)

We live with the consequences of this work, responsibly and responsively. The character of ethics is relationship. People, particularities, differences, commitments, and obligations inhabit ethics. It is the relationship between these contingencies that converge to constitute and occupy the rigors of an ethical examination of hermeneutic research. Decision-making, beliefs, feelings, and actions are complexly woven together, fraught with consequences and ramifications, costs and benefits. The rigor in this attention to ethical comportment is a constant attention to the potential to do harm and the potential to make a difference that is a good difference, something that must be done with integrity and harmony.

Integrity and Harmony

We have grounded this book about the conduct of hermeneutic research on a philosophical foundation and one of the measures of rigor is to maintain that grounding. For example, if researchers base a study on Gadamer's philosophical hermeneutics and then describe how they have used software to count the number of times a particular theme arose and thus determined this as an interpretation, there is an apparent contradiction of Gadamer's honoring of the particular. Of course, Gadamer never addressed questions like whether or not to use software in research, but it would at the very least call for a reasoned explanation in terms of his philosophy.

As much as hermeneutics can have a charming, ebullient, and seemingly effortless face, this is not the case. The work must have literacy and scholarship. When something is not guided by a strict methodological procedure, its strength and credibility lies in good scholarly judgment, in being citatious and accountable. One characteristic of hermeneutic work is its embrace of plurality and difference, so that although agreement is not the goal, the credibility and integrity of the work do require a sense of cohesion. Gadamer (1960/1997) suggested that "the harmony of all details with the whole is the criterion of correct understanding… failure to achieve this harmony means that understanding has failed" (p. 291). We interpret this as meaning that research ought to have consistency between its philosophical assumptions, its conduct, and the expression of its conclusions. This is not to say that there cannot be contradiction, disagreement, or differences in terms of the content or findings—in fact we should look for the expression of complexity as hermeneutic research takes up a topic and, in Caputo's (1987) words, "restores [it] to its original difficulty" (p. 1).

Integrity, then, of the work lies in part in its ability to hold tension, to be "not quite this and not quite that," in recognizing that with every opening, there is a closing of something else, in knowing that openings are invitations and portals to understanding, not dark rabbit holes where the topic disappears. Integrity lies in the hermeneutic humility of knowing that truth is a flexible encounter with something that offers room for many views.

Hermeneutic research, in its openness to possibilities also runs the risk of being misinterpreted that "anything goes" and anyone can do it well. There *can* be bad examples of research done under the name of hermeneutics and there are some mistakes that can occur. Field (2017) wrote of how we can slip into making the obvious inescapable, there can be uniformed and disrespectful mixing of methods, and the research can devolve into "little t" truth. Further, we offer that we see hermeneutic researchers sometimes fall into the trap of thinking that, if the writing is creative, poems are inserted, metaphors employed, and there is saturation in etymological tracing, the work is hermeneutic. On the contrary, hermeneutic research must demonstrate a discernment in how topics are approached and how interpretations are presented. To arrive at something that is tentative but not timid requires great judgment, tact, discernment, and recognition of what works to best represent understanding of a topic.

Limitations of Hermeneutic Research

> And to say for myself, just once,
> without embarrassment, *bless*,
> thrown out as to some lightness
> that I actually believe in,
> surprised (as I believe
> they were) to find it
> here, where it seems impossible
> that one life even matters, though
> like them, I'll argue
> the stubborn argument of the particular,
> right now, in the midst of things, *this*
> and *this*. (Wallace, 1987, p. 111)

A part of the integrity of any research lies in recognizing and acknowledging that no one method provides all the answers, and every method has strengths and limitations. It is the nature of hermeneutics to allow a topic to show itself, while knowing that it will exceed any single interpretation. The very thing that adds merit to this kind of research is that which restricts it. Hermeneutics is a study and honoring of the particular, discovering how the particular lives in its connectedness in the world (Moules et al., 2013). In every well-conducted hermeneutic study, there are rich, vibrant, and expansive opportunities for understanding. It is the depth of these particulars that offers the gifts and strengths that surround this kind of research, but it could be argued that hermeneutic research is sometimes constrained by its very openness that resists solid conclusion. A research study of this kind does not have "power" in the traditional, quantitative sense, so what power does it bring?

We would suggest that it is rooted in the power of the particular—in the recognition of one voice, one experience, one mattering of human life, one diminishment of suffering, one experience of healing, one moment of seeing education come alive in the classroom—that the practice professions have always found their "real" power. It is in the moment of being present at the death of one child; or watching one child "get it" while learning math; or the privilege of being present while one family makes peace in troubled relationships; *or* in watching a family learn to laugh and play while attending a cancer camp where their own child can no longer attend, as he is no longer alive. It is in the richness of the power of these individual, particular moments of grace, kinship, and human relationship that our human practices have always found their own graceful and powerful place—in the context of one human life, here and now, in *this*, and *this*, and *this*.

Summary

In this chapter, we have spoken to some of the complexity of accounting for and recognizing rigor in hermeneutic research. We have discussed some of the distinctive traits of rigor in hermeneutic research, as well as issues that are shared with all research in contemporary academic institutions. We offer an advocacy for the value of interpretive research, which is not defense or apology:

> It is as if, in our quasi-militaristic zeal to neutralize bias and defend our projects against threats to validity, we were more preoccupied with building fortifications against attack than with creating the evocative, true-to-life, and meaningful portraits, stories, and landscapes of human experience that constitute the best test of rigor in qualitative work. (Sandelowski, 1993, p. 1)

Although, as Nicholas Davey has written, "hermeneutics is not always its own best advocate" (2006, p. xi), researchers in the hermeneutic tradition need to and must advocate *for* it, persuasively without apology and with confidence in the integrity of the process and the outcome of conducting this work well. In the next chapter, we discuss the "so what?" issue that is often asked of hermeneutic research.

References

Angen, M. J. (2000). Evaluating interpretive inquiry: Reviewing the validity debate and opening the dialogue. *Qualitative Health Research, 10*(3), 378–395. <https://doi.org/10.1177/104973230001000308>

Bergum, V., & Dossetor, J. (2005). *Relational ethics: The full meaning of respect.* University Publishing Group.

Caputo, J. D. (1987). *Radical hermeneutics: Repetition, deconstruction and the hermeneutic project*. Indiana University Press.

Caputo, J. D. (1993). *Against ethics: Contributions to a poetics of obligation with constant reference to deconstruction*. Indiana University Press.

Davey, N. (2006). *Unquiet understanding: Gadamer's philosophical hermeneutics.* SUNY.

Field, J. C. (2017). Losing the so-called paradigm war: Does our confusion, disarray, and retreat contribute to the advance? *Journal of Applied*

Hermeneutics, Article 4. <https://journalhosting.ucalgary.ca/index.php/jah/article/view/53308>

Gadamer, H.-G. (1960/1997). *Truth and method* (2nd rev. ed.; J. Weinsheimer & D. G. Marshall, Trans.). Continuum.

Gadamer, H.-G. (1984). The hermeneutics of suspicion. In G. Shapiro & A. Sica (Eds.), *Hermeneutics: Questions and prospects* (pp. 54–65). University of Massachusetts.

Gadamer, H.-G. (1977). *Philosophical hermeneutics* (D. E. Linge, Trans.). University of California Press.

Gadow, S. (2009). Relational narrative: The postmodern turn in nursing ethics. In P. Reed & N. Crawford-Shearer (Eds.), *Perspectives on nursing theory* (pp. 571–580). Lippincott Williams & Wilkins.

George, T. (2020). *The responsibility to understand: Hermeneutical contours of ethical life*. Edinburgh University Press.

Kitchener, K. S. (1984). Intuition, critical evaluation, and ethical principles: The foundation for ethical decisions in counseling psychology. *The Counseling Psychologist, 12*(3–4), 43–55. <https://doi.org/10.1177/0011000084123005>

Kvale, S., & Brinkmann, S. (2009). *InterViews: Learning the craft of qualitative research interviewing* (2nd ed.). SAGE.

Lather, P. (1993). Fertile obsession: Validity after poststructuralism. *The Sociological Quarterly, 334*(4), 673–693. <https://doi.org/10.1111/j.1533-8525.1993.tb00112.x>

Madison, G. B. (1988). *The hermeneutics of postmodernity: Figures and themes*. Indiana University Press.

Moules, N. J. (2002). Hermeneutic inquiry: Paying heed to history and Hermes. An Ancestral, substantive, and methodological tale. *International Journal of Qualitative Methods, 1*(3), 1–21. <https://doi.org/10.1177/160940690200100301>

Moules, N. J. (2020). Book review: "The responsibility to understand: Hermeneutical contours of ethical life" by Professor Theodore George. *Journal of Applied Hermeneutics*, Article 6, 1–9. <https://doi.org/10.11575/jah.vi0.71086>

Moules, N. J., Jardine, D. W., McCaffrey, G, & Brown, C. (2013). Isn't all of oncology hermeneutic? *Journal of Applied Hermeneutics*, Article 3. <https://doi.org/10.11575/jah.v0i2.53221>

Moules, N. J., Venturato, L., Laing, C. M., & Field, J. C. (2017). Is it really "yesterday's war"? What Gadamer has to say about what gets counted.

Journal of Applied Hermeneutics, Article 1. <https://journalhosting.ucalgary.ca/index.php/jah/article/view/53302>

Sandelowski, M. (1986). The problem of rigor in qualitative research. *Advances in Nursing Science, 8*(3), 27–37. <https://doi.org/10.1097/00012272-198604000-00005>

Sandelowski, M. (1993). Rigor or rigor mortis: The problem of rigor in qualitative research revisited. *Advances in Nursing Science, 16*(2), 1–8. <http://dx.doi.org/10.1097/00012272-199312000-00002>

Smith, D. G. (1991). Hermeneutic inquiry: The hermeneutic imagination and the pedagogic text. In E. Short (Ed.), *Forms of curriculum inquiry* (pp. 187–209). SUNY.

Stewart, K., & Amundson, J. (1995). The ethical postmodernist: Or not everything is relative all at once. *Journal of Systemic Therapies, 14*(2), 70–78. <https://doi.org/10.1521/jsyt.1995.14.2.70>

Wallace, B. (1987). Particulars. In B. Wallace, *The stubborn particulars of grace* (pp. 110–111). McClelland & Stewart.

"So What?"—Implications of Hermeneutic Research

In 2011, Dr. Catherine Laing, a doctoral candidate at the time, presented to board members of a local children's cancer care foundation on her proposed study of children's cancer camps. She described her intent to study the cancer camp run by the foundation and her goal to attempt to reach some understanding of the meaning of the camp for children and families. The board members wholeheartedly supported this research, but they asked what the findings would bring them to support their requests for individual and corporate donor contributions to the running of the camp. "Will you get evidence to prove that camp makes a difference?" "What kind of statistics will you get from your study that will convince people to donate?" Laing responded that she would not have statistics or the kind of data that they thought they needed to be convincing. A cancer researcher sitting at the table, who held the role of the Scientific Director of the Canadian Institute of Health Research, Dr. Stephen Robbins, astutely asked the questions: "Do you really want those numbers, that kind of measurement? Because what if you measured and you found out that camp made NO difference in the trajectory of the cancer, or that it even increased the possibility of infection, and then compromised treatment? What if all you found out was that camp was fun and it diminished the kids' suffering a bit for one week?"

To these poignant questions, the room of people had no response, *but hermeneutics does*. Hermeneutics is not about measuring, quantifying, explaining, providing proof, or answering once and for all the questions of how and why or cause and effect. Instead, it offers an answer to a question that could have been answered differently, and it offers an answer that cannot be ignored.

A year later, Laing, having completed her Ph.D., returned to the foundation's board and presented her findings. In the room were healthcare professionals and very high-powered corporate leaders, well connected in the community. As the group listened, visibly moved, there was an awakening that what this study said was important and that, in it, was all the evidence they needed to convince people (i.e., donors) that camp matters and why it matters, and it is not numbers alone that convinces but rather the understanding that children have cancer, people go to camp, and camp does, in fact, as Dr. Robbins suggested, make a difference in suffering.

As mentioned at the end of our last chapter, hermeneutics is an honoring of the particular; it is not necessarily attentive to or interested in the aggregate. This by no means negates the fact that evidence provided through quantitative means is important and makes a relevant contribution to practice and knowledge. It in fact has, and continues to, save lives. This is not a competitive venture nor an either/or but a both/and. As cited earlier in Chapter 3, Gadamer reminded us that "what is established by statistics seems to be a language of facts, but which questions these facts answer and which facts would begin to speak if other questions are asked are hermeneutical questions" (Gadamer, 2007, p. 84). In this chapter, we discuss what it is that hermeneutic research can bring to practice—from "philosophy to research to practice," as the title of our book suggests.

The Utility of Hermeneutic Research Findings

There is an obligation in hermeneutic work that is immense. Davey (2006) suggested that hermeneutics is not just about understanding and interpretation but holds a commitment to change.

In 2004, Margarete Sandelowski wrote a seminal paper about the "use" of qualitative research in general. In this paper, she offered an attempt to respond to the demand and urgency of end user communities about the utility or what she called the "actionability" (p. 1367) of qualitative research, an urgency driven by the call for "evidence-based practice." Hermeneutic research, along with its fellow qualitative research methods, is constantly being called to account for its utility and actionability, for how and in what ways it adds value, knowledge, and change directly to the practice professions in which it is located (at least in the context of this book). Writing theses and dissertations, grant proposals, or research reports all call for the answer to the questions of "So what does this research tell us? What are the implications for practice?"

Eastabrooks (1999, 2001) offered a classification of levels of utilization that serves as way to examine what it is that hermeneutic research brings to practice. We borrow these categories to speak to the utility of hermeneutic work.

Instrumental Utility

Instrumental utilization refers to the concrete application of research findings in a very practical sense that is tangible and visible. Sandelowski (2004) offered the examples of "clinical guidelines, care standards, appraisal tools, pathways, intervention protocols, or algorithms" (p. 1371), which are all material forms that are directed to achieve particular outcomes. This kind of utilization is evident to both the users and the ends users (the practitioners and the recipients of the practice—patients, students, clients, etc.). Because of the outcome of this level of utilization, one can anticipate that it most often arises from forms of research that are quite empirical. However, we argue that hermeneutic research can have an instrumental utility as well.

An example of this is that, as a result of a hermeneutic study conducted by Moules (2002, 2003, 2009a, 2009b) on therapeutic letters (described earlier in Chapter 5), there was a tangible and instrumental change in the practice of writing letters. This change first happened in the practice unit from which the data arose, but as a result of dissemination through research publications, it accounted for changes in the practices of others, even in the practice of the originator of therapeutic letters (Epston, 2009).

In the same vein, Laing (2013a, 2013b, 2014a, 2014b) drew from her findings in her research on children's cancer camps, offering that camp should be viewed as a necessity, not a luxury. If, in fact, this recommendation was accepted by health authorities, it could evolve into a part of the treatment protocol for some children with cancer and this would be reflective of an instrumental utilization, therefore attesting to the instrumental utility of the hermeneutic research.

Symbolic Utility

Less tangible and visible, symbolic utilization is not necessarily about making changes in practice directly, but rather "the use of research findings as a persuasive or political tool to legitimate a position or practice" (Sandelowski, 2004, p. 1371). Sandelowski further claimed that the "actionability resides largely in talk" (p. 1371), though it may in fact ultimately lead to instrumental changes.

The persuasive power of hermeneutic research is part of its symbolic potential. Laing's study on children's cancer camps is one such example. As discussed at the beginning of this chapter, potential donors for the camps were "swayed," persuaded and convinced that camp matters, simply by listening to the stories and interpretations that came out of her research. This research legitimized camp as a healing and helpful intervention for children and families facing childhood cancer and therefore as a persuasive piece of research to present to potential donors.

Conceptual Utility

The utility of research findings at a purely conceptual level appears to evoke no observable changes at all, no changes in practices, policies, or positions. Instead, change happens at the level of thinking about something—about people, practices, problems, or relationships. It has been well documented in therapeutic fields, however, that changes in thinking and in beliefs result in changes in behavior. Wright and Bell (2021) argued that changes in behaviors and practices are not sustainable if there are no changes in the thinking or the beliefs practitioners hold. For example, if teachers, because of research evidence, change their teaching practices to something they do not really believe will work with students, it is inevitable that the practice will not be sustained, and the teachers will come to see what they originally believed to be true, reverting back to old practices.

In the beginning, the change happens quietly, often internally and often …

> in the user who is newly informed or enlightened, but this change in the user may not be obvious to anyone nor have any obvious impact on anyone or anything else. Indeed, the users who experienced this change may be unable to articulate the change experience even to themselves. Yet, like symbolic utilization, conceptual utilization may be a precursor to instrumental utilization as users develop the capacity to articulate the change experience and to translate it into more observable or material form. (Sandelowski, 2004, p. 1372)

The study mentioned in earlier chapters on grandparents' experiences of childhood cancer stands as an example of hermeneutic research that can make changes at a conceptual level that leads to behavioral/practice changes.

The KT Challenge

Currently, there is a demand for research to live up to promises of actionability and no more so than in the focus on knowledge translation (KT). Knowledge translation movements evolved out of the acknowledgment that, although there is much happening in research, there is an evident gap between the research and the findings and what happens in practice. Goals of a KT focus include improving how research results are communicated, utilized, and have impact at various levels of end users (Knowledge Translation Canada, <http://ktclearinghouse.ca/ktcanada>).

Doane and Varcoe (2008) [6] raised questions about the epistemological limits of KT as it is usually presented, under various related but effectively interchangeable

---

6 They also touched on the idea of translation as a form of interpretation (p. 293)—there is a hermeneutic study to yet to be written about the difficulties and nuances of translation in terms of KT, where the term is used naively.

terms such as "research utilization, knowledge transfer, research dissemination, research uptake, innovation diffusion, and so forth" and their similar focus on the use of knowledge with the goal of "'how to get knowledge used' and 'translated' into practice" (p. 284). These authors drew on "deconstructive hermeneutics" (p. 283) to highlight the absence in conventional KT of sensitivity to the multi-layered contexts of how knowledge finds its way into practice. Inherent in this limitation is the privileging of empirically based findings with the simultaneous diminishment of knowledge that cannot be empirically verified, including the subjectivity of practitioners using knowledge within ideologically loaded institutional settings. When knowledge is developed to meet existing horizons of knowledge gaps, the restricted goal of knowledge is to "confirm and refine prediction and hypothesis" (Doane & Varcoe, 2008, p. 287).

We argue that hermeneutics is not focused on a pre-set horizon and part of the difficulty of meeting KT expectations is because hermeneutics is in search of new horizons of knowledge and understanding: "it is possible, and sometimes necessary that the horizon undergo revision … a reorganization of the whole field of disciplinary activity" (Caputo, 2000, p. 164). By keeping open to what might arrive as new, we do not and cannot prescribe in advance how this new knowledge will be translated. That it should be translated into practice is not in debate, but rather the decision of when or how it is located might be at a different juncture than current KT directives dictate.

The KT focus is undeniably important, but it presents a unique challenge within hermeneutic work in the way that granting agencies are organized and focused. To apply for funding for research requires a declaration in advance of what the KT strategies will involve and how outcomes of results will be actualized in practice. This is difficult in hermeneutic studies in many ways. In hermeneutics, we attempt to remain open to the newness that comes to meet us; we do not attempt to hypothesize or anticipate in advance what the findings will be. It is therefore very difficult to declare in advance what our KT strategies will be in dissemination and utilization of the results. We might speculate on possibilities, but not until the study is completed, and the analysis done, do the implications for practice and dissemination arise.

Learning how to write grant applications that promise a plan for KT becomes then a juggling act of discussing possibilities while keeping the research itself open to what the findings have to teach the researcher. In this sense, the KT portions of grant applications need to be written tentatively, fleshing out potential strategies, but being clear that the strategies are only possibilities and will be determined by the findings of the study. In many ways, the focus in this part of the application needs to be on strategies for dissemination that are creative and inclusive and do not only target an academic audience. A decision cannot even be made in advance about who really is the end user of the research. The audiences that emerge as the interpretations develop may require different dissemination strategies, and this can be discussed in advance of conducting the research, however, the specifics of this dissemination cannot be anticipated.

For hermeneutic research, we caution against the somewhat lazy practice of simplifying implications for practice, as a "catch all" of recommendations that basically say: "requires further research on the topic." This is not to say that studies do not indicate the need for future research, but the researcher must dig deeper into the implications of the current study to understand how the interpretations do have something to say to practice and to articulate what that something might be. Another common claim of implications for practice is that of "education" which works under the assumption that if people just "knew more or were taught better," the problem will be solved. This assumption flies in the face of years of practice and research that asserts that instructive interaction (i.e., educational strategies) do not always (or more boldly stated—rarely!) equate to behavioral change. A clear example of this is the failure of the years of anti-smoking campaigns in schools and the subsequent increase in teen and young adult smoking rates (Farrelly et al., 2003; Paek & Gunther, 2007; University of Georgia, 2007).

Because hermeneutics is attuned to the need to deconstruct taken-for-granted assumptions about human experience and practices, researchers in this tradition are cautioned against falling prey to prescriptive and taken-for-granted prescriptions of implications for practice. Professor James Risser is known for his philosophical engagement with understanding what is "at stake" in what and how we understand (Risser, 1997, 2012, 2019). "With respect to the living word, hermeneutics cannot escape from an operation of memory—an operation of memory that is undoubtedly quite complex, for in the movement of its reproduction what is at stake is a central tenet of Gadamerian hermeneutics, namely, the sharing of meaning" (Risser, 2012, p. 92). In our research, then there is constant vigilance for remaining attentive to "what is at stake" in it and a recognition that all any research can do is offer advice for better practice; it cannot guarantee it.

What Is at Stake? Research as a Giver of Advice

It is my belief that it is in the explanation, in the interpretation of events, in the way we use them in our personal lives that history begins to matter…
—Wallace (1992, p. 27)

If we listen carefully to the interpretations found in hermeneutic work, we hear invitations and, in some invitations, we might be beckoned by something that sounds like advice on how to proceed in our practices and lives. Advice can be audacious, bold, and certain, but it can also be subtle and embedded, couched within speculation and wonder—*and* it can also, always, be turned down.

One of the tasks of hermeneutics lies in making visible the value of symbolic and conceptual utility. Understanding is the imperative of hermeneutic research, not explanation. The persuasion of it lies in its ability to meaningfully convince others of the truth of it and how, within truth, there is usually utility and meaning to be found. As Davey (2006) asserted, hermeneutics is not aimed at simply understanding or interpreting events in the world, but as a result of such understanding, the world (or parts of it) are necessarily changed. Creating space for possibilities of change demands discernment in deciding what is at stake in the topic and the study. We study things that matter in human lives and in our disciplines' work. Articulating why it matters often serves to lead us to implications for practice. For example, it matters that we understand issues of integration of disabilities in schools because it has impact on human lives and requires one to "live well with and for others in just institutions" (Ricoeur, 1992, p. 352). This mattering, then, means that we have to think about why we do what we do in the school system around disabilities, and ask the question: do we need to re-think this and do it differently and better? When something is at stake, when something matters, the conceptual utility of research results cannot help but lead to instrumental and practical utility.

A central question in hermeneutic work is to consider if the results are useful and, if so, for what purpose and for whom. Once determined, the pragmatic decision is to make choices of the delivery method of the knowledge; in other words, how might the findings be best disseminated to the audience who most could use them? Greenhalgh (2002) suggested that what makes qualitative research (which includes hermeneutic research) distinctive, in part, is its ability to narrow the gap between understanding and action as well as making the connection between efficacy of what works in research with effectiveness, which is what works in practice. Producers of research and users of research have a relationship, but the line is not as clear as these terms suggest. Producers also use research to inform future directions of research, and users of research "by virtue of their use alone, re-produce and re-create" the results of research (Sandelowski, 2004, p. 1380).

> Qualitative research ... could improve as a knowledge producing social practice by not just being reflexive about what individual researchers bring to the research process ... but also by being reflexive about what this social practice of knowledge production ... presupposes about the human reality, and how it affects human reality. (Kvale & Brinkmann, 2009, p. 315)

Summary

Hermeneutics is in search of understanding of human reality. Through understanding, through interpretation that brings understanding of the complexity of human reality, invitations for change most often reside and this understanding compels us. As Humberto Maturana, the Chilean neurobiologist, offered:

> The knowledge of knowledge compels. It compels us to adopt an attitude of permanent vigilance against the temptation of certainty. It compels us to recognize that certainty is not a proof of truth. It compels us to realize that the world everyone sees is not the world but *a* world we bring forth with others. It compels us to see that the world will be different only if we live differently. It compels us because, when we know that we know, we cannot deny (to ourselves or to others) that we know…(This) implies an ethics that we cannot evade … an ethics that springs from human reflection and puts human reflection right at the core as a constitutive social phenomenon. (Maturana & Varela, 1992, p. 245)

The "so what" of hermeneutic research is inherently a social endeavor. Though questions that guide hermeneutic research are vitally important, no less important is to answer these questions—tentatively, openly, and with the hermeneutic humility that recognizes that no one question can be answered definitively once and for all. Rather, hermeneutics "concentrates on the question of what happens to us when we 'understand'" (Davey, 2006, p. xi).

Hermeneutics compels us as researchers and users of research to live in the world differently, to realize that understanding is not, as Davey (2006) invoked, just about interpreting the world but also about changing it. Herein, lies the "so what" of this work, premised on the insight that when we know what we know, we cannot deny that we know, and we are ethically obligated to do something about it.

References

Caputo, J. D. (2000). *More radical hermeneutics: On not knowing who we are.* Indiana University Press.

Davey, N. (2006). *Unquiet understanding: Gadamer's philosophical hermeneutics.* SUNY.

Doane, G. H., & Varcoe, C. (2008). Knowledge translation in everyday nursing: From evidence-based to inquiry-based practice. *Advances in Nursing Science, 31*(4), 283–295. <https://doi.org/10.1097/01.ANS.0000341409.17424.7f>

Epston, D. (2009). The legacy of letter writing as a clinical practice: Introduction to the special issue on therapeutic letters. *Journal of Family Nursing, 15*(1), 3–5. <https://doi.org/10.1177/1074840708331150>

Estabrooks, C. A. (1999). The conceptual structure of research utilization. *Research in Nursing and Health, 22*, 203–216. <https://doi.org/10.1002/(SICI)1098-240X(199906)22:3<203::AID-NUR3>3.0.CO;2-9>

Estabrooks, C. A. (2001). Research utilization and qualitative research. In J. M. Morse, J. M. Swanson, & A. J. Kuzel (Eds.), *The nature of qualitative evidence* (pp. 275–298). SAGE.

Farrelly, M. C., Niederdeppe, J., & Yarsevich, J. (2003). Youth tobacco prevention mass media campaigns: Past, present, and future directions. *Tobacco Control, 12*, 35–47. <https://doi.org/10.1136/tc.12.suppl_1.i35>

Gadamer, H.-G. (2007). *The Gadamer reader: A bouquet of later writings* (R. E. Palmer, Ed. & Trans.). Northwestern University Press.

Greenhalgh, T. (2002). Integrating qualitative research into evidence-based practice. *Endocrinology and Metabolism Clinics of North America, 31*, 583–601. <https://doi.org/10.1016/s0889-8529(02)00009-9>

Kvale, S., & Brinkmann, S. (2009). *InterViews: Learning the craft of qualitative research interviewing* (2nd ed.). SAGE.

Laing, C. M. (2013a). *"It's not just camp": Understanding the meaning of children's cancer camps for children and families*. Unpublished doctoral research, University of Calgary, Calgary, AB, Canada.

Laing, C. M., & Moules, N. J. (2013b). The island of misfit toys. *Journal of Applied Hermeneutics, Article 8*, <https://doi.org/10.11575/jah.v0i2.53228>

Laing, C. M., & Moules, N. J. (2014a). Stories from cancer camp: Tales of glitter and gratitude. *Journal of Applied Hermeneutics*, Article 3, <https://doi.org/10.11575/jah.v0i0.53235>

Laing, C. M., & Moules, N. J. (2014b). Children's cancer camps: A sense of community, a sense of family. *Journal of Family Nursing, 20*(2), 185–203. <https://doi.org/10.1177/107484071452071>

Maturana, H. R., & Varela, F. (1992). *The tree of knowledge: The biological roots of human understanding* (rev. ed.). Shambhala.

Moules, N. J. (2002). Nursing on paper: Therapeutic letters in nursing practice. *Nursing Inquiry, 9*(2), 104–113. <https://doi.org/10.1046/j.1440-1800.2002.00133.x>

Moules, N. J. (2003). Therapy on paper: Therapeutic letters and the tone of relationship. *Journal of Systemic Therapies, 22*(1), 33–49. <https://doi.org/10.1521/jsyt.22.1.33.24091>

Moules, N. J. (2009a). Therapeutic letters in nursing: Examining the character and influence of the written word in clinical work with families experiencing illness. *Journal of Family Nursing, 15*(1), 31–49. <https://doi.org/10.1177/1074840709331639>

Moules, N. J. (2009b). The past and future of therapeutic letters: Family suffering and healing words. *Journal of Family Nursing, 15*(1), 102–111. <https://doi.org/10.1177/1074840709332238>

Paek, H.-J., & Gunther, A. C. (2007). How peer proximity moderates indirect media influence on adolescent smoking. *Communication Research, 34*(4), 407–432. <https://doi.org/10.1177/0093650207302785>

Ricoeur, P. (1992). *Oneself as another.* University of Chicago Press.

Risser, J. (1997). *Hermeneutics and the voice of the other.* SUNY.

Risser, J. (2012). *The life of understanding: A contemporary hermeneutics.* Indiana University Press.

Risser, J. (2019). When words fail: On the power of language in human experience. *Journal of Applied Hermeneutics.* Article 6, 1–11. <https://doi.org/10.111575/jah.v0i0.68706>

Sandelowski, M. (2004). Using qualitative research. *Qualitative Health Research, 14*(10), 1366–1386. <https://doi.org/10.1177/1049732304269672>

University of Georgia. (2007). Why some anti-smoking ads succeed and others backfire. *ScienceDaily*, July 20, 2007. <www.sciencedaily.com/releases/2007/07/070719170315.htm>

Wallace, B. (1992). *Arguments with the world.* Quarry Press.

Wright, L. M., & Bell, J. M. (2021). *Illness beliefs: The heart of healing with families and individuals* (3rd ed.). 4th Floor Press.

Conclusion—Firsts and Lasts

If there can be no last word in philosophical hermeneutics, there can be no first. The question is how and where to join a continuing "conversation."
—DAVEY (2006, P. XI)

We have returned our voices to the continuing conversation in a particular way, expanding on our interpretation of the historical philosophical tradition's influence on hermeneutics as a research method in applied disciplines. In this 2nd edition of this book, we again traced the German school of hermeneutic scholars leading to the work of Hans-Georg Gadamer's philosophical hermeneutics. From this standpoint, we re-engaged in the methodological dilemmas of proceeding with research in a way that is consistent with the philosophy that guides it. We followed with an exploration of aspects of hermeneutic research including the address of the topic; the conduct of interviews; interpretation (data analysis) in hermeneutics; examples of interpretive writing of research findings; rigor and integrity of this kind of research; and ending with the call to be accountable to the research in terms of its utility and usefulness.

In this endeavor, we have challenged the notion that hermeneutic research is an unguided research approach and shown rather that it is a rigorous practice of attentiveness, openness, discernment, tact, discipline, and dis-position.

> … hermeneutics does not constitute a "philosophical position" but a philosophical dis-position. It is a practice of disposing or orientating oneself toward the other and the different with the consequence of experiencing a dis-positioning of one's initial expectancies … If philosophical hermeneutics is a practice of attentiveness, then like all reflective and spiritual disciplines it inhabits and articulates a tense space, the space of being in between. Openness to the other requires a particular refinement: the skill of being critically distant while remaining involved, attentive, and caring. Hermeneutic practice is indeed difficult. It involves the testing discipline of not residing in the quietness of a single interpretation. (Davey, 2006, p. xvi)

Being in-between is a tension that requires the ability to suspend certain things while holding other things in attention. In disclosing and unconcealing in efforts to understand, it covers some things while exposing others. There is a hermeneutic humility being "not quite this or quite that" and in remembering that truth is always a tenuous encounter with something that leaves room for other things. This is not an easy adventure, and it is necessarily one navigated personally; "for everything that understanding mediates is mediated through ourselves" (Gadamer, 2007, p. 244). Gadamer (2007) suggested that "understanding is an adventure, and like any other adventure, is dangerous" (p. 243), but we offer that *understanding is the ultimate hermeneutic wager*: that understanding matters and will make a difference. When we practice hermeneutics as a research tradition, we do so with the conviction that what we come to understand through its conduct are matters of human consequence of living well in conditions where suffering often exists. Research that involves the practice professions of nursing, education, psychology, or social work as examples, is research that touches on human conditions of living: illness, schools, children, health, relationships, suffering, healing, and hope.

As mentioned in earlier chapters, Davey suggested that "philosophical hermeneutics is not always its own best advocate" (Davey, 2006, p. xi), however, in this book, we argue that hermeneutic researchers need to advocate for the rigor and integrity of this kind of research. Hermeneutic research is buoyed and guided by philosophy, but it ends up becoming something much more practical, tethered to praxis and phronesis.

The reality that there are no firsts and lasts is at the heart of understanding as Davey (2006) suggested, and it is often what lies in between that matters most and is most at stake in understanding.

References

Davey, N. (2006). *Unquiet understanding: Gadamer's philosophical hermeneutics*. SUNY.

Gadamer, H.-G. (2007). *The Gadamer reader: A bouquet of the later writings* (R. Palmer, Ed. & Trans). Northwestern University Press.

Index

critical qualitative research

Shirley R. Steinberg, *General Editor*

The Critical Qualitative Research series examines societal structures that oppress and exclude so that transformative actions can be generated. This transformed research is activist in orientation. Because the perspective accepts the notion that nothing is apolitical, research projects themselves are critically examined for power orientations, even as they are used to address curricular, educational, or societal issues.

This methodological work challenges modernist orientations and universalist impositions, asking critical questions like: Who/what is heard? Who/what is silenced? Who is privileged? Who is disqualified? How are forms of inclusion and exclusion being created? How are power relations constructed and managed? How do different forms of privilege and oppression intersect to affect educational, societal, and life possibilities for various individuals and groups?

We are particularly interested in manuscripts that offer critical examinations of curriculum, policy, public communities, and the ways in which language, discourse practices, and power relations prevent more just transformations.

For additional information about this series or for the submission of manuscripts, please contact:

Shirley R. Steinberg | msgramsci@gmail.com

To order other books in this series, please contact our Customer Service Department:

peterlang@presswarehouse.com (within the U.S.)
order@peterlang.com (outside the U.S.)

Or browse online by series:

www.peterlang.com

www.ingramcontent.com/pod-product-compliance
Ingram Content Group UK Ltd.
Pitfield, Milton Keynes, MK11 3LW, UK
UKHW020259051026
15470UKWH00021B/1468